Understanding
OPEN SOURCE & FREE SOFTWARE LICENSING

Other Linux resources from O'Reilly

Related titles

The Cathedral & The Bazaar

Free as in Freedom

Open Sources: Voices from the Open Source Revolution

Linux Unwired

Exploring the JDS Linux Desktop

Learning Red Hat Enterprise Linux & Fedora

Linux Security Cookbook

Building Secure Servers with Linux

Building Embedded Linux Systems

Linux Cookbook

Linux Books Resource Center

linux.oreilly.com is a complete catalog of O'Reilly's books on Linux and Unix and related technologies, including sample chapters and code examples.

ONLamp.com is the premier site for the open source web platform: Linux, Apache, MySQL and either Perl, Python, or PHP.

Conferences

O'Reilly brings diverse innovators together to nurture the ideas that spark revolutionary industries. We specialize in documenting the latest tools and systems, translating the innovator's knowledge into useful skills for those in the trenches. Visit *conferences.oreilly.com* for our upcoming events.

Safari Bookshelf (*safari.oreilly.com*) is the premier online reference library for programmers and IT professionals. Conduct searches across more than 1,000 books. Subscribers can zero in on answers to time-critical questions in a matter of seconds. Read the books on your Bookshelf from cover to cover or simply flip to the page you need. Try it today with a free trial.

Understanding
OPEN SOURCE & FREE SOFTWARE LICENSING

Andrew M. St. Laurent

O'REILLY®

Beijing · Cambridge · Farnham · Köln · Paris · Sebastopol · Taipei · Tokyo

Understanding Open Source and Free Software Licensing
by Andrew M. St. Laurent

Published by O'Reilly Media, Inc., 1005 Gravenstein Highway North, Sebastopol, CA 95472.

O'Reilly books may be purchased for educational, business, or sales promotional use. Online editions are also available for most titles (*safari.oreilly.com*). For more information, contact our corporate/institutional sales department: (800) 998-9938 or *corporate@oreilly.com*.

Editor:	Simon St.Laurent
Production Editor:	Marlowe Shaeffer
Cover Designer:	Emma Colby
Interior Designer:	David Futato

Printing History:

August 2004:	First Edition.

 This book uses RepKover™, a durable and flexible lay-flat binding.

ISBN: 0-596-00581-4

[M]

To Tamara

Table of Contents

Preface

Free and open source development models have made tremendous contributions to computing, sustaining both research and commercial projects and making it easier for large groups of people, who may not even be acquainted, to help each other. While this growing activity has a promising future, all of this work is built on top of licenses—legal documents—that often seem arcane or difficult to understand. Businesses and individuals aren't always sure what is at stake in their decisions to participate, and deciding which license to use for a particular project can be a project of its own.

This book is designed to simplify those decisions, explaining the different licenses and their effects on projects, including both commercial and non-commercial projects. It explores how licenses can be used as glue to bind groups of people together in common, and how the different styles of license interact with different kinds of projects.

The licenses and projects covered include:

- MIT
- BSD
- Apache, Versions 1.0 and 2.0
- Academic Free License (AFL)
- GNU General Public License (GPL)
- GNU Lesser General Public License (LGPL)
- Mozilla Public License (MPL)
- Qt License
- Artistic License
- Creative Commons Licenses
- Sun Community Source License and Commercial Use Supplement
- Microsoft Shared Source Initiative

Each license is examined clause by clause, including both the original license text and explanation. This book also looks at issues affecting all of these licenses, including the formation of a contract, enforceability of warranty and other disclaimers, and cross-licensing.

Audience

A few lawyers will undoubtedly read this book, and hopefully find it useful, but you don't need to be a lawyer to read this book. Whether you're a programmer deciding what license to use in publishing a personal code library, a manager deciding if and how you can use open source code in your business, or a lawyer evaluating rules for integrating open source code with proprietary code, you should find the information you need here.

Organization

This book starts with the basics of contracts and licensing, proceeds through the details of the licenses, and concludes with a discussion of the implications of these licenses for organizations and for projects. You don't need to read the book from start to finish, and it's quite reasonable in some cases to read only the parts that apply to the licenses that interest you. This book has seven chapters:

Chapter 1, *Open Source Licensing, Contract, and Copyright Law*
> This chapter takes a look at the traditional foundations below open source licensing, including contracts and copyrights, with a brief look at patents and warranties.

Chapter 2, *The MIT, BSD, Apache, and Academic Free Licenses*
> This chapter takes a close look at licenses that specify terms, which allow the redistribution of source code but place few limits on its commercial use.

Chapter 3, *The GPL, LGPL, and Mozilla Licenses*
> These licenses specify terms that are designed to keep source code and derivations of that code openly available for further community development.

Chapter 4, *Qt, Artistic, and Creative Commons Licenses*
> This chapter looks at some licenses that take their own paths, reserving rights to the creator of a project, and, in the case of Creative Commons, licensing content that isn't necessarily code.

Chapter 5, *Non-Open Source Licenses*
> While free and open source licenses are the focus of this book, understanding proprietary licenses can also be important, especially as companies like Sun and Microsoft work on approaches that reserve many of their rights while attempting to reap some of the benefits of more open development models.

Chapter 6, *Legal Impacts of Open Source and Free Software Licensing*
Using or publishing software under a license creates obligations. This chapter examines how those obligations work and what their consequences may be, as well as questions of mixing licenses or publishing software under multiple licenses.

Chapter 7, *Software Development Using Open Source and Free Software Licenses*
The licenses are important, but their use makes them valuable. This chapter looks at how these licenses have been used and are being used on software projects, as well as how to choose from the many licenses available and what to do if you feel you must draft your own license.

Appendix, *Creative Commons Attribution-NoDerivs License*
The Appendix contains the Creative Commons Attribution-NoDerivs 2.0 License, which sets terms under which this book may be freely distributed.

If you want to get an overview of all of the options in free and open source licensing and development, then it probably makes sense to read the book straight through. If you just want to look up a few licenses, it may make sense to pick up foundations in Chapter 1 and read the relevant sections in Chapters 2 through 5, and then look over Chapters 6 and 7.

Conventions Used in This Book

The following typographical conventions are used in this book:

Plain text
Indicates menu titles, menu options, menu buttons, and keyboard accelerators (such as Alt and Ctrl).

Italic
Indicates new terms, URLs, email addresses, filenames, file extensions, pathnames, directories, and Unix utilities.

Indented quotations
Indicate the text of the original licenses and separate them from the commentary.

This icon signifies a tip, suggestion, or general note.

This icon indicates a warning or caution.

Comments and Questions

Please address comments and questions concerning this book to the publisher:

O'Reilly Media, Inc.
1005 Gravenstein Highway North
Sebastopol, CA 95472
(800) 998-9938 (in the United States or Canada)
(707) 829-0515 (international or local)
(707) 829-0104 (fax)

We have a web page for this book, where we list errata, examples, and any additional information. You can access this page at:

http://www.oreilly.com/catalog/osfreesoft

To comment or ask technical questions about this book, send email to:

bookquestions@oreilly.com

For more information about our books, conferences, Resource Centers, and the O'Reilly Network, see our web site at:

http://www.oreilly.com

Acknowledgments

I want to thank my editor, Simon St.Laurent, without whom this book would never have been written; Eben Moglen, who introduced me to open source and free software; and Mitchell Baker, Danese Cooper, David Stutz, and John Cowan for their invaluable help in reviewing and correcting this book. I also want to thank John Urda, for his help and encouragement; and Jason Yung, for his last-minute assistance. All the mistakes remain the property of the author.

CHAPTER 1

Open Source Licensing, Contract, and Copyright Law

Open source licensing and development approaches have been challenging and transforming software development for decades. Although open source licensing is often described as radical, it is built on solid, traditional legal foundations, including the rights granted by copyright under the law of the United States (and elsewhere), and the ways in which basic contract principles can alter and supersede those rights.

Basic Principles of Copyright Law

Under the laws of the United States (and of European countries, through the Berne Convention, and of members of the World Trade Organization through the WTO Agreement on Trade-Related Aspects of Intellectual Property Rights), copyright is automatically attached to every novel expression of an idea, whether through text, sounds, or imagery. For example, the words in this paragraph are protected by copyright as soon as they are written. This also applies to diary entries, letters, song lyrics, and drawings, even if they are only done "off the cuff," in the most casual of circumstances.

For example, a drawing of a dog made on a café napkin is copyrighted simultaneously with its creation and is the sole property—barring any contractual abrogation of the copyright—of its creator. This drawing cannot be copied, displayed, or otherwise commercially exploited by any person other than the creator for the life of the copyright. Among other things, no person other than the creator has the right under copyright law to create "derivative works"—works that depend upon or develop from the original, copyrighted work. This limitation is of particular significance to open source licensing, as will be explained later. In the United States, the period protected by copyright is very long indeed: the life of the creator plus 70 years, or in the case of works made "for hire" or by creators who are not identified, 95 years from the date of publication or 120 years from the date of creation, whichever is shorter.

This does not mean, of course, that the creator of this drawing has a monopoly on the depiction of dogs. Copyright law does not protect any particular idea. Rather, copyright protects only the *expression* of that idea. The creator of the dog drawing has a right to the commercial exploitation of only that particular expression of "dog." This right is no limitation on the right of others to create, and to commercially exploit, their own expressions of "dog," whether through drawing or other media. This limitation to expressions excludes protection from copyright of creations that are not expressed in a tangible, reproducible medium. For example, a dramatic monologue read on a street corner is not protected by copyright. However, if a reading of that monologue is recorded, whether on audio or videotape or paper, it is subject to copyright protection.

This limitation to the expressions of an idea is the principal distinction between the applications of patent and copyright. Unlike copyright, a valid patent does not protect the expression of an idea but the underlying substance of it. For example, a patent applicable to a microchip protects not the expression of the chip itself, or the electrical diagram describing it, but the idea that given circuits can be organized and made to operate in a particular way. Because of their potentially vast scope, patents are construed more strictly, require a registration process, and last for shorter periods than copyrights.

A copyright does not need to be registered to be legally effective. As already noted, a copyright comes into force when the protected work is created. While registration of the work with the United States Copyright Office has some effect on the rights of the copyright holder, it is not required. Moreover, while works published previous to March 1, 1989 need to bear explicit notice of copyright protection or risk losing that protection, works published after that date do not. Nonetheless, use of a copyright notice alerts potential infringers that the work falls under the protection of copyright.

The vesting of copyright protection in the creator of a work is subject to two important limitations: the doctrines of "work for hire" and "fair use." Works that are made "for hire" are made by an employee in the scope of his or her employment by another, including those that are specially commissioned for use in another work or as a supplement to another work, such as a translation. Works that are created "for hire" are still subject to copyright protection, under the same terms as described above, but the copyright belongs to the employer of the creator, or the person who commissioned the work, not the creator.

The doctrine of "fair use" defines certain uses of copyrighted material as non-infringing. "Fair use" allows persons other than the creator to make certain limited uses of the copyrighted material for purposes of commenting upon or criticizing the work, reporting, or teaching related to the copyrighted material. "Fair use" is a flexible standard, and whether a particular use is considered "fair" depends in substantial part on the extent to which that use impedes the copyright holder's exclusive rights to commercially exploit the work. In addition, one additional category of work is held to be non-infringing. A "transformative derivative work" is one that, although based on a copyrighted work, so fundamentally alters it that a new work results. Such a "transformative derivative work" is considered a new work for copyright purposes, and the holder of the copyright of the work—from which such a "transformative derivative work" is derived—has no rights over it.

Finally, the protections of copyright are subject to one more important limitation: time. Copyrighted works are protected for a set period of time, measured either from the death of their creator or from the date of their creation. After the expiration of that period of time, the copyright protection on the work lapses as the work goes into the "public domain."

Works currently in the public domain include thousands of songs and musical works, novels, poems, stories, and histories written before the twentieth century. Anyone is free to commercially exploit such works by selling copies of those works, creating derivative works based upon them, and by distribuing or displaying the work publicly.

Contract and Copyright

In the United States, all of the rights belonging to the creator of a work become theirs at the time of the completion of that work in a fixed medium. No registration is required, nor does any signed writing need to be executed in order to preserve those rights. Rather, these rights arise entirely from the operation of the statutory law.

Creators rarely take advantage of these rights by themselves, however. The production and distribution of works on a large scale has historically been capital-intensive, so creators of works have generally relied on others to produce the physical copies of their works and distribute them. The idea of copyright developed in parallel with the development of the printing press in the fifteenth century, and it originally protected the rights of printers to exclusively exploit works that they had commissioned. Legal enforcement, and, in particular, international legal enforcement, being what it was in the fifteenth and sixteenth centuries, copyrights were frequently disregarded. Of course, given the systematic violation of copyrights in many parts of the world today, it can be argued that the situation has not changed that much.

The relationship between the creator of a work and its publisher is often an uneasy one. The creator, naturally, wishes to retain both control over the use of the work and the income stream derived from commercial exploitation of the work. The publisher, whether a book company, a record label, or a film studio—to take three common examples—similarly wishes to retain exactly those same things: control over and income from the work. Because publishing (in whatever format) is a capital-intensive business, the dynamic tends to strongly favor the publisher over the creator of the work, except in the exceptional case of creators who have both a proven track record of generating income from their work and, perhaps more importantly, the ability to negotiate without restriction. The case of musicians and their battles with record labels is particularly well-known.

The most typical trade made between creators and publishers is the licensing of the work in exchange for payments, known as royalties. In the case of books, authors are generally entitled to royalties on every copy sold by the publisher. Music royalties are more complicated because there are more venues in which music can be sold or publicly performed, but the principle is the same. Royalties are generally owed to the songwriter for every copy of an album sold (mechanical royalties), for play on jukeboxes or on the radio (performance royalties), and for use on television or in films (synchronization royalties).

Software publishing, the subject with which this book is primarily concerned, generally does not involve the payment of royalties to individuals. Because commercial software is made, as a general matter, by large teams of people and requires the substantial expenditure of capital, the resulting work is "work for hire." As already discussed, the copyright of such works belongs to the employer, which, in the case of software, is usually also the publisher and the distributor of the software itself.

In general, under the American copyright system an effective monopoly is vested in the creator of each work, subject to relatively few limitations. However, for a number of reasons, most of them having to do with the substantial costs of developing and distributing work in a mass-market medium, rights held under copyright are rarely enforced by the work's creator and very little, if any, of the benefit of the copyright goes to that person. Rather, because of the negotiation of contracts by publishers with the creator or through the doctrine of work for hire, the benefits of copyright flow to the corporations that distribute the work, not the people who create it.

Open Source Software Licensing

In part as a reaction to this distributor-driven model of copyright licensing, programmers developed what is now known popularly as "Open Source" licensing. The development of this manner of software development and licensing has been described well elsewhere and will not be repeated here. For more details on the history, read *Free As In Freedom* (Sam Williams, O'Reilly 2002), *The Cathedral & The Bazaar* (Eric S. Raymond, O'Reilly 2001), and *Open Sources: Voices from the Open Source Revolution* (DiBona et al., O'Reilly, 1999).

The fundamental purpose of open source licensing is to deny anybody the right to *exclusively* exploit a work. Typically, in order to permit their works to reach a broad audience, and, incidentally, to make some sort of living from making works, creators are required to surrender all, or substantially all, of the rights granted by copyright to those entities that are capable of distributing and thereby exploiting that work.

Because these entities, by their very nature, do not see work as *work* in the first instance, but rather as the source of an income stream flowing from its exploitation, they are jealous of their right to exclusive exploitation of the work. They are similarly reluctant to share any part of the value of the work with others. While the potential consumers of a literary or musical work will be limited by the costs of acquiring the work—costs that are set exclusively by the person or entity that controls the right to distribute it—market forces will tend to reduce prices so as to maximize returns to that person or entity. Because the marginal costs of mechanical reproduction are relatively low, selling more copies of a work (at lower prices) will generally result in a larger stream of income to the publisher.

As a result, publishers fiercely defend the copyrighted work from unauthorized distribution of copies of the work itself or creation of derivative works based on the work. In the case of artistic works, the problem of unauthorized distribution of the original work is more common. While unauthorized derivative works occasionally result in lawsuits or other disputes, the value of artistic or aesthetic works relies on their original form of expression: they are "non-dynamic." Consumers want to hear Bruce Springsteen's *Born To Run* and to read Dave Eggers' *Heartbreaking Work of Staggering Genius*; they most likely do not want to hear Dave Eggers' *Born To Run* or read Bruce Springsteen's *Heartbreaking Work of Staggering Genius*.

By contrast, software is both functional and dynamic. Each program contains code that is both functional, in the sense that it does work,* and dynamic, in the sense that it can perform those functions in an entirely different context. As a result, each program that is created presents two distinct types of value. The first is its formal purpose as a database or another application. The second is a potential source of code for use in performing other functions.

When a consumer purchases a piece of software, say, Microsoft Excel, she acquires, along with the physical copy of the software and the manual (if there are such physical copies), the right to use the software for its intended purpose—in this case, as a spreadsheet program. By opening the plastic wrap on the box, the consumer becomes bound by the so-called "shrinkwrap license" under which she is bound not to copy the work (beyond the single copy made for her own use), not to make derivative works based on the work, and not to authorize anyone else to do either of these two things.† The elimination of these three restrictions is the foundation of open source licensing.

---

* The value of work that simply inspires pleasure in the observer is self-evident. However, the fact that software essentially operates like a tool—it is more like a handsaw than a sunset—makes it fundamentally different than a purely aesthetic creation.

† Such "shrinkwrap licenses" are provided with virtually every copy of commercial software sold today. Although such licenses do not present the formalities that people usually associate with contracts, they are generally enforced as binding contracts. *Specht v. Netscape Comm. Corp.*, 00 Civ. 4871 (AKS), 2001 WL 755396 (S.D.N.Y. July 5, 2001). The enforceability of shrinkwrap licenses is discussed in Chapter 6.

A comparable consumer of open source licensed software is in an entirely different position. She can freely distribute (in exchange for payment or not) copies of the work because of the "open distribution" principle. She can freely modify the work and distribute those derivative works (again, whether in exchange for payment or not), because of the "open modification" principle. The only substantial limitation upon her exercise of these rights that an open source license is likely to impose is that the copies of the work that she distributes, whether the original work or her own derivative work, be themselves licensed in a manner consistent with the original license.

For example, an open source license may require that derivative works be distributed on the same terms under which the licensee was permitted access to the work under the original license. This means that those people who receive copies of these works must themselves be able to redistribute the original and to make derivative works from the original, subject only to the limitation that they allow others to do the same. This principle is called "generational limitation."* This limitation may, depending on the terms of the original license, prevent open source code from "going closed" and require that users and contributors to the code abide by the communitarian values of open source.

While open source differs from the operation of traditional copyright licensing by permitting both open distribution and open modification, the removal of the second type of limitation is probably the more important one. By requiring that copyright holders both make available a user-modifiable source code for programs that they distribute and by requiring that they permit the development and distribution of derivative works, open source licensing makes possible three substantial improvements over traditional proprietary commercial software licensing models.

The first, and perhaps the greatest, of these benefits is innovation. It is now well-demonstrated that programmers are willing to contribute to open source projects for no reward other than that of making a program more useful. Open source works. The more programmers that can contribute to a given work, the more value that work is likely to have.†

The second benefit is reliability. Many programmers means many people who are available to debug a given program. Moreover, the benefit is not simply one of numbers. A knowledgeable user, who has witnessed firsthand the limitations of a particular application or the effects of a bug on a program's operation, is generally in a better position to address that limitation or to fix a given bug than an employee of

---

* The term "copyleft" has been used to describe this type of restriction of redistributions of such a work and derivative works. Copyleft is described in more detail in Chapter 3. Because licensors can (and do) impose other types of limitations on second and succeeding generations of derivative works, copyleft is not the equivalent to a generational limitation but is rather one example of such a limitation.

† This may be another meaningful distinction between software and aesthetic works. Aesthetic works may benefit less from contributions from many participants.

the creator of the original software. Such a user almost certainly has a greater incentive to correct such a shortcoming in a given piece of code than a software publisher, where suggestions to make such corrections must compete not only with other perhaps more pressing corrections, but also with the publisher's own financial or organizational limitations.

The third benefit is longevity. When commercially licensed software goes "out of print" and is no longer supported by its publisher, there is generally no way that software can be updated or adapted to new uses. Such software comes to an evolutionary dead end. By contrast, open source licensed software can fall into disuse for some period but still be revived, adapted, or rewritten by a subsequent user who finds a use for it—a use that may be completely different from the use originally intended.

Issues with Copyrights and Patents

All of the licenses described in this book can be broken up into two parts. The first part asserts that the person granting the license, the licensor, has the right to license the work to which the license applies. This representation may be implicit or explicit, and may be limited to specific types of rights. A licensor may, for example, assert that he has only applicable rights under copyright to the licensed work and makes no representation about patent rights that may apply to it. The second part of every license is a grant (again, however limited) by the licensor to the licensee of rights to that licensed work.

Obviously, both parts of the license need to be there in order for the license to be effective. When the first part of the license is there and the licensor has all of the rights necessary to grant them to the licensee, the only question is the relationship between the licensor and the licensee under the terms of the license. However, significant complications arise when a third party has legitimate legal claims to the work purporting to be licensed.

In the case of copyrights, a creator of an original work (defined in the legal, not the artistic sense), can confidently license that work, at least to the extent to which it may be governed by copyright law. The creator (hopefully) knows that he or she has not plagiarized the work from another and therefore has the right to license it.

Patents, however, present more complicated issues. It is more difficult to obtain and retain a patent in the first place, and there is always a risk of possible, and possibly unknowing, infringement of a patented process by the licensor, and, accordingly, by his or her licensees.

Unlike copyright protection, which does not even require filing or a formal notice on the copyrighted work, obtaining a patent from the Office of Patent and Trademark requires filing of relatively complex and laborious paperwork, including, most importantly, some explanation of the novelty of the patent in question and how it differs from processes or mechanisms already known. This generally requires the participation of an experienced patent lawyer. But obtaining the patent is not even half the struggle. Because of the profitability of patent royalties, patent holders tend to be very jealous of their rights and patrol the boundaries of their patents vigorously, attempting through the courts to extend the boundaries of their patents as much as possible and at the same time to narrow the scope of patents held by others. This can be, as you may imagine, an extremely expensive and time-consuming ordeal.

Even if a patent holder has licensed that patent for use in open source software, they may not have the inclination or the resources to defend that patent. This may have substantially negative consequences for the licensees of that patent. Although the licensee may have, in good faith, undertaken the use of the licensor's patent in full compliance with the terms of the license, at some point in the future, that patent may be narrowed or eliminated through litigation by a rival patent holder. Because of the continuing use of that narrowed or eliminated patent, the licensee of the original patent may be liable to a competing patent holder for a claim of infringement. It is possible that such a licensee would want to take action to protect the licensor's patent, by initiating or participating in patent litigation in situations in which the licensor is unwilling or unable to defend the patent. This can, of course, get expensive.

A larger problem is that there may be patent claims that apply to the licensed software but are known to neither the licensor nor the licensee. Because licensors can only license works that belong to them, the existence of a particular software license is no protection for the licensee against claims of infringement that are not brought by the licensor but by a third-party patent holder. There are no easy solutions to this problem. Software patents are frequently granted and often maddeningly vague.*

The Open Source Definition

Now that we have examined the basic principles of copyright and contract and contrasted the operation of those principles with those of open source licensing, it is worth discussing in some detail the definition of open source licensing.

The Open Source Definition is the definition propounded by the Open Source Initiative, used to describe which licenses qualify as "Open Source" licenses. The Open Source Initiative also certifies licenses as OSI Certified to indicate that they fall within the Open Source Definition. We have already seen the basic principles of open source licensing: open source licenses must permit non-exclusive commercial exploitation of the licensed work, must make available the work's source code, and must permit the creation of derivative works from the work itself. Each of these principles is expressed in the Open Source Definition, and, as we will see later, in the open source licenses discussed later in the book.

---

* For a more thorough discussion on the effects of patent laws and licensing on open source and free source software, and a compelling argument for limiting the application of patent law to software, see "The Danger Of Software Patents" in *Free Software Free Society: Selected Essays of Richard M. Stallman* (Free Software Foundation, 2002).

The Open Source Definition* begins as follows:

Introduction

Open source doesn't just mean access to the source code. The distribution terms of open-source software must comply with the following criteria:

1. Free Redistribution

The license shall not restrict any party from selling or giving away the software as a component of an aggregate software distribution containing programs from several different sources. The license shall not require a royalty or other fee for such sale.

This requirement embodies the open distribution principle discussed a moment ago, with the variation that free distribution is required only as part of an "aggregate software distribution." This relatively minor modification of the open distribution principle was made to include the Perl Artistic License described in Chapter 4, under the umbrella of open source. This modification may well be removed in future versions of the Open Source Definition.

2. Source Code

The program must include source code, and must allow distribution in source code as well as compiled form. Where some form of a product is not distributed with source code, there must be a well-publicized means of obtaining the source code for no more than a reasonable reproduction cost–preferably, downloading via the Internet without charge. The source code must be the preferred form in which a programmer would modify the program. Deliberately obfuscated source code is not allowed. Intermediate forms such as the output of a preprocessor or translator are not allowed.

In order to make the open modification principle effective in software, users must have access to source code. The preferred method of distribution is for source code to come with the compiled code. As a general matter, however, distributors prefer to make source code available separately from the compiled code to limit file sizes and ease distribution.

3. Derived Works

The license must allow modifications and derived works, and must allow them to be distributed under the same terms as the license of the original software.

This paragraph concisely describes the open modification principle that is fundamental to open source licensing. This paragraph also *permits*, but does not require, the imposition of a generational limitation (such as copyleft) by the license. As will be made clear in the next chapter, such a generational limitation, even if present in a particular license, may not necessarily bar software from "going closed"—being incorporated into proprietary code—depending, of course, on the terms of the particular license.

---

* The quoted sections are from v1.9 of the Open Source Definition. The definition is frequently updated. Check *www.opensource.org* for updates.

4. Integrity of The Author's Source Code

The license may restrict source-code from being distributed in modified form only if the license allows the distribution of "patch files" with the source code for the purpose of modifying the program at build time. The license must explicitly permit distribution of software built from modified source code. The license may require derived works to carry a different name or version number from the original software.

This is a permissive, not a mandatory, part of the definition. Licenses may limit the open modification principle by requiring distributions of modified source code as original source code plus patches, as described, and still fall within the definition. This license provision allows creators to protect the integrity of their work (and presumably of their reputations) by requiring that modifications be provided and identified as separate from the original work. Such a limitation, however, can apply only to the source code. In order to fall within the definition, the license must permit the free distribution of compiled code as modified, although the license may require a distinct name or number for the modified program.

Because of the logistical complications created by the distribution of source code with patch files, licenses that require such distribution are not recommended.

5. No Discrimination Against Persons or Groups

The license must not discriminate against any person or group of persons.

6. No Discrimination Against Fields of Endeavor

The license must not restrict anyone from making use of the program in a specific field of endeavor. For example, it may not restrict the program from being used in a business, or from being used for genetic research.

These anti-discrimination provisions ban restrictions on the use or modification of code by selected persons or for particular uses. The motivations behind such restrictions tend to be moral or political: abortion rights activists might oppose the use of their code by those opposed to abortion; oil companies might object to environmental activists using their work, or vice versa. However well-intentioned such restrictions may be, they are antithetical to the notion of open source and, in practice, are damaging to its objectives. Every limitation on the use of a given piece of code restricts the number of potential contributors, and thereby limits the flexibility, reliability, and longevity of that code.

7. Distribution of License

The rights attached to the program must apply to all to whom the program is redistributed without the need for execution of an additional license by those parties.

This requires that licenses have legally effective provisions that give the identical rights to and enforce the generational limitations, if any, on second and subsequent generations of users.

8. License Must Not Be Specific to a Product

The rights attached to the program must not depend on the program's being part of a particular software distribution. If the program is extracted from that distribution and used or distributed within the terms of the program's license, all parties to whom the program is redistributed should have the same rights as those that are granted in conjunction with the original software distribution.

This provision is included to close a loophole under which individual parts of an aggregation of software would be distributed under a different license than the aggregate package, which would be licensed under open source. This loophole allows a fairly obvious end-run around open source principles and is therefore inconsistent with the purposes of open source licensing.

9. The License Must Not Restrict Other Software

The license must not place restrictions on other software that is distributed along with the licensed software. For example, the license must not insist that all other programs distributed on the same medium must be open-source software.

This is not really an open source licensing question at all, but a question of the manner in which software may be distributed. It is included not to directly further the goals of open source but to ensure the freedom of software distributors and to maximize the availability of products licensed under open source licensing.

10. The License must be technology-neutral

No provision of the license may be predicated on any individual technology or style of interface.

This is a housekeeping provision. Some licenses required, as a precaution, that a user take an affirmative action to assent to the license, such as mouse-clicking on a particular box. Because such provisions effectively prohibit the distribution of the program in media (like paper) that are not capable of interpreting acceptance by the user, these licenses effectively limit the free transmission of the code.

Warranties

Warranty disclaimers, while not a part of the open source definition and not necessary for a license to function as an open source license, are nonetheless very common in licenses.

To understand the effect of the warranty disclaimer, it helps to have some understanding of what the terms used in it are and what it means to have a warranty associated with or implied by the acquisition of a particular work. The most obvious form of warranty is an *express warranty*. If upon the sale of a particular item, the seller explicitly states to the buyer that the item being sold, say, an answering machine, will perform a particular function, say, automatically answer incoming calls, the warranty is part of the sale. In the event the product does not perform as stated, the buyer has a remedy against the seller, generally either to have the price of purchase returned or to receive an equivalent but functioning item in exchange for the defective one. Express warranties are very common in sales of consumer goods. My stereo speakers, for example, were warrantied against defects for 10 years from the date of sale.

A *warranty of merchantability* is not an express warranty, but rather a variety of *implied warranty*, a warranty created by the operation of law, not by the seller's decision to make a particular representation. This type of warranty is generally applicable only to merchants, persons who make a business in the sale of particular goods. This warranty operates as a general guarantee that goods sold by a merchant are suitable for use as generally intended. A purchaser who buys rope from a hardware store, even if there is no express warranty, is nonetheless guaranteed that the rope will function as rope generally does. By contrast, if you buy a car from your cousin, who is not a car dealer, you have no guarantee that the car will run in a particular way, or even that it will run at all.

A *warranty of fitness for a particular purpose* lies somewhere between a warranty of merchantability and an express warranty. Like a warranty of merchantability, it is implied by law, and not by express guarantee; but like an express warranty, it applies to a particular function. Its name describes its function. For example, if you buy rope in a hardware store, and prior to the purchase you say to the person selling the rope, "oh and by the way I am using this rope to pull the car I just bought from my cousin out of a ditch," and the person selling it says, "oh yeah, it's strong enough for that," a warranty of fitness for a particular purpose is implied. If the rope does not work, the buyer, again, has a remedy against the seller.

A *warranty against infringement* is a type of warranty unique to intellectual property. Such a warranty is a guarantee by the seller, say, a writer or a musician, that the work that she is selling is in fact a work that she has copyright to, generally because she is the creator of the work.

This is probably a good moment to address *consequential damages*. As described above, the remedies for a breach of one of the warranties just described include the familiar ones of the return of the price of purchase or the exchange of the defective item. However, under at least some circumstances, a seller of a defective product may be liable for more than just the sale price of the item. If the defect in the item causes damages of a type that were reasonably foreseeable at the time of the sale, the seller of the item could be liable for damages that flowed from the defect. These damages are often far greater than the sale price of the item and are known as *consequential damages*. Suppose, for example, the manufacturer of a brand of coffeemakers makes a particular model of coffeemaker that, contrary to its warranty, will start a fire if left on for more than four hours. If one of those coffeemakers starts a fire that burns down the house of the unfortunate purchaser of that coffeemaker, the manufacturer may be responsible not only for reimbursing the price of the coffeemaker, the so-called *direct damages*, but also for the value of the house and contents, the reasonably foreseeable consequential damages flowing from the defect.

As described in Chapter 7, warranty disclaimers can also produce business opportunities for developers willing to sign contracts to provide support for products that come without a warranty otherwise. However, these contracts are usually in addition to the open source license, not a part of it.

In light of the potential liability, disclaimers of warranties like that in the MIT License, described in Chapter 2, are commonly found in open source licenses. The use of such disclaimers is not necessarily foolproof, however. A contrary representation or agreement, particularly one made as part of a sale, may end up nullifying the disclaimer and result in liability attaching at least to the person making the relevant representation or entering into the particular agreement. In addition, state or federal law may limit the enforcement or the effectiveness of such disclaimers. Accordingly, licensors should consult with an experienced lawyer before relying on such disclaimers.

CHAPTER 2

The MIT, BSD, Apache, and Academic Free Licenses

The MIT and BSD Licenses were two of the earliest open source licenses. Because these licenses are relatively straightforward and illustrate some of the basic principles of open source licensing, they are described here first. The MIT (or X), BSD, and Apache Licenses are classic open source licensing software licenses and are used in many open source projects. The most well-known of these are probably the BSDNet and FreeBSD Unix-like operating systems and the Apache HTTP Server.

These licenses, as applied to the original licensed code, allow that code to be used in proprietary software and do not require that open source versions of the code be distributed. Code created under these licenses, or derived from such code, may go "closed" and developments can be made under that proprietary license, which are lost to the open source community. For the same reason, however, these licenses are very flexible and compatible with almost every form of open source license.

 If you're interested in licenses that keep code from being used in proprietary software, look ahead to Chapter 3.

The Academic Free License is a somewhat more elaborate license, embodying many of the same provisions found in the MIT, BSD, and Apache Licenses; in addition, it includes certain clauses addressing the application of patent rights to open source software.

The MIT (or X) License

The MIT License, the simplest license in this book, begins as follows:

> Copyright (c) <year> <copyright holders>
>
> Permission is hereby granted, free of charge, to any person obtaining a copy of this software and associated documentation files (the "Software"), to deal in the Software without restriction, including without limitation the rights to use, copy, modify,

merge, publish, distribute, sublicense, and/or sell copies of the Software, and to permit persons to whom the Software is furnished to do so, subject to the following conditions:

The <year> and <copyright holder> tags obviously refer to the date of publication of the code and the person in whom copyright is vested, which is generally going to be the creator of the code. This part of the license essentially surrenders all of the rights that the copyright holder typically receives, including, as discussed in the previous chapter, the exclusive right to commercially exploit the work and to develop derivative works from the work. In addition, the licensee may, but need not, permit its own licensees to exercise these same rights.

This grant of rights is subject to two conditions:

The above copyright notice and this permission notice shall be included in all copies or substantial portions of the Software.

And:

THE SOFTWARE IS PROVIDED "AS IS", WITHOUT WARRANTY OF ANY KIND, EXPRESS OR IMPLIED, INCLUDING BUT NOT LIMITED TO THE WARRANTIES OF MERCHANTABILITY, FITNESS FOR A PARTICULAR PURPOSE AND NONINFRINGEMENT. IN NO EVENT SHALL THE AUTHORS OR COPYRIGHT HOLDERS BE LIABLE FOR ANY CLAIM, DAMAGES OR OTHER LIABILITY, WHETHER IN AN ACTION OF CONTRACT, TORT OR OTHERWISE, ARISING FROM, OUT OF OR IN CONNECTION WITH THE SOFTWARE OR THE USE OR OTHER DEALINGS IN THE SOFTWARE. [all caps in original]

The first of these two conditions is almost universal in open source licensing and serves the straightforward and necessary purpose of alerting future users of the work of the restrictions on it. (Copyright laws used to require that copyrighted works carry an explicit notice in published forms to receive copyright protection.) The second of the two conditions provides the warranty disclaimer described in the previous chapter.

The BSD License

The BSD License, which is only slightly more restrictive than the MIT License, exists in a number of substantially similar forms. The following example is the UCB/LBL form, named after the University of California at Berkeley and the Lawrence Berkeley Laboratory.

This license, like the MIT License, begins:

Copyright (c) <YEAR>, <OWNER>

All rights reserved.

Redistribution and use in source and binary forms, with or without modification, are permitted provided that the following conditions are met:

The copyright notice and the attribution are substantially the same as those in the MIT License. Again, the license should reflect the actual year of copyright and the correct name of the creator.

Prior to 1999, the BSD License contained the following provision:

> All advertising materials mentioning features or use of this software must display the following acknowledgement: This product includes software developed by the University of California, Lawrence Berkeley Laboratory.

This provision seems relatively innocuous. It seems both reasonable and natural that the creator, having surrendered the exclusive right to commercially exploit a work, should receive credit not only in the acknowledgment of rights but in the advertising as well. It does not challenge the essential premises of open source, as it does not limit the scope of the use of the software in any direct way. Nonetheless, the pre-1999 BSD License sometimes causes problems because of this clause. The principles of open source endorse the commercial exploitation of software, including the sale of software, manuals, and support for profit. Such commercial exploitation very well may include advertising and when an open source project draws from a number of predecessors, the requirement of including such references can become a real burden. The BSD License, however, was amended in 1999 and this clause was removed. The University of California rescinded this clause and to the extent it may still be found in BSD files licensed by the University of California, it no longer has any legal effect.

The remainder of the license largely mirrors the effect of the provisions of the MIT License already described, by conditioning distribution—whether in modified form or not—on the maintenance of the conditions already described:

> Redistribution and use in source and binary forms, with or without modification, are permitted provided that the following conditions are met:
>
> Redistributions of source code must retain the above copyright notice, this list of conditions and the following disclaimer.
>
> Redistributions in binary form must reproduce the above copyright notice, this list of conditions and the following disclaimer in the documentation and/or other materials provided with the distribution.
>
> Neither the name of the <ORGANIZATION> nor the names of its contributors may be used to endorse or promote products derived from this software without specific prior written permission.

With the clause about advertising removed (formerly, the third clause in the license), the only substantial difference between this license and the MIT License is the non-attribution provision in the last clause. This provision requires prior permission for use of the name of the creator, and it protects the reputation of the creator from being explicitly associated with derivative versions of the program. Such restrictions permit creators to protect themselves from the injury to their reputations that can result from association with a defective or poorly written program, while still allowing others to use or modify a work.

The final provision is a disclaimer of warranties:

> THIS SOFTWARE IS PROVIDED BY THE REGENTS AND CONTRIBUTORS "AS IS" AND ANY EXPRESS OR IMPLIED WARRANTIES, INCLUDING, BUT NOT LIMITED TO, THE IMPLIED WARRANTIES OF MERCHANTABILITY AND FITNESS

FOR A PARTICULAR PURPOSE ARE DISCLAIMED. IN NO EVENT SHALL THE REGENTS OR CONTRIBUTORS BE LIABLE FOR ANY DIRECT, INDIRECT, INCIDENTAL, SPECIAL, EXEMPLARY, OR CONSEQUENTIAL DAMAGES (INCLUDING, BUT NOT LIMITED TO, PROCUREMENT OF SUBSTITUTE GOODS OR SERVICES; LOSS OF USE, DATA, OR PROFITS; OR BUSINESS INTERRUPTION) HOWEVER CAUSED AND ON ANY THEORY OF LIABILITY, WHETHER IN CONTRACT, STRICT LIABILITY, OR TORT (INCLUDING NEGLIGENCE OR OTHERWISE) ARISING IN ANY WAY OUT OF THE USE OF THIS SOFTWARE, EVEN IF ADVISED OF THE POSSIBILITY OF SUCH DAMAGE.

This provision specifically disclaims any express warranty, as well as the warranties of merchantability and fitness for a particular purpose, and it operates much like the disclaimer in the MIT License.

The Apache License, v1.1 and v2.0

The Apache License is very similar to the BSD and MIT Licenses already described. The Apache License, Version 1.1, follows substantially the same pattern as the BSD License in premising distribution and modification upon compliance with relatively unrestrictive terms. Version 2.0, a top-down rewriting of the license, was first published in 2004 and is described in detail later.

The Apache License, v1.1

Version 1.1 is slightly longer than the licenses discussed earlier in the chapter, but it operates in much the same way.

Copyright (c) 2000 The Apache Software Foundation.

All rights reserved.

Redistribution and use in source and binary forms, with or without modification, are permitted provided that the following conditions are met:

1. Redistributions of source code must retain the above copyright notice, this list of conditions and the following disclaimer.

2. Redistributions in binary form must reproduce the above copyright notice, this list of conditions and the following disclaimer in the documentation and/or other materials provided with the distribution.

The copyright notice, the clause introducing the limitations on distribution, and the first two limitations are substantially identical to those in the BSD License.

3. The end-user documentation included with the redistribution, if any, must include the following acknowledgment: "This product includes software developed by the Apache Software Foundation (http://www.apache.org/)."

Alternately, this acknowledgment may appear in the software itself, if and wherever such third-party acknowledgments normally appear.

The Apache License does not have the cumbersome advertising clause in the rescinded version of the BSD License, but it requires an acknowledgment of the creator's contribution to the work being distributed.

> 4. The names "Apache" and "Apache Software Foundation" must not be used to endorse or promote products derived from this software without prior written permission. For written permission, please contact apache@apache.org.

Like the BSD License, the Apache License contains a non-attribution provision, which protects the reputation of the creator.

> 5. Products derived from this software may not be called "Apache" nor may "Apache" appear in their name, without prior written permission of the Apache Software Foundation.

Like the provision just discussed, this provision prevents the possibly damaging association of the creator with derivative works created from the original code.

Finally, the Apache License includes a warranty disclaimer provision substantially similar to those already described.

> THIS SOFTWARE IS PROVIDED "AS IS" AND ANY EXPRESSED OR IMPLIED WARRANTIES, INCLUDING, BUT NOT LIMITED TO, THE IMPLIED WARRANTIES OF MERCHANTABILITY AND FITNESS FOR A PARTICULAR PURPOSE ARE DISCLAIMED. IN NO EVENT SHALL THE APACHE SOFTWARE FOUNDATION OR ITS CONTRIBUTORS BE LIABLE FOR ANY DIRECT, INDIRECT, INCIDENTAL, SPECIAL, EXEMPLARY, OR CONSEQUENTIAL DAMAGES (INCLUDING, BUT NOT LIMITED TO, PROCUREMENT OF SUBSTITUTE GOODS OR SERVICES; LOSS OF USE, DATA, OR PROFITS; OR BUSINESS INTERRUPTION) HOWEVER CAUSED AND ON ANY THEORY OF LIABILITY, WHETHER IN CONTRACT, STRICT LIABILITY, OR TORT (INCLUDING NEGLIGENCE OR OTHERWISE) ARISING IN ANY WAY OUT OF THE USE OF THIS SOFTWARE, EVEN IF ADVISED OF THE POSSIBILITY OF SUCH DAMAGE.

The license closes with clauses identifying the contributors to the code being distributed. These are not, strictly speaking, parts of the license as they impose no obligation on the user.

> This software consists of voluntary contributions made by many individuals on behalf of the Apache Software Foundation. For more information on the Apache Software Foundation, please see <http://www.apache.org/>.

> Portions of this software are based upon public domain software originally written at the National Center for Supercomputing Applications, University of Illinois, Urbana-Champaign.

The Apache License, v2.0

Released in January, 2004, the Apache License, v2.0, is a thorough revision of the Apache License. While the Apache License, v1.1, operates much like a BSD or MIT License with a non-endorsement provision barring the use of the Apache name without permission, v2.0 is a fuller and more complex license, laying out in more specific detail the rights granted. In particular, v2.0 differs in that it expressly addresses both patent rights being granted by the license and the use of other licenses for derivative works based on works licensed under v2.0. Perhaps most importantly, v2.0 provides for "Contributions" to the licensed work that are made with the express understanding that they will become part of the licensed work and will be governed by v2.0.

After the introductory phrases, definitions appear.

> Apache License
>
> Version 2.0, January 2004
>
> *http://www.apache.org/licenses/*
>
> TERMS AND CONDITIONS FOR USE, REPRODUCTION, AND DISTRIBUTION
>
> 1. Definitions.
>
> "License" shall mean the terms and conditions for use, reproduction and distribution as defined by Sections 1 through 9 of this document.
>
> "Licensor" shall mean the copyright owner or entity authorized by the copyright owner that is granting the License.

These terms are both self-explanatory. The "License" is this document. The Licensor is that person with ability and inclination to grant the rights described in the License.

> "Legal Entity" shall mean the union of the acting entity and all other entities that control, are controlled by, or are under common control with that entity. For the purposes of this definition, "control" means (i) the power, direct or indirect, to cause the direction or management of such entity, whether by contract or otherwise, or (ii) ownership of fifty percent (50%) or more of the outstanding shares, or (iii) beneficial ownership of such entity.

"Legal Entity", substantially similar to the Mozilla Public License described in the next chapter, provides that complexly structured organizations, such as many large corporations, are considered to be one entity for the purposes of this license.*

> "You" (or "Your") shall mean an individual or Legal Entity exercising permissions granted by this License.

"You" is equivalent to the licensee, i.e., the party that is bound by the license.

> "Source" form shall mean the preferred form for making modifications, including but not limited to software source code, documentation source, and configuration files.

This definition is a slightly more expansive form of the term "source code," expanded to include documentation, source, and configuration, including all information necessary or useful in modifying or creating a derivative work from a piece of code.

---

* As discussed in Chapter 3, such a provision may simplify compliance by the licensee with the terms of the license but may not be enforceable in every case.

"Object" form shall mean any form resulting from mechanical transformation or translation of a Source form, including but not limited to compiled object code, generated documentation, and conversions to other media types.

This definition is also a more expansive form of what is generally referred to as the executable form of code, compiled so that, when run, the code performs a function or functions.

"Work" shall mean the work of authorship, whether in Source or Object form, made available under the License, as indicated by a copyright notice that is included in or attached to the work (an example is provided in the Appendix below).

This term "Work" is substantially similar to work as that term is used in copyright law and throughout this book. "Work" is the copyrighted work that is the subject of the license.

"Derivative Works" shall mean any work, whether in Source or Object form, that is based on (or derived from) the Work and for which the editorial revisions, annotations, elaborations, or other modifications represent, as a whole, an original work of authorship. For the purposes of this License, Derivative Works shall not include works that remain separable from, or merely link (or bind by name) to the interfaces of, the Work and Derivative Works thereof.

This definition, "Derivative Works," is also substantially similar to the term derivative work as used in copyright law and in this book. It means a work that is a modification of or otherwise derived from the original work. This definition excludes certain combinations of works: when another work merely links to the interfaces of the "Work" it does not become a "Derivative Work," as that term is used in this license. This is an important distinction, as specific limitations apply under the License to Derivative Works, explained later.

"Contribution" shall mean any work of authorship, including the original version of the Work and any modifications or additions to that Work or Derivative Works thereof, that is intentionally submitted to Licensor for inclusion in the Work by the copyright owner or by an individual or Legal Entity authorized to submit on behalf of the copyright owner. For the purposes of this definition, "submitted" means any form of electronic, verbal, or written communication sent to the Licensor or its representatives, including but not limited to communication on electronic mailing lists, source code control systems, and issue tracking systems that are managed by, or on behalf of, the Licensor for the purpose of discussing and improving the Work, but excluding communication that is conspicuously marked or otherwise designated in writing by the copyright owner as "Not a Contribution."

A "Contribution" is a specific modification to the Work that is provided to the original Licensor for the explicit purpose of being included in the Work. A Licensee under the License may choose to modify the Work and to create a separate Derivative Work subject to the terms of the License. A licensee may also choose to submit that modification to the Licensor in the form of a Contribution, and, if accepted, that Contribution becomes part of the original Work, under the copyright and control of the Licensor. The original work with any such "Contributions," obviously, will continue to be licensed under v2.0.

"Contributor" shall mean Licensor and any individual or Legal Entity on behalf of whom a Contribution has been received by Licensor and subsequently incorporated within the Work.

This is a common sense reflection of Contribution: a Licensee who makes a Contribution is a Contributor. The original Licensor is also a Contributor, as that term is used in the License.

2. Grant of Copyright License.

Subject to the terms and conditions of this License, each Contributor hereby grants to You a perpetual, worldwide, non-exclusive, no-charge, royalty-free, irrevocable copyright license to reproduce, prepare Derivative Works of, publicly display, publicly perform, sublicense, and distribute the Work and such Derivative Works in Source or Object form.

This provision is, as described in its title, the grant of copyright license. The license granted is irrevocable and royalty free and grants Licensees all the rights available under copyright, including the right to reproduce and distribute the Work and Derivative Works. As part of making a Contribution, a Contributor has consented to making a grant of rights as to the Contribution on the same terms as the original Work.

Unlike the BSD, MIT, and the Apache License, v1.1, the Apache License, v2.0, also explicitly grants rights under a patent claims that may exist in the original Work.

3. Grant of Patent License.

Subject to the terms and conditions of this License, each Contributor hereby grants to You a perpetual, worldwide, non-exclusive, no-charge, royalty-free, irrevocable (except as stated in this section) patent license to make, have made, use, offer to sell, sell, import, and otherwise transfer the Work, where such license applies only to those patent claims licensable by such Contributor that are necessarily infringed by their Contribution(s) alone or by combination of their Contribution(s) with the Work to which such Contribution(s) was submitted. If You institute patent litigation against any entity (including a cross-claim or counterclaim in a lawsuit) alleging that the Work or a Contribution incorporated within the Work constitutes direct or contributory patent infringement, then any patent licenses granted to You under this License for that Work shall terminate as of the date such litigation is filed.

This patent license only grants the irrevocable, royalty-free license to the extent that such patent rights are necessary to use the original Work (and Contributions thereto). This grant does not extend to patent rights that may inhere in the Work separate and apart from the Work itself. Like the Academic Free License, described in the next section, in the event that a Licensee initiates patent litigation against any Contributor on the basis that any part of the Work infringes on a patent, the License terminates as to that Licensee as of the date that litigation is filed. This prevents the situation in which a party is getting the benefit of the rights to the Work under the License while at the same time suing the Licensor or Contributor under a claim of patent infringement.[*]

---

[*] This treatment of patent litigation renders v2.0 incompatible with the GNU General Public License described in the next chapter. See *http://www.apache.org/licenses/GPL-compatibility.html*.

Redistribution of the Work or Derivative Works created by the licensee therefrom is permitted to that licensee subject to certain, relatively limited, restrictions.

> 4. Redistribution.
>
> You may reproduce and distribute copies of the Work or Derivative Works thereof in any medium, with or without modifications, and in Source or Object form, provided that You meet the following conditions:
>
> > 1. You must give any other recipients of the Work or Derivative Works a copy of this License; and
> >
> > 2. You must cause any modified files to carry prominent notices stating that You changed the files; and
> >
> > 3. You must retain, in the Source form of any Derivative Works that You distribute, all copyright, patent, trademark, and attribution notices from the Source form of the Work, excluding those notices that do not pertain to any part of the Derivative Works; and
> >
> > 4. If the Work includes a "NOTICE" text file as part of its distribution, then any Derivative Works that You distribute must include a readable copy of the attribution notices contained within such NOTICE file, excluding those notices that do not pertain to any part of the Derivative Works, in at least one of the following places: within a NOTICE text file distributed as part of the Derivative Works; within the Source form or documentation, if provided along with the Derivative Works; or, within a display generated by the Derivative Works, if and wherever such third-party notices normally appear. The contents of the NOTICE file are for informational purposes only and do not modify the License. You may add Your own attribution notices within Derivative Works that You distribute, alongside or as an addendum to the NOTICE text from the Work, provided that such additional attribution notices cannot be construed as modifying the License.

These terms give fair notice to the licensee's distributees—those people receiving a copy of the Work or a Derivative Work from a licensee—of the terms of the license applicable to the Work; the modifications, if any, made to the Work; the copyright, patent, and trademark notices present in the original Work; and, if applicable, the Notice file distributed with the Work.

The last paragraph of this section makes explicit what is implicit in the MIT, BSD, and Apache License, v1.1, which is that the creator of a Derivative Work based on the Work may license that Derivative Work under a license other than that applicable to the original work.

> You may add Your own copyright statement to Your modifications and may provide additional or different license terms and conditions for use, reproduction, or distribution of Your modifications, or for any such Derivative Works as a whole, provided Your use, reproduction, and distribution of the Work otherwise complies with the conditions stated in this License.

The application of different license terms (which may include proprietary license terms) is permitted so long as the terms of that license comply with the License. There is no requirement that the Licensor of such a Derivative Work make available the source code for the Derivative Work or otherwise license it under an open source or free software license.

---

5. Submission of Contributions.

Unless You explicitly state otherwise, any Contribution intentionally submitted for inclusion in the Work by You to the Licensor shall be under the terms and conditions of this License, without any additional terms or conditions. Notwithstanding the above, nothing herein shall supersede or modify the terms of any separate license agreement you may have executed with Licensor regarding such Contributions.

This section makes clear what was implicit in the definition of Contribution already described. By making a Contribution, the Contributor agrees that the Contribution shall be governed by the terms of the License unless another, specific agreement is made with the Licensor.

6. Trademarks.

This License does not grant permission to use the trade names, trademarks, service marks, or product names of the Licensor, except as required for reasonable and customary use in describing the origin of the Work and reproducing the content of the NOTICE file.

As was the case with the Apache License, v1.1, licensees are not granted any trademark rights and are prohibited from associating the name of the Licensor with their Derivative Works (or their distribution of the original Work), except as necessary to give notice of the source of the work.

7. Disclaimer of Warranty.

Unless required by applicable law or agreed to in writing, Licensor provides the Work (and each Contributor provides its Contributions) on an "AS IS" BASIS, WITHOUT WARRANTIES OR CONDITIONS OF ANY KIND, either express or implied, including, without limitation, any warranties or conditions of TITLE, NON-INFRINGEMENT, MERCHANTABILITY, or FITNESS FOR A PARTICULAR PURPOSE. You are solely responsible for determining the appropriateness of using or redistributing the Work and assume any risks associated with Your exercise of permissions under this License.

8. Limitation of Liability.

In no event and under no legal theory, whether in tort (including negligence), contract, or otherwise, unless required by applicable law (such as deliberate and grossly negligent acts) or agreed to in writing, shall any Contributor be liable to You for damages, including any direct, indirect, special, incidental, or consequential damages of any character arising as a result of this License or out of the use or inability to use the Work (including but not limited to damages for loss of goodwill, work stoppage, computer failure or malfunction, or any and all other commercial damages or losses), even if such Contributor has been advised of the possibility of such damages.

These two provisions operate the same way as those provisions in the MIT, BSD, and Apache License, v1.1, in disclaiming warranties and limiting liabilities, except under circumstances where a Contributor has explicitly undertaken to provide a warranty.

9. Accepting Warranty or Additional Liability.

While redistributing the Work or Derivative Works thereof, You may choose to offer, and charge a fee for, acceptance of support, warranty, indemnity, or other liability obligations and/or rights consistent with this License. However, in accepting such obligations, You may act only on Your own behalf and on Your sole responsibility, not on behalf of any other Contributor, and only if You agree to indemnify, defend, and hold each Contributor harmless for any liability incurred by, or claims asserted against, such Contributor by reason of your accepting any such warranty or additional liability.

This section explicitly permits a licensee to enter into a separate warranty arrangement with others for the Work or Derivative Works. This makes clear what is implicit in Sections 7 and 8, that such a warranty obligation only extends to the party making that warranty and not to any Contributor. Any licensee making such a warranty agrees to "indemnify, defend, and hold harmless" any Contributor in connection with any claim against such a Contributor. This means that the party giving the warranty agrees to pay any and all costs associated with defending such a claim, including attorney's fees and the costs of paying a judgment, if a judgment is entered against such a Contributor.

Following the end of the "terms and conditions" is a short appendix with a boilerplate notice indicating that a given Work is subject to the terms of this License.

The Apache License, v2.0, operates substantially like the MIT, BSD, and Apache License, v1.1, with some additional benefits. First, it makes clear that the licensing of Derivative Works under other licenses is permitted so long as the terms of the Apache License, v2.0, are complied with. This is implied but not specifically spelled out in the MIT and BSD Licenses. Second, the Apache License, v2.0, provides clearly marked pathways for both open development and non-open development of code licensed under it. By making a Contribution, a licensee is agreeing to have that addition to the Work licensed under the same, open, terms applicable to the original Work. Particularly for dynamic well-organized open developments like Apache, this is likely a common result for modifications to the Work. But there is no obligation to make a Contribution: licensees are free to take their Derivative Work and license it under a different license. While this approach does not resolve the tension between open and closed development of software, at least it makes what the options are clear.

The Academic Free License

The Academic Free License is substantially similar to the Apache License, v1.1, in forbidding claims of endorsement by the work's creator, in requiring attribution to the creator, in disclaiming warranties, and in permitting distribution of the original work and derivative works subject only to certain limitations. The Academic Free License adds four more provisions that are not in the Apache or BSD Licenses, two of them pertaining to patent law, and two of them governing choice of law and shifting of attorneys fees.

As discussed in Chapter 1, the intellectual property rights at play in software licenses derive for the most part from copyright, protecting the expression of particular ideas. The Academic Free License also addresses the case in which a patent holder chooses to permit the open source use of that patent.

Paragraph 1 of the Academic Free License (v2.0) provides:[*]

> 1) **Grant of Copyright License.** Licensor hereby grants You a world-wide, royalty-free, non-exclusive, perpetual, sublicenseable license to do the following: a) to reproduce the Original Work in copies; b) to prepare derivative works ("Derivative Works") based upon the Original Work; c) to distribute copies of the Original Work and Derivative Works to the public; d) to perform the Original Work publicly; and e) to display the Original Work publicly.

This is essentially the same bundle of rights granted by the Apache and BSD Licenses already discussed. Paragraph 2 distinguishes the Academic License by making it clear that patent claims owned or controlled by the Licensor are licensed to those working with this software.

> 2) **Grant of Patent License.** Licensor hereby grants You a world-wide, royalty-free, non-exclusive, perpetual, sublicenseable license, under patent claims owned or controlled by the Licensor that are embodied in the Original Work as furnished by the Licensor, to make, use, sell and offer for sale the Original Work and Derivative Works.

This paragraph grants the licensee a license to exercise patent rights without payment of royalties, so long as a) those patent rights are held by the licensor, and b) those patent rights are exercised in connection with the Original Work or a Derivative Work. Accordingly, this may be an appropriate license (or license provision) to be used for a work that its creator intends to be open source licensed that includes property subject to one or more patents.

While this license explicitly provides for the granting of rights under both copyright and patent, some of the licenses previously described in this book (and some of the ones that follow) implicitly provide such a grant. Because the granting of patent rights involves a number of issues distinct from those in granting rights under copyright law, you may want to review the discussion of patents in Chapter 1.

Paragraph 3 of the license states that the Licensor will make the source code of the licensed program available in some form, a term that is common to the open source licenses described later in this book.

> 3) **Grant of Source Code License.** The term "Source Code" means the preferred form of the Original Work for making modifications to it and all available documentation describing how to modify the Original Work. Licensor hereby agrees to provide a machine-readable copy of the Source Code of the Original Work along with each copy of the Original Work that Licensor distributes. Licensor reserves the right to satisfy this obligation by placing a machine-readable copy of the Source Code in an information repository reasonably calculated to permit inexpensive and convenient access by You for as long as Licensor continues to distribute the Original Work, and by publishing the address of that information repository in a notice immediately following the copyright notice that applies to the Original Work.

---

[*] The text of the Acadmic License can be found at *http://www.opensource.org/licenses/afl-2.0.php*. It is copyright 2003 by Lawrence E. Rosen.

Paragraph 4 of the license delineates the limitations of the license and includes a non-endorsement provision similar to the one in the Apache License.

> 4) **Exclusions From License Grant.** Neither the names of Licensor, nor the names of any contributors to the Original Work, nor any of their trademarks or service marks, may be used to endorse or promote products derived from this Original Work without express prior written permission of the Licensor. Nothing in this License shall be deemed to grant any rights to trademarks, copyrights, patents, trade secrets or any other intellectual property of Licensor except as expressly stated herein. No patent license is granted to make, use, sell or offer to sell embodiments of any patent claims other than the licensed claims defined in Section 2. No right is granted to the trademarks of Licensor even if such marks are included in the Original Work. Nothing in this License shall be interpreted to prohibit Licensor from licensing under different terms from this License any Original Work that Licensor otherwise would have a right to license.
>
> 5) This section intentionally omitted.

Paragraph 5 speaks for itself. Paragraph 6 requires attribution of the Licensor in the source code of any derivative works. The utility of this paragraph is limited by the fact that the Academic License may not, as explained later, require Licensees to distribute source code along with derivative works.

> 6) **Attribution Rights.** You must retain, in the Source Code of any Derivative Works that You create, all copyright, patent or trademark notices from the Source Code of the Original Work, as well as any notices of licensing and any descriptive text identified therein as an "Attribution Notice." You must cause the Source Code for any Derivative Works that You create to carry a prominent Attribution Notice reasonably calculated to inform recipients that You have modified the Original Work.

Paragraphs 7 and 8 disclaim warranties and limit liabilities in ways substantially similar to provisions in the MIT, BSD, and Apache Licenses. The first full sentence of Paragraph 7 explicitly warrants that the copyright and patent rights granted by the Licensor are owned by the Licensor.

> 7) **Warranty of Provenance and Disclaimer of Warranty.** Licensor warrants that the copyright in and to the Original Work and the patent rights granted herein by Licensor are owned by the Licensor or are sublicensed to You under the terms of this License with the permission of the contributor(s) of those copyrights and patent rights. Except as expressly stated in the immediately proceeding sentence, the Original Work is provided under this License on an "AS IS" BASIS and WITHOUT WARRANTY, either express or implied, including, without limitation, the warranties of NON-INFRINGEMENT, MERCHANTABILITY or FITNESS FOR A PARTICULAR PURPOSE. THE ENTIRE RISK AS TO THE QUALITY OF THE ORIGINAL WORK IS WITH YOU. This DISCLAIMER OF WARRANTY constitutes an essential part of this License. No license to Original Work is granted hereunder except under this disclaimer.
>
> 8) **Limitation of Liability.** Under no circumstances and under no legal theory, whether in tort (including negligence), contract, or otherwise, shall the Licensor be liable to any person for any direct, indirect, special, incidental, or consequential damages of any character arising as a result of this License or the use of the Original Work including, without limitation, damages for loss of goodwill, work stoppage, computer failure or

malfunction, or any and all other commercial damages or losses. This limitation of liability shall not apply to liability for death or personal injury resulting from Licensor's negligence to the extent applicable law prohibits such limitation. Some jurisdictions do not allow the exclusion or limitation of incidental or consequential damages, so this exclusion and limitation may not apply to You.

The next paragraph, Paragraph 9, is an example of a license provision imposing, or attempting to impose, a generational limitation that puts substantial limitations on the licensing of derivative works, as opposed to requiring an attribution or prohibiting putative endorsements. Because of ambiguous drafting, it is not immediately apparent what this paragraph is attempting to accomplish, but it appears that the requirement that it imposes on licensees to ensure that licensees of their own, derivative, works are similarly bound is not as stringent as that of other licenses discussed later in this book. The paragraph begins:

> 9) **Acceptance and Termination.** If You distribute copies of the Original Work or a Derivative Work, You must make a reasonable effort under the circumstances to obtain the express assent of recipients to the terms of this License.

There are problems with this first sentence. First, it is not immediately clear that the licensor intends that the provisions of this license also govern the derivative works created by the licensee and derivative works created by the licensee's licensees and so forth. This sentence should probably be interpreted to mean that licensees assent to the proposition that the original work is in fact governed by the license; not necessarily that any derivative work be governed by the terms of that license. Second, and perhaps no less importantly, this sentence requires only that the licensee use "reasonable effort under the circumstances" to obtain assent of future licensees to the terms of the license, with regard both to the original and derivative works. A putative licensee, even one generation removed, could argue that because a previous licensee had not communicated these restrictions, the putative licensee believed that the work was bound by fewer than all the restrictions of the license or by no restrictions at all. The following sentence attempts to address this second problem.

> Nothing else but this License (or another written agreement between Licensor and You) grants You permission to create Derivative Works based upon the Original Work or to exercise any of the rights granted in Section 1 herein, and any attempt to do so except under the terms of this License (or another written agreement between Licensor and You) is expressly prohibited by U.S. copyright law, the equivalent laws of other countries, and by international treaty.

As already noted, the statutory rights created by copyright bar any but limited use of a given work. The fact that a particular work is open source licensed does not remove its protection by the copyright laws. As the second sentence of this paragraph states, without the grant of rights by the license (along with the restrictions coupled thereto), no use of the copyrighted work is permitted. This "saves" the license and supports the argument that a putative licensee is bound by the terms of the license even if that licensee has not expressly assented to the terms of the license. Without some knowledge of the license, the putative licensee would have no reason to believe that he or she had any right at all to the work. Accordingly, such a putative licensee could be presumed to be "on notice" of the possibility of license restrictions and accordingly could be found to have legal liabilty for violating the terms of the license if he or she does not make sufficient efforts to determine the restrictions of the license. As discussed in Chapter 6, this provision, and similar ones in the licenses, is critical to the legal enforcement of open source licenses. The final sentence of this paragraph largely reiterates the effect of the second sentence: that use of the work is bound by the terms of the license and that exercise of rights under the license indicates consent to the restrictions imposed by it:

> Therefore, by exercising any of the rights granted to You in Section 1 herein, You indicate Your acceptance of this License and all of its terms and conditions.

Paragraph 10 creates a disincentive for licensees to sue licensors for patent infringement. It is questionable how much this adds to the license, insofar as it seems unlikely that any person believing that he had or would have a legitimate claim for patent infringement against the creator of the work would use that work. Nonetheless, the license includes it, perhaps to avoid the unlikely, but undeniably awkward, situation in which the same person is suing the licensor and profiting in some manner from the use of the licensor's work.

> 10) **Termination for Patent Action.** This License shall terminate automatically and You may no longer exercise any of the rights granted to You by this License as of the date You commence an action, including a cross-claim or counterclaim, for patent infringement (i) against Licensor with respect to a patent applicable to software or (ii) against any entity with respect to a patent applicable to the Original Work (but excluding combinations of the Original Work with other software or hardware).

The remainder of the license provisions consists largely of terms common to commercial contracts. Paragraph 11 provides for choice of the jurisdiction in which suits under the license may be brought:

> 11) **Jurisdiction, Venue and Governing Law.** Any action or suit relating to this License may be brought only in the courts of a jurisdiction wherein the Licensor resides or in which Licensor conducts its primary business, and under the laws of that jurisdiction excluding its conflict-of-law provisions. The application of the United Nations Convention on Contracts for the International Sale of Goods is expressly excluded. Any use of the Original Work outside the scope of this License or after its termination shall be subject to the requirements and penalties of the U.S. Copyright Act, 17 U.S.C. 101 et seq., the equivalent laws of other countries, and international treaty. This section shall survive the termination of this License.

In general, choice of venue and choice of law provisions specifically identify the court and law that govern. For example, a typical provision might specify that "Claims arising under this contract may only be brought before courts of competent jurisdiction within the State of New York. The law governing the resolution of such claims shall be the law of the State of New York without giving effect to the choice of laws provisions thereof." Because of the open source nature of the license, however, and so that derivative works can be licensed under it without changing the text, the license tracks the jurisdiction in which suits can be brought (and the law that applies to the interpretation of the license) to follow the place in which the licensor resides or conducts its primary business. While this open-ended provision is somewhat problematic in that a licensee may face some uncertainty because the residence of a given licensor might be unknown to the licensee, it seems likely that this provision would likely be enforced by a court as long as the licensor's residence could be readily determined.

Paragraph 12 contains a provision also fairly common in commercial contracts:

> 12) **Attorneys Fees.** In any action to enforce the terms of this License or seeking damages relating thereto, the prevailing party shall be entitled to recover its costs and expenses, including, without limitation, reasonable attorneys' fees and costs incurred in connection with such action, including any appeal of such action. This section shall survive the termination of this License.

In all United States jurisdictions, parties to a suit bear their own costs for bringing the suit in most cases. Fee shifting provisions like this one, however, are generally enforced. While there is considerable debate about the social utility of this rule, known as the American rule (in contrast to the British rule, in which the prevailing party has historically been able to collect attorneys fees along with other damages), the balancing of the benefits of it are beyond the scope of this book. This provision is a fairly common one in contracts, but it has nothing to do with open source, except perhaps that it may encourage licensors to more vigorously pursue licensees who clearly violate the terms of a given license.

Paragraph 13 is also typical to commercial contracts, and it makes clear that the license is the only agreement between the parties.

> 13) **Miscellaneous.** This License represents the complete agreement concerning the subject matter hereof. If any provision of this License is held to be unenforceable, such provision shall be reformed only to the extent necessary to make it enforceable.

Such provisions, known as "merger clauses," are generally included in contracts to make clear that pre-existing written agreements or oral agreements are superseded by the particular contract. This provision operates on an open source license as it would in any other agreement. The second sentence is a severability clause, preserving the effect of other sections of the license if a section is found to be invalid.

Paragraph 14 defines "You" as it is used in the license to include agents of the licensee or other persons within the control of the licensee.

> 14) **Definition of "You" in This License.** "You" throughout this License, whether in upper or lower case, means an individual or a legal entity exercising rights under, and complying with all of the terms of, this License. For legal entities, "You" includes any entity that controls, is controlled by, or is under common control with you. For purposes of this definition, "control" means (i) the power, direct or indirect, to cause the direction or management of such entity, whether by contract or otherwise, or (ii) ownership of fifty percent (50%) or more of the outstanding shares, or (iii) beneficial ownership of such entity.

This provision is probably not necessary. To the extent that any person or entity not under the control of a particular licensee exercises any of the rights described in Paragraph 1 of the license, they would likely be found to be directly bound by the license. The fact that they are associated with or controlled by another licensee would accordingly not matter.*

Finally, Paragraph 15 of the license provides that:

> 15) **Right to Use.** You may use the Original Work in all ways not otherwise restricted or conditioned by this License or by law, and Licensor promises not to interfere with or be responsible for such uses by You.

This paragraph adds no restrictions on licensees not already articulated by the license, but rather adds an additional restriction on the licensor, i.e., non-interference in uses permitted by the license. This is a somewhat problematic provision, as it could be interpreted to create legal liability for licensors in situations in which the drafter of this license probably did not intend to create liability. For example, a licensor whose work competes directly with that of a licensee could, at least in theory, be liable for "interference" with sales of the licensed work. While this is probably unlikely, it is not impossible that such a lawsuit could be maintained. It is almost certainly not the result contemplated by the drafter of the license.

The final un-numbered paragraph of the license sets out that while licensors can use the license, they cannot modify its terms without permission.

> This license is Copyright (C) 2003 Lawrence E. Rosen. All rights reserved. Permission is hereby granted to copy and distribute this license without modification. This license may not be modified without the express written permission of its copyright owner.

Application and Philosophy

All of these licenses have been used in practice, both in licensing software maintained in the open source community and in providing the basis for commercial applications of programs derived from open source models. The BSD, MIT, and Apache Licenses, longer established and more frequently adopted than the Academic Free License, provide the examples described in this section.

Each of these three licenses has contributed to the widespread commercial adoption of the programs they license, frequently (though not always) through incorporation into products distributed under a proprietary license. This is completely consistent with the language and intent of the licenses. This also reflects their place of origin. For example, both Berkeley Unix and the X Window System were research projects; the goal of their creators was to explore technology, to provide a proof-of-concept implementation, and then to permit others to build on that work. Commercial applications readily followed successful implementations of research ideas.

---

* This provision is discussed further in Chapter 3 in connection with the Mozilla Public License.

BSD Unix became the basis for commercial versions of Unix ranging from Sun's Solaris to Apple's Mac OS X. BSD-derived proprietary versions of Unix outstripped the commercially licensed AT&T versions relatively quickly, and they dominated the commercial Unix market until the 1990s when Unix was challenged by GPL-licensed Linux distribution. The TCP/IP software stack that was part of the Berkeley networking release became the basis for almost all commercial TCP/IP stacks, including Microsoft's. The X Window System became the standard GUI platform for the Unix workstation market, displacing Sun's proprietary NeWS windowing system. In addition, even as these commercial implementations became available at the same time, open sourced implementations continued to be widely available and accessible for modifications and improvements by programmers.

Despite setbacks from a lawsuit from AT&T that was ultimately settled out of court in 1992, Berkeley Unix still has many million installations, running such well-known sites as Yahoo!, and it continues to be modified and improved. Moreover, and partly as a result, later commercial entrants such as Apple have tried to keep a better defined line between the open source foundations of their programs and their proprietary extensions.

Other individual parts of Berkeley Unix continued to flourish as parts of the free software ecosystem. For example BIND, the Berkeley Internet Name Daemon, continued to be maintained by its original author, Paul Vixie* under the auspices of the Internet Software Consortium. Despite many commercial implementations, the open source version of BIND continues to be the definitive version that runs the Internet's Domain Name System (DNS), the single most mission-critical piece of software in the Internet infrastructure. Sendmail, another piece of Berkeley Unix, continues to be maintained by its creator, Eric Allman, who founded a company in 1998 to commercialize the software. He adopted a hybrid proprietary/open source strategy, completely consistent with the licenses, in which some new features of interest to commercial clients are released in proprietary software, while the open source version is also still maintained.

In short, research-style licenses, like the BSD and MIT Licenses, are ideal for situations in which you want wide deployment of your ideas and do not care whether this results in open source software or proprietary software. Because of their openness to commercial use, the programs they license can be, by many metrics, more influential. Red Hat maintains a Linux business that makes approximately $90 million in annual revenues, while Sun Microsystems has revenues of approximately $18 billion. There are literally billions of dollars of economic activity associated just with the Internet software stack originally released under the Berkeley License.

Nonetheless, the very success of the commercial developments premised on programs distributed under these licenses could be said to undermine the purpose of

---

* The specifications for this program were written by Paul Mockapetris.

open source licensing. The argument could be made, for example, that the widespread adoption of commercial versions of such programs discourages open source development and encourages the creation of code closed off to the open source community by proprietary licenses. It could be regarded as a failure that the highly sophisticated Solaris software was developed as proprietary software,* that Microsoft was able to build a version of MIT's Kerberos security software that contains proprietary extensions for communicating with Microsoft servers, or that Microsoft was able to build so easily on the Internet infrastructure software.

It cannot be said, however, that such a result is inconsistent with the text and the intent of these licenses or that such types of commercial uses were not foreseen by their drafters. The original BSD and X Window System developers intended their software to be used in this way. Some of these developers even built their own companies based on the open source software that they had originally written. Bill Joy was one of the founders of Sun Microsystems; Eric Allman was able to found Sendmail, Inc.

The one well-known case in which the software authors were unhappy with their choice was the licensing of the MIT Kerberos security program. As Microsoft appeared to embrace and extend Kerberos, the authors wished they had used a more stringent license like the GPL. Of course, in that case, Microsoft would have chosen another basis for their security software, and Kerberos would have been less widely used. Nonetheless, the authors may have reasonably felt that a more restrictive license might have better protected the development of the software that they had anticipated.

Moreover, at least for certain types of programs, the nature of the function performed by the software makes additional license restrictions unnecessary to maintain an open development model. The Apache license provides one such example. While there have been several proprietary commercializations of Apache (such as the SSL-enabled Stronghold), the free version of Apache has retained its dominant market share as the result of two dynamics:

1. Strong branding. The Apache License's requirement that derived works cannot use the Apache name gives a significant degree of protection.
2. Standards-compliance. Because Apache is communications-oriented software, its need to adhere to standards such as the HTTP protocol prevents proprietary extensions. Of course, this protection remains only as long as Apache or other standards-compliant web servers retain dominant market share. Were Apache to lose its dominant market share, its protocols would no longer control, and this advantage would disappear.

---

* Sun has recently announced that it will release Solaris under an open source license, a major victory for open source.

These licenses, like all open source and free software licenses, permit forking and the subsequent fragmentation of projects. The multiple, and mutually incompatible, versions of BSD (FreeBSD, NetBSD, OpenBSD) provide one such example. However, this is less a result of the dynamic of the license itself than it is of the complex social dynamic involved in large software projects. The original BSD project leaders moved on to other activities, and the software was taken up by new people with different goals. This dynamic is discussed in more detail in Chapter 7.

CHAPTER 3
The GPL, LGPL, and Mozilla Licenses

The licenses described in this chapter are very different from those described in Chapter 2. These licenses impose substantial limitations on those who create and distribute derivative works based on works that use these licenses. The GNU General Public License (the GPL License) explicitly requires that derivative works be distributed under the terms of the GPL License and also that derivative works may *only* be permitted to be distributed under the terms of the license. The Mozilla License imposes different and less restrictive terms on the licensing of derivative works. Both of these licenses (and a variation of the GPL License) are described in some detail in the following sections.

Before going into detailed descriptions of these licenses and their effects, it's a good idea to re-examine the limitations imposed by the licenses described in the previous chapter, if only for contrast.

The MIT License, probably the simplest of those licenses, imposes almost no restrictions on licensees and no meaningful restriction at all on licensees distributing derivative works. When the original work or "substantial portions" of it are distributed, the licensee is required to include a copyright notice and the notice giving permission to potential licensees of their rights to use the work. The licensee is not even required to include the disclaimer of warranties that was part of the original license. (Such licensees may, however, have good reason to include that disclaimer—in particular, to protect themselves from potential liability.)

The MIT License does not impose even these restrictions on licensees who choose not to distribute it or "substantial portions" of it, but rather only works derived from it. Such licensees need not include the copyright notice, the disclaimer of warranties, or the permission notice. As described in the previous chapter, this allows the creator of a derivative work to license that new work in any way that he may choose, whether under a proprietary license or under the MIT or another open source license.

By contrast, the BSD License, both pre- and post-1999, imposes explicit limitations on distribution of both the original and derivative works.* These limitations include the inclusion of the enumerated terms of the license so that these limitations will also govern the use of the derivative work: the non-endorsement provision, the copyright notice, the acknowledgment of the creator of the original work, and the inclusion of the disclaimer of warranties. These enumerated limitations, however, do not require that the creator of the derivative work license under terms no more restrictive than those applicable to the original work. Accordingly, as noted in the previous chapter, so long as these conditions are complied with, the creator of the derivative work may then license that work under a proprietary license, under another open source license, or under the BSD License, so long as the terms of that license do not conflict with the limitations of the BSD License. There is no requirement, for example, that the creator of the derivative work make the source code of that work available to others.

The licenses discussed in this chapter impose much more specific limitations on the way in which derivative works may be licensed. Essentially, by using a work licensed under the GPL, the LGPL, or the Mozilla Licenses, the licensee is agreeing not only to respect those limitations with regard to his or her own use of the licensed work but to impose those limitations (and with regard to the GPL and LGPL Licenses *only* those limitations) on licensees of any derivative work that he or she may choose to create from the original work.

GNU General Public License

The GNU's General Public License, or GPL, is one of the foundation open source licenses. Created by the Free Software Foundation (FSF), which has made many contributions to open source coding, it is the preferred license for projects authorized by the FSF, including the GNU Emacs Editor and the GNU C Compiler, among literally scores of others, including the GNU/Linux kernel.

The intentions behind the license and the premise underlying it are explained in the license's preamble, which is included here in its entirety. The preamble follows the copyright notice,† and a notice that prevents modifications, ironically enough, to the license itself: "Everyone is permitted to copy and distribute verbatim copies of this license document, but changing it is not allowed." While the license permits the creation of derivative works from the licensed *code*, it does not permit the creation of derivative licenses from the license itself.

---

* The BSD license phrases this as "Redistribution and use [of the work] in source and binary forms, with or without modification," a clause that seems intended to govern the distribution of both the original and derivative works. Whether a derivative work that incorporated only a small part of the BSD licensed work could reasonably be described as a "work . . . with modification" is, admittedly, arguable. A better reading of the license would bring derivative works within the enumerated restrictions, as this appears to be the intent of the license's drafters.

† The license described is Version 2.0 of the GPL and is Copyright © 1989, 1991 Free Software Foundation, Inc., 59 Temple Place, Suite 330, Boston, MA 02111-1307 USA.

Preamble

The licenses for most software are designed to take away your freedom to share and change it. By contrast, the GNU General Public License is intended to guarantee your freedom to share and change free software—to make sure the software is free for all its users. This General Public License applies to most of the Free Software Foundation's software and to any other program whose authors commit to using it. (Some other Free Software Foundation software is covered by the GNU Library General Public License* instead.) You can apply it to your programs, too.

When we speak of free software, we are referring to freedom, not price. Our General Public Licenses are designed to make sure that you have the freedom to distribute copies of free software (and charge for this service if you wish), that you receive source code or can get it if you want it, that you can change the software or use pieces of it in new free programs; and that you know you can do these things.

To protect your rights, we need to make restrictions that forbid anyone to deny you these rights or to ask you to surrender the rights. These restrictions translate to certain responsibilities for you if you distribute copies of the software, or if you modify it.

For example, if you distribute copies of such a program, whether gratis or for a fee, you must give the recipients all the rights that you have. You must make sure that they, too, receive or can get the source code. And you must show them these terms so they know their rights.

We protect your rights with two steps: (1) copyright the software, and (2) offer you this license which gives you legal permission to copy, distribute and/or modify the software.

Also, for each author's protection and ours, we want to make certain that everyone understands that there is no warranty for this free software. If the software is modified by someone else and passed on, we want its recipients to know that what they have is not the original, so that any problems introduced by others will not reflect on the original authors' reputations.

Finally, any free program is threatened constantly by software patents. We wish to avoid the danger that redistributors of a free program will individually obtain patent licenses, in effect making the program proprietary. To prevent this, we have made it clear that any patent must be licensed for everyone's free use or not licensed at all.

The precise terms and conditions for copying, distribution and modification follow.

This preamble clearly and concisely sets out the three main purposes of the GPL. The first, and by far the most important, is to keep software free, in the sense that it can be distributed and modified without additional permission of the licensor. This imposes a mirror-image restriction on the licensee: while the licensee has free access to the licensed work, the licensee must distribute any derivative works subject to the

---

* The most current GNU Library General Public License is now known as the GNU Lesser General Public License (LGPL) and is described in more detail later in this chapter.

same limitations and restrictions as the licensed work. The second purpose of the GPL is to ensure that licensees are aware that software under the license is distributed "as is" and without warranty. This purpose is not unique to the GPL, as we have seen. The third purpose (which is really a variant of the first) is that the licensed software be free of restrictive patents: to the extent that a patent applies to the licensed software, it must be licensed in parallel with the code. As we discussed in Chapter 1, a given piece of code may be subject to both a copyright and a patent. In order for the GPL to function properly, both copyright and patent licenses must be subject to the terms of the GPL.

The individual provisions of the license articulate each of these purposes in some detail. The GPL License is written with a great deal more specificity and in substantially more detail than the licenses described in the previous chapter. This meticulousness is obvious in the license's first provision, which defines the scope of the license and its critical terms.

GNU GENERAL PUBLIC LICENSE

TERMS AND CONDITIONS FOR COPYING, DISTRIBUTION AND MODIFICATION

0. This License applies to any program or other work which contains a notice placed by the copyright holder saying it may be distributed under the terms of this General Public License. The "Program", below, refers to any such program or work, and a "work based on the Program" means either the Program or any derivative work under copyright law: that is to say, a work containing the Program or a portion of it, either verbatim or with modifications and/or translated into another language. (Hereinafter, translation is included without limitation in the term "modification".) Each licensee is addressed as "you".

Activities other than copying, distribution and modification are not covered by this License; they are outside its scope. The act of running the Program is not restricted, and the output from the Program is covered only if its contents constitute a work based on the Program (independent of having been made by running the Program). Whether that is true depends on what the Program does.

The term "Program" is roughly equivalent to what this book has described previously as "work," the term "work based on the Program" to derivative work, and the term "you" to licensee.* The exclusion of activities other than copying, modifying, or distributing the program or a work based on it is typical of the meticulousness of this license. This exclusion could reasonably be assumed to apply to the licenses discussed in Chapter 2, but only here is it specifically described.

The next provision describes all of the limitations that apply to distribution of the licensed work.

1. You may copy and distribute verbatim copies of the Program's source code as you receive it, in any medium, provided that you conspicuously and appropriately publish on each copy an appropriate copyright notice and disclaimer of warranty; keep intact

---

* The terms "work" and "derivative work" are terms of art defined by copyright law.

all the notices that refer to this License and to the absence of any warranty; and give any other recipients of the Program a copy of this License along with the Program.

You may charge a fee for the physical act of transferring a copy, and you may at your option offer warranty protection in exchange for a fee.

This provision embodies the most important principles with regard to the distribution of the original work. The original licensed work can be distributed or sold by a licensee. This provision by itself creates the opportunity for a profitable business—any person can simply acquire and package GPL-licensed software, perhaps bundle it with an appropriate manual,* market it, and sell it. There is no need to "add value" other than by making the work available in a format convenient to consumers. The limitation, obviously, to this business model is that any other person is equally free to start a business on the same principles and distribute the same work or works. This is not necessarily fatal to such businesses. Businesses do not need to be monopolies in order to prosper. The FSF itself derives a substantial amount of income from distributing its own "free" works.

The other business model identified by this provision is the warrantying of a particular work. Any person can take a GPL-licensed work and sell a guarantee that the work will perform a particular function and make whatever changes or modifications to the work are necessary to achieve that goal. As previously noted, most open source licenses, including the GPL, expressly disclaim warranties of any kind. However, businesses strongly prefer to have reliable software, and, in particular, to have software that is backed up by knowledgeable professionals who are capable of adapting it to particular purposes and situations. This type of "value-adding" is expressly authorized by the GPL.

The second paragraph of the GPL is its most important, as it embodies the FSF idea of "copyleft," a variety of the generational limitation described in Chapter 1, which requires that derivative works be subject to the terms of the GPL and only the terms of the GPL.

2. You may modify your copy or copies of the Program or any portion of it, thus forming a work based on the Program, and copy and distribute such modifications or work under the terms of Section 1 above, provided that you also meet all of these conditions:

This is the first part of copyleft: subject to certain restrictions, modifications to the work or any part of it are permitted.

a) You must cause the modified files to carry prominent notices stating that you changed the files and the date of any change.

Like the restriction imposed by the BSD license, this provision serves to ensure that users are aware that the derivative work is not identical to the original work and to

---

* The application of open source licensing principles to works other than software, including manuals, is described in Chapter 5.

identify the person or persons who are responsible for the changes. This is intended to protect users and to protect the reputations of creators of work against injury arising from flawed derivative works.

> b) You must cause any work that you distribute or publish, that in whole or in part contains or is derived from the Program or any part thereof, to be licensed as a whole at no charge to all third parties under the terms of this License.

This key part of the second paragraph of the GPL is the most important provision of the license. Derivative works must be licensed under the GPL and be subject to all of its restrictions. Unlike works licensed under the MIT or the BSD License, works derivative of work licensed under the GPL (or the original work itself) may not be made proprietary or otherwise limited in their distribution. If a programmer is looking to create proprietary works, the entire universe of GPL-licensed software is closed off to her. Indeed, as described in Chapter 6, the inclusion of any GPL-licensed code in purportedly proprietary software could prevent the creator of that software from enforcing any of the rights otherwise available under copyright: any person could distribute, sell, or modify that software, in disregard of any rights that would otherwise be granted the creator under the copyright laws.*

> c) If the modified program normally reads commands interactively when run, you must cause it, when started running for such interactive use in the most ordinary way, to print or display an announcement including an appropriate copyright notice and a notice that there is no warranty (or else, saying that you provide a warranty) and that users may redistribute the program under these conditions, and telling the user how to view a copy of this License. (Exception: if the Program itself is interactive but does not normally print such an announcement, your work based on the Program is not required to print an announcement.)

This provision is a necessary complement to provision 2(b). The fact that licensees of the derivative work may freely exercise rights under the GPL is of little importance unless those licensees *know* that they can exercise those rights. This provision attempts to inform those licensees of those rights.

> These requirements apply to the modified work as a whole. If identifiable sections of that work are not derived from the Program, and can reasonably be considered independent and separate works in themselves, then this License, and its terms, do not apply to those sections when you distribute them as separate works. But when you distribute the same sections as part of a whole which is a work based on the Program, the distribution of the whole must be on the terms of this License, whose permissions for other licensees extend to the entire whole, and thus to each and every part regardless of who wrote it.

> Thus, it is not the intent of this section to claim rights or contest your rights to work written entirely by you; rather, the intent is to exercise the right to control the distribution of derivative or collective works based on the Program.

---

* Whether such a person would in turn be bound by the GPL is discussed in more detail in Chapter 6.

It is not uncommon for a particular program to be capable of both integration with other software to form a unified whole, such as into a calculator program that performs a variety of functions, and also functioning with minimal or no modifications as a separate entity, such as a program that only calculates square roots. This provision of the GPL allows the author of such software to license the software under another license (typically, a proprietary one) when distributed by itself and under the GPL when the program is distributed as part of a larger work, including GPL-licensed programs. This may provide some benefit to the software developer, but probably not if the developer chooses to distribute the GPL-licensed software publicly. In general, consumers would prefer to acquire the GPL-licensed work, which will likely have greater functionality and be more cheaply available, than to acquire the more limited proprietary work.

This provision may be of some comfort to software developers who are creating software primarily for their own use "in-house." Presumably, such developers could write programs or functions designed to work with GPL-licensed programs and simply limit the distribution of that GPL-licensed code to persons within the organization. If the developers' own code got to the point where it could be commercially distributed on its own, the developers could, with confidence, "disengage" that code from the GPL-licensed code and distribute it as part of standalone programs under a proprietary license or otherwise.

> In addition, mere aggregation of another work not based on the Program with the Program (or with a work based on the Program) on a volume of a storage or distribution medium does not bring the other work under the scope of this License.

This provision serves as a safeguard against overly broad interpretations of the GPL. This makes explicit what is implicit in the rest of the license: the provisions of the GPL are not contagious, like a cold. Mere proximity does not cause the license to govern a particular piece of code. To fall under the copyleft, the code must be integral to and/or derivative of a program that is GPL-licensed.

The following provisions of the GPL require that the licensees of the GPL-licensed code make available in one of two ways the source code to the program. The right to create derivative works from a program is obviously limited in practice if the source code is not available.

> 3. You may copy and distribute the Program (or a work based on it, under Section 2) in object code or executable form under the terms of Sections 1 and 2 above provided that you also do one of the following:

Note that this requirement is equally applicable to derivative works created under Section 2 of the GPL.

> a) Accompany it with the complete corresponding machine-readable source code, which must be distributed under the terms of Sections 1 and 2 above on a medium customarily used for software interchange; or,

This is the most favored way to make source code available. It requires no additional effort from the distributee and is not time-limited. This is the best way to comply with Section 3 for all but the largest programs.

> b) Accompany it with a written offer, valid for at least three years, to give any third party, for a charge no more than your cost of physically performing source distribution, a complete machine-readable copy of the corresponding source code, to be distributed under the terms of Sections 1 and 2 above on a medium customarily used for software interchange; or,

This option furthers the purposes of open source and free software but does so in a way that imposes additional costs on both licensors and licensees. The licensor must maintain a facility for providing copies of the source code; the licensee interested in creating the derivative work must contact and pay for the copying of the source code. Moreover, this provision is limited to three years, which could result in potentially useful software "going closed" as a practical matter (at least for the creation of derivative works) once the licensor ceases making the source code available.

> c) Accompany it with the information you received as to the offer to distribute corresponding source code. (This alternative is allowed only for noncommercial distribution and only if you received the program in object code or executable form with such an offer, in accord with Subsection b above.)

Section 3(c) allows noncommercial distributors of GPL-licensed software to "piggyback" on the original licensor's offer to make the source code available, if the source code of such software was originally made available under Section 3(b).

The following paragraph of the GPL defines "source code" as that term is used in the license.

> The source code for a work means the preferred form of the work for making modifications to it. For an executable work, complete source code means all the source code for all modules it contains, plus any associated interface definition files, plus the scripts used to control compilation and installation of the executable. However, as a special exception, the source code distributed need not include anything that is normally distributed (in either source or binary form) with the major components (compiler, kernel, and so on) of the operating system on which the executable runs, unless that component itself accompanies the executable.

This limits the size of the source code that needs to be provided by narrowing the definition of program to exclude major components, like the operating system the program is intended to run on. Obviously, if the GPL-licensed programs being distributed (or one or more of them) are themselves major components of an operating system, the source code for those components must be made available, as described in 3(a–c).

> If distribution of executable or object code is made by offering access to copy from a designated place, then offering equivalent access to copy the source code from the same place counts as distribution of the source code, even though third parties are not compelled to copy the source along with the object code.

This is another provision that explains in greater detail something already implicitly stated elsewhere in the license. Offering access to copy the source in the same manner and with the same degree of ease as the executable code is sufficient to comply with the requirements of Section 3(a).

The first part of Section 4 of the GPL identifies the license as the exclusive license for use of the licensed software.

> 4. You may not copy, modify, sublicense, or distribute the Program except as expressly provided under this License. Any attempt otherwise to copy, modify, sublicense or distribute the Program is void, and will automatically terminate your rights under this License.

In the event that a licensee violates any term of the GPL by, for example, distributing a proprietary derivative work based on GPL-licensed code, all rights under the GPL are voided. This brings back into play the ordinary protections of copyright law (and of patent law, if applicable) described in Chapter 1. In the event of such a breach, the ex-licensee would become legally liable to the licensor for violation of the copyright. The licensor could enjoin the ex-licensee from distributing the derivative work and could sue for damages, which could include, among other things, any and all profits the ex-licensee made from distributing the derivative work. This scenario is described in more detail in Chapter 7.

> However, parties who have received copies, or rights, from you under this License will not have their licenses terminated so long as such parties remain in full compliance.

This sentence acts as a savings clause, preventing liability from attaching to those persons who received the licensed work or a GPL-distributed derivative work from the ex-licensee.

Section 5 addresses a problem that applies to almost all software licenses: the uncertainty as to whether a binding contract is in fact created between the licensor and licensee.

> 5. You are not required to accept this License, since you have not signed it. However, nothing else grants you permission to modify or distribute the Program or its derivative works. These actions are prohibited by law if you do not accept this License. Therefore, by modifying or distributing the Program (or any work based on the Program), you indicate your acceptance of this License to do so, and all its terms and conditions for copying, distributing or modifying the Program or works based on it.

While no court has yet ruled on the effect of this provision, it is likely enforceable. As noted in Chapter 1, courts have found that "shrinkwrap" licenses—proprietary licenses that the licensee accepts by breaking the shrinkwrap on commercial software—are enforceable. The GPL can rest firmly on the fundamental (and intrinsic) protection of copyright. The licensor owns every part of the work and any use of it (excepting "fair use") is infringement. The potential licensee is thus faced with a choice: either refuse the GPL, which bars almost every use of the licensed work, or accept it, and use the work as permitted by the GPL. As described in more detail in

Chapter 6, knowledge of the applicable license should be implied even as to putative licensees who have no actual knowledge of the license. Some degree of diligence should be required of such users: if they truly believed that there was "no license" applicable to the program, they should have made no use of it at all other than the very limited uses permitted by copyright law.

Section 6 of the GPL creates a relationship between the licensor and each of the licensees, regardless of the number of generations of distribution that may lay between them.

> 6. Each time you redistribute the Program (or any work based on the Program), the recipient automatically receives a license from the original licensor to copy, distribute or modify the Program subject to these terms and conditions.

The GPL should be effective, regardless of the number of distributions through which it passes, because of the limitations and requirements of Sections 1 through 4. This provision, therefore, acts in some way as a back-up to those sections. More importantly, however, it also tries to create *contractual privity* between the licensor of the original work and all the licensees of that work.

Contractual privity is the legal state between two (or more) parties in which they are bound by contractual obligations to each other. In the GPL, it safeguards the *standing* of the licensor to bring a lawsuit against all the licensees of the work. *Standing* is a legal term of art, but, in simple terms, it means essentially that the person with standing to sue has been directly injured in some way by another such that that person has the right to bring an action for relief. Without this contractual privity creating the standing on the part of the licensor to sue, a licensee of the work could argue that she did not receive the license to use the work from the original licensor, but rather from some intermediate distributor (who may have no interest at all in defending the terms of the license), and that, accordingly, only that intermediate distributor has standing to sue for putative violations of the license. Section 6 attempts to head off this argument, by creating a relationship between the original licensor and all licensees of the work, regardless of the number of distributors.

The second sentence of Section 6 is the mirror image of Section 2(b). As that section required that derivative works be distributed subject to the restrictions of the license, so this sentence prohibits the addition of any restrictions to those present in the GPL.

> You may not impose any further restrictions on the recipients' exercise of the rights granted herein.

As described in Chapter 6, this limitation has significant consequences on the compatibility of the GPL with other licenses.

The third sentence prevents liability from attaching to innocent distributors for license violations committed by distributees or any other person.

> You are not responsible for enforcing compliance by third parties to this License.

Section 7 prevents any outside act, including court judgments premised on patent rulings or otherwise, from limiting or altering the terms of the license.

> 7. If, as a consequence of a court judgment or allegation of patent infringement or for any other reason (not limited to patent issues), conditions are imposed on you (whether by court order, agreement or otherwise) that contradict the conditions of this License, they do not excuse you from the conditions of this License. If you cannot distribute so as to satisfy simultaneously your obligations under this License and any other pertinent obligations, then as a consequence you may not distribute the Program at all. For example, if a patent license would not permit royalty-free redistribution of the Program by all those who receive copies directly or indirectly through you, then the only way you could satisfy both it and this License would be to refrain entirely from distribution of the Program.

This section is constructed so that in the event that any court attempts to limit or modify the license by imposing obligations or restrictions inconsistent with the GPL, the license for all practical purposes ceases to exist.* Because of this, patent issues remain something GPL developers need to watch.

In practice, this could have dire consequences on the consumers of GPL-licensed software. Say, for example, that a small software company determines that part of a widely distributed and used GPL-licensed program, such as the GNU/Linux kernel, infringes on a software patent that it holds. The company brings suit and a court determines that the program infringes on the patent. Because the infringing part of the program is relatively trivial, the court determines that the appropriate remedy is for every licensee to pay a one-time fee of one dollar to the company. While both current and future licensees (or at least some of them) would gladly pay the fee and continue to use the software, this payment, because it is a restriction not part of the GPL license, is inconsistent with the license. Accordingly, Section 7, were it to be enforced, would bar any distribution of the program after the court judgment.†

Like the rest of the GPL, this section has not been interpreted by a court. However, it is unlikely that a court would allow this section to limit its own power to grant relief. It is certainly not impossible that a court in adjudicating such a dispute would give notice to the licensor and permit the licensor to make appropriate arguments concerning the license, but would then grant relief that would essentially rewrite the GPL in favor of the injured party and permit licensees to continue to copy, distribute, and modify the affected program. This is, of course, only my speculation.

---

* For an interesting discussion of the effects of the bringing of a patent infringement action on a licensor's ability to continue to distribute under the GPL a work that the licensor itself claims violates its own patent rights and the subsequent effect of this on the GPL's compatibility with the Apache License, v2.0, see *http://www. apache.org/licenses/GPL-compatibility.html*. As of this writing, the FSF has taken the position that the Apache License, v2.0, is incompatible with the GPL because the Apache License, v2.0, has a slightly different treatment of this scenario.

† Because Section 7 refers only to distribution, and because Section 0 limits the application of the license to "copying, distribution and modification," the licensees could continue to run the affected program. However, the licensees could not copy, distribute, or modify the program, drastically limiting its usefulness in the open source/free software model.

> If any portion of this section is held invalid or unenforceable under any particular cir-
> cumstance, the balance of the section is intended to apply and the section as a whole is
> intended to apply in other circumstances.

This sentence is another variety of the savings clause, intended to preserve the remaining parts of this section even if some part of it is invalidated by a court. It is hard to see, however, what effect any part of this section could have if the critical part of it is superseded by a court, as described earlier.

The following part of the section does not really apply a legal limitation on licensees as much as it articulates a defense of Section 7.

> It is not the purpose of this section to induce you to infringe any patents or other prop-
> erty right claims or to contest validity of any such claims; this section has the sole pur-
> pose of protecting the integrity of the free software distribution system, which is
> implemented by public license practices. Many people have made generous contribu-
> tions to the wide range of software distributed through that system in reliance on con-
> sistent application of that system; it is up to the author/donor to decide if he or she is
> willing to distribute software through any other system and a licensee cannot impose
> that choice.
>
> This section is intended to make thoroughly clear what is believed to be a conse-
> quence of the rest of this License.

The thesis is that the licensor's choice to use the GPL license is, in some sense, a political one, and that choice should be protected and defended against encroachment. Licensees, obviously, may see the situation differently.

Although the potential results from the application of Section 7 may seem draconian, Section 7 is probably necessary to protect the integrity of the GPL and of the GPL distribution model. The license prevents licensees from altering the GPL contractually, through provisions that are very likely to be enforced. However, private parties are not the only entities capable of altering legal obligations. Courts have an even greater power, to alter, to cancel, and to rewrite contracts to effect appropriate relief on any number of grounds. The GPL's use of a strategy of "if we're not playing my game, I'm taking my ball and going home" is probably necessary to prevent the model from being undermined by courts. How the courts will react to the restriction of Section 7, however, is still unknown.

Section 8 addresses a similar problem, where the laws of certain jurisdictions would limit or otherwise modify the GPL.

> 8. If the distribution and/or use of the Program is restricted in certain countries either
> by patents or by copyrighted interfaces, the original copyright holder who places the
> Program under this License may add an explicit geographical distribution limitation
> excluding those countries, so that distribution is permitted only in or among countries
> not thus excluded. In such case, this License incorporates the limitation as if written in
> the body of this License.

To the extent that there are jurisdictions in which the licensor is limited from licensing the program due by pre-existing patents or copyrights, the licensor is free to carve them out from the area in which the GPL is effective. This gives the licensor maximum flexibility, by permitting the GPL-licensed software to spread as widely as possible, if it is restricted in certain jurisdictions. This is an example of an area in which the GPL can itself be modified, at least under one set of circumstances.

Section 9 of the GPL gives notice that the FSF may issue updated or revised versions of the license.

> 9. The Free Software Foundation may publish revised and/or new versions of the General Public License from time to time. Such new versions will be similar in spirit to the present version, but may differ in detail to address new problems or concerns.

Unlike most of the other parts of the GPL, this provision really serves to give notice to potential licensors—i.e., those who choose to use the GPL to license a new program—not to licensees.

> Each version is given a distinguishing version number. If the Program specifies a version number of this License which applies to it and "any later version", you have the option of following the terms and conditions either of that version or of any later version published by the Free Software Foundation. If the Program does not specify a version number of this License, you may choose any version ever published by the Free Software Foundation.

This paragraph makes clear that in order to preserve specific guarantees or rights, licensors should identify the GPL version used by version number. If they do not, the licensee can exercise rights under *any* of the GPL licenses. Moreover, if the licensor adds the language "and any later license" following the identification of the version number, the licensee can exercise the rights under that version and any subsequent version of the GPL.

A different option, albeit not one permitted by the GPL, would be the inclusion of language to the effect that "this software is licensed under GPL Version X.Y. This license is subject to periodic revision and amendment by the Free Software Foundation. Upon publication of such a revised or amended license by the Free Software Foundation, such revised or amended license is deemed to have superseded the license previously applicable to this software, and such revised or amended license shall from that time govern the contractual relationship between licensors and licensees. Accordingly, any further copying, distribution, or modification of this software after that time will be subject to the terms of the revised and amended license. You have the obligation to track such revisions and amendments to the GPL."*

This option was not included in the GPL, most likely because it further complicates the already somewhat thorny issues related to providing notice of the license to licensees and forming a binding contract between licensor and licensee described in Chapter 6. It is one thing to expect a licensee to be bound by the terms of a license, which are made clear to the licensee upon the first use of the program; it may be something entirely different to require that licensee to track the actions of the FSF

---

* A similar provision is contained in the Mozilla Public License described later in this chapter.

and conform behavior accordingly. Nonetheless, if those issues could be addressed, this option could offer some benefits, particularly in allowing the FSF to address threats to the GPL, such as those described in Section 8.

Section 10 is less a binding provision than an explanation to licensees as to how to address the GPL's incompatibility with other licenses.

> 10. If you wish to incorporate parts of the Program into other free programs whose distribution conditions are different, write to the author to ask for permission. For software which is copyrighted by the Free Software Foundation, write to the Free Software Foundation; we sometimes make exceptions for this. Our decision will be guided by the two goals of preserving the free status of all derivatives of our free software and of promoting the sharing and reuse of software generally.

As we have seen, the second sentence of Section 6 of the GPL bars licensees from imposing any additional restrictions on recipients' exercise of rights under the license, and Section 4 terminates all rights under the license in the event that any provision is not complied with. The effect of these two sections is to make the GPL incompatible with most other open source licenses.* Section 10 provides a possible solution, although one that may be impractical in many situations. The original licensor of the program, holding the copyright to the software and having licensed the software under the GPL, cannot withdraw or alter the terms of the license already granted; the licensor, however, in addition to licensing the software under the GPL License, can also license it under another license, such as the Artistic License. If the original licensor is willing to undertake such parallel licensing, the code can be made available under a non-GPL compatible license and thereby avoid the problem.

The rest of the license consists substantially of disclaimers of warranty similar to those in the licenses described in the previous chapters. These disclaimers are also in all-caps.

> NO WARRANTY

> 11. BECAUSE THE PROGRAM IS LICENSED FREE OF CHARGE, THERE IS NO WARRANTY FOR THE PROGRAM, TO THE EXTENT PERMITTED BY APPLICABLE LAW. EXCEPT WHEN OTHERWISE STATED IN WRITING THE COPYRIGHT HOLDERS AND/OR OTHER PARTIES PROVIDE THE PROGRAM "AS IS" WITHOUT WARRANTY OF ANY KIND, EITHER EXPRESSED OR IMPLIED, INCLUDING, BUT NOT LIMITED TO, THE IMPLIED WARRANTIES OF MERCHANTABILITY AND FITNESS FOR A PARTICULAR PURPOSE. THE ENTIRE RISK AS TO THE QUALITY AND PERFORMANCE OF THE PROGRAM IS WITH YOU. SHOULD THE PROGRAM PROVE DEFECTIVE, YOU ASSUME THE COST OF ALL NECESSARY SERVICING, REPAIR OR CORRECTION.

> 12. IN NO EVENT UNLESS REQUIRED BY APPLICABLE LAW OR AGREED TO IN WRITING WILL ANY COPYRIGHT HOLDER, OR ANY OTHER PARTY WHO MAY MODIFY AND/OR REDISTRIBUTE THE PROGRAM AS PERMITTED

---

* Not all licenses are incompatible, however. For a list of licenses the Free Software Foundation considers compatible with the GPL, which include the MIT (or X license) and the post-1999 BSD license, see *http:// www.gnu.org/licenses/license-list.html*.

ABOVE, BE LIABLE TO YOU FOR DAMAGES, INCLUDING ANY GENERAL, SPE-CIAL, INCIDENTAL OR CONSEQUENTIAL DAMAGES ARISING OUT OF THE USE OR INABILITY TO USE THE PROGRAM (INCLUDING BUT NOT LIMITED TO LOSS OF DATA OR DATA BEING RENDERED INACCURATE OR LOSSES SUSTAINED BY YOU OR THIRD PARTIES OR A FAILURE OF THE PROGRAM TO OPERATE WITH ANY OTHER PROGRAMS), EVEN IF SUCH HOLDER OR OTHER PARTY HAS BEEN ADVISED OF THE POSSIBILITY OF SUCH DAMAGES.

END OF TERMS AND CONDITIONS

One interesting, potentially significant distinction between this disclaimer of liability and those discussed in the previous chapter is that the disclaimer does not expressly disclaim liability for "direct damages." As discussed in the previous chapter, direct damages are measured by the price of the software alleged to be defective. This deci-sion to exclude direct damages may be deliberate—it would not be inconsistent with the ideas underlying the GPL to hold distributors liable for the price of the software, for example, if it was poorly copied. However, the better reading of the provision is that it disclaims all damages, and that the list of "general, specific [etc.]" damages that are disclaimed is illustrative, not definitive.

More importantly, Sections 11 and 12 permit one kind of modification to the GPL, in that they permit a separate written agreement between two parties to establish war-ranties or permit suits for damages. One business model that is available for open source is the provision of warranties and maintenance of open source and free soft-ware. The GPL does not prohibit the provision of such services by inserting these exceptions into Sections 11 and 12. Such services are also explicitly authorized in Section 1.

As noted in the notice immediately following Section 12, this is the close of the pro-visions of the license. The remainder of the GPL text is instructions for implement-ing the license, which follow here:

How to Apply These Terms to Your New Programs

If you develop a new program, and you want it to be of the greatest possible use to the public, the best way to achieve this is to make it free software which everyone can redistribute and change under these terms.

To do so, attach the following notices to the program. It is safest to attach them to the start of each source file to most effectively convey the exclusion of warranty; and each file should have at least the "copyright" line and a pointer to where the full notice is found.

one line to give the program's name and a brief idea of what it does.
Copyright (C)

This program is free software; you can redistribute it and/or modify it under the terms of the GNU General Public License as published by the Free Software Foun-dation; either version 2 of the License, or (at your option) any later version.

This program is distributed in the hope that it will be useful, but WITHOUT ANY WARRANTY; without even the implied warranty of MERCHANTABILITY or FIT-NESS FOR A PARTICULAR PURPOSE. See the GNU General Public License for more details.

You should have received a copy of the GNU General Public License along with this program; if not, write to the Free Software Foundation, Inc., 59 Temple Place, Suite 330, Boston, MA 02111-1307 USA

Also add information on how to contact you by electronic and paper mail.

If the program is interactive, make it output a short notice like this when it starts in an interactive mode:

Gnomovision version 69, Copyright (C) year name of author Gnomovision comes with ABSOLUTELY NO WARRANTY; for details type 'show w'. This is free software, and you are welcome to redistribute it under certain conditions; type 'show c' for details.

The hypothetical commands 'show w' and 'show c' should show the appropriate parts of the General Public License. Of course, the commands you use may be called something other than 'show w' and 'show c'; they could even be mouse-clicks or menu items—whatever suits your program.

You should also get your employer (if you work as a programmer) or your school, if any, to sign a "copyright disclaimer" for the program, if necessary. Here is a sample; alter the names:

Yoyodyne, Inc., hereby disclaims all copyright interest in the program 'Gnomovision' (which makes passes at compilers) written by James Hacker.

signature of Ty Coon, 1 April 1989
Ty Coon, President of Vice

This General Public License does not permit incorporating your program into proprietary programs. If your program is a subroutine library, you may consider it more useful to permit linking proprietary applications with the library. If this is what you want to do, use the GNU Library General Public License instead of this License.

GNU Lesser General Public License

The GNU Lesser General Public License (LGPL) is another license created by the FSF for the purpose of permitting a certain class of programs, generally subroutine libraries, to be licensed under an FSF license but be permitted to link with non-GPL software programs. Subroutine libraries provide various functions to other programs, and because as part of their function they link with such programs, the resulting program plus library could be considered as a legal matter to be a derivative work. Accordingly, if the other program were licensed under a proprietary license and the library under the GPL and the program and library were distributed together under the proprietary license, the GPL would be violated, as the program plus library would be considered a derivative work that would be subject to limitations on copying, distribution, and modification that are inconsistent with the GPL.*

---

* The *use* of a GPL-licensed program with a proprietary-licensed library (or any other program, whether under a proprietary license or some other non-GPL license) is not a violation of the GPL license. Rather, the GPL license comes into play only when the GPL-licensed software is copied, distributed, or modified—none of which is implicated by the simple use of the software. As explained in more detail later, libraries present some unique technical problems for licensing in that their use may result in the "modification," as that term is defined in the GPL, of the program that uses them.

The LGPL provides an alternative license that preserves many of the benefits of the GPL model for such libraries—in fact, the Lesser General Public License was in its first incarnation known as the Library General Public License. LGPL-licensed libraries can be linked with non-GPL licensed programs, including proprietary software. However, libraries need not be licensed under the LGPL, and as the following preamble to the license points out, the preferable way to license libraries, at least under some circumstances, is under the GPL.

Preamble

The licenses for most software are designed to take away your freedom to share and change it. By contrast, the GNU General Public Licenses are intended to guarantee your freedom to share and change free software—to make sure the software is free for all its users.

This license, the Lesser General Public License, applies to some specially designated software packages—typically libraries—of the Free Software Foundation and other authors who decide to use it. You can use it too, but we suggest you first think carefully about whether this license or the ordinary General Public License is the better strategy to use in any particular case, based on the explanations below.

When we speak of free software, we are referring to freedom of use, not price. Our General Public Licenses are designed to make sure that you have the freedom to distribute copies of free software (and charge for this service if you wish); that you receive source code or can get it if you want it; that you can change the software and use pieces of it in new free programs; and that you are informed that you can do these things.

To protect your rights, we need to make restrictions that forbid distributors to deny you these rights or to ask you to surrender these rights. These restrictions translate to certain responsibilities for you if you distribute copies of the library or if you modify it.

For example, if you distribute copies of the library, whether gratis or for a fee, you must give the recipients all the rights that we gave you. You must make sure that they, too, receive or can get the source code. If you link other code with the library, you must provide complete object files to the recipients, so that they can relink them with the library after making changes to the library and recompiling it. And you must show them these terms so they know their rights.

We protect your rights with a two-step method: (1) we copyright the library, and (2) we offer you this license, which gives you legal permission to copy, distribute and/or modify the library.

To protect each distributor, we want to make it very clear that there is no warranty for the free library. Also, if the library is modified by someone else and passed on, the recipients should know that what they have is not the original version, so that the original author's reputation will not be affected by problems that might be introduced by others.

Finally, software patents pose a constant threat to the existence of any free program. We wish to make sure that a company cannot effectively restrict the users of a free program by obtaining a restrictive license from a patent holder. Therefore, we insist that any patent license obtained for a version of the library must be consistent with the full freedom of use specified in this license.

Most GNU software, including some libraries, is covered by the ordinary GNU General Public License. This license, the GNU Lesser General Public License, applies to certain designated libraries, and is quite different from the ordinary General Public License. We use this license for certain libraries in order to permit linking those libraries into non-free programs.

When a program is linked with a library, whether statically or using a shared library, the combination of the two is legally speaking a combined work, a derivative of the original library. The ordinary General Public License therefore permits such linking only if the entire combination fits its criteria of freedom. The Lesser General Public License permits more lax criteria for linking other code with the library.

We call this license the "Lesser" General Public License because it does Less to protect the user's freedom than the ordinary General Public License. It also provides other free software developers Less of an advantage over competing non-free programs. These disadvantages are the reason we use the ordinary General Public License for many libraries. However, the Lesser license provides advantages in certain special circumstances.

For example, on rare occasions, there may be a special need to encourage the widest possible use of a certain library, so that it becomes a de-facto standard. To achieve this, non-free programs must be allowed to use the library. A more frequent case is that a free library does the same job as widely used non-free libraries. In this case, there is little to gain by limiting the free library to free software only, so we use the Lesser General Public License.

In other cases, permission to use a particular library in non-free programs enables a greater number of people to use a large body of free software. For example, permission to use the GNU C Library in non-free programs enables many more people to use the whole GNU operating system, as well as its variant, the GNU/Linux operating system.

Although the Lesser General Public License is Less protective of the users' freedom, it does ensure that the user of a program that is linked with the Library has the freedom and the wherewithal to run that program using a modified version of the Library.

The precise terms and conditions for copying, distribution and modification follow. Pay close attention to the difference between a "work based on the library" and a "work that uses the library". The former contains code derived from the library, whereas the latter must be combined with the library in order to run.*

Much of this preamble parallels the language in the GPL described earlier. There are two new points, however, worth identifying. The first is the decision on the part of the developer as to which license to use for a particular library. The Preamble posits this choice as if it were between the GPL on one hand and the LGPL on the other. To begin with, obviously, developers can choose to license their programs, including their libraries, under any license, FSF-approved or not. For those who are interested in using the GPL-distribution model, however, the Preamble identifies those situations in which LGPL may be favored, such as when the library is intended to replace an already available commercially licensed product.

---

* This version of the LGPL is 2.1, distributed February, 1999. It is copyright © 1991, 1999 by the Free Software Foundation, Inc., 59 Temple Place, Suite 330, Boston, MA 02111-1307 USA. As was the case with the GPL, "Everyone is permitted to copy and distribute verbatim copies of this license document, but changing it is not allowed."

The second point worthy of mention is the distinction in the LGPL between "work based on the library," which is subject to essentially the same restrictions as imposed by the GPL, and "work that is used with the library," which is not. This distinction is explained in more detail later.

As was the case with the GPL, the first section after the "Terms and Conditions for Copying, Distribution, and Modification" is Section 0, which defines the basic terms used in the license and sets out its fundamental premises.

> 0. This License Agreement applies to any software library or other program which contains a notice placed by the copyright holder or other authorized party saying it may be distributed under the terms of this Lesser General Public License (also called "this License"). Each licensee is addressed as "you".

The next full paragraph defines small-l "library" as it is used in the LGPL.

> A "library" means a collection of software functions and/or data prepared so as to be conveniently linked with application programs (which use some of those functions and data) to form executables.

The next paragraph defines capital-L "Library," a term of art used to refer to the licensed program, and "work based on the Library," another term of art that is equivalent to this book's use of "derivative work."

> The "Library", below, refers to any such software library or work which has been distributed under these terms. A "work based on the Library" means either the Library or any derivative work under copyright law: that is to say, a work containing the Library or a portion of it, either verbatim or with modifications and/or translated straightforwardly into another language. (Hereinafter, translation is included without limitation in the term "modification".)

In contrast to the GPL, the LGPL also includes a definition of "source code" in this section; the parallel definition is in Section 3(c) of the GPL.

> "Source code" for a work means the preferred form of the work for making modifications to it. For a library, complete source code means all the source code for all modules it contains, plus any associated interface definition files, plus the scripts used to control compilation and installation of the library.

This is most likely included here to include a number of files related to the library—modules, interfaces, and scripts—to maximize the functionality of the source code.

The final paragraph of Section 0 is substantially identical to the paragraph found at the end of the GPL's Section 0.

> Activities other than copying, distribution and modification are not covered by this License; they are outside its scope. The act of running a program using the Library is not restricted, and output from such a program is covered only if its contents constitute a work based on the Library (independent of the use of the Library in a tool for writing it). Whether that is true depends on what the Library does and what the program that uses the Library does.

Many of the provisions of the LGPL are identical or near-identical to provisions in the GPL. Accordingly, the annotations in the section focus on those provisions in which significant changes have been made. Examine the earlier discussion of the GPL if you have questions about any of the provisions that are not thoroughly discussed here.

Section 1 of the LGPL is substantially identical to Section 1 of the GPL, except that it refers to the "Library" instead of to the Program.

> 1. You may copy and distribute verbatim copies of the Library's complete source code as you receive it, in any medium, provided that you conspicuously and appropriately publish on each copy an appropriate copyright notice and disclaimer of warranty; keep intact all the notices that refer to this License and to the absence of any warranty; and distribute a copy of this License along with the Library.
>
> You may charge a fee for the physical act of transferring a copy, and you may at your option offer warranty protection in exchange for a fee.

Section 2 of the LGPL appears to be substantially identical to the equivalent section of the GPL. There are, however, a few noteworthy changes relating to the specific qualities of libraries, including one that sharply limits the LGPL's applicability to programs other than libraries.

> 2. You may modify your copy or copies of the Library or any portion of it, thus forming a work based on the Library, and copy and distribute such modifications or work under the terms of Section 1 above, provided that you also meet all of these conditions:

This paragraph reads substantially like the first paragraph of the GPL's Section 2, again with the distinction that it uses "Library" in place of "Program."

The first of the clauses of this section, however, imposes a limitation absent from the GPL, i.e., it limits the type of derived work that can come from an LGPL-licensed program.

> a) The modified work must itself be a software library.

In Section 0, the LGPL had noted that the license applied to "any software library or other program." This provision, however, limits the ability to create derivative works to those circumstances in which the resulting work is a library, as that term is defined in the LGPL. This may complicate, or, more likely, entirely prevent the creation of derivative works from programs that are licensed under the LGPL but are not software libraries. If the LGPL were to permit such derivative works to be made from programs other than software libraries, Section 2(a) should have read something like "The modified work must itself be a software library if the Library [i.e., the original work] is itself a library." Note that the definition of big-L Library under the LGPL includes both small-l libraries and "work" that has been distributed under the license. This bar on the creation of derivative works other than libraries from LGPL-licensed works makes the LGPL essentially useless as a license for such works. Creators of such works should look to the GPL or another open source license.

Sections 2(b) and 2(c) mirror equivalent provisions in the GPL.

> b) You must cause the files modified to carry prominent notices stating that you changed the files and the date of any change.
>
> c) You must cause the whole of the work to be licensed at no charge to all third parties under the terms of this License.

Section 2(d) adds specific limitations on licensed libraries' use of tables or other functionality provided by the program with which the library is intended to function.

> d) If a facility in the modified Library refers to a function or a table of data to be supplied by an application program that uses the facility, other than as an argument passed when the facility is invoked, then you must make a good faith effort to ensure that, in the event an application does not supply such function or table, the facility still operates, and performs whatever part of its purpose remains meaningful.
>
> (For example, a function in a library to compute square roots has a purpose that is entirely well-defined independent of the application. Therefore, Subsection 2d requires that any application-supplied function or table used by this function must be optional: if the application does not supply it, the square root function must still compute square roots.)

This maximizes the utility (and the value to other open source and free software developers) of the library by encouraging them to be as portable as possible. The closer a given library comes to standing alone, the easier it is to conform it to function with an application other than the one for which it was originally written.

The last three paragraphs of Section 2 are substantially identical to the parallel provisions in the GPL.

> These requirements apply to the modified work as a whole. If identifiable sections of that work are not derived from the Library, and can be reasonably considered independent and separate works in themselves, then this License, and its terms, do not apply to those sections when you distribute them as separate works. But when you distribute the same sections as part of a whole which is a work based on the Library, the distribution of the whole must be on the terms of this License, whose permissions for other licensees extend to the entire whole, and thus to each and every part regardless of who wrote it.
>
> Thus, it is not the intent of this section to claim rights or contest your rights to work written entirely by you; rather, the intent is to exercise the right to control the distribution of derivative or collective works based on the Library.
>
> In addition, mere aggregation of another work not based on the Library with the Library (or with a work based on the Library) on a volume of a storage or distribution medium does not bring the other work under the scope of this License.

Section 3 of the LGPL addresses a change in licensing from the LGPL to the GPL.

> 3. You may opt to apply the terms of the ordinary GNU General Public License instead of this License to a given copy of the Library. To do this, you must alter all the notices that refer to this License, so that they refer to the ordinary GNU General Public License, version 2, instead of to this License. (If a newer version than version 2 of the ordinary GNU General Public License has appeared, then you can specify that version instead if you wish.) Do not make any other change in these notices.

This part of the section apparently addresses the bar inherent in the LGPL or creating derivative works that are not libraries from an LGPL-licensed work. This provision is interesting in that it permits any licensee to "upgrade" the license to the GPL license. It operates as a savings clause, in that it would provide an escape in the event that any interpretation of the LGPL or the GPL prevented a program licensed under one from being used with a program licensed under the other.

This change in the license applicable to a given copy of a library is a one-way street. Once a program is re-licensed as a GPL program, it cannot go back to licensing under the LGPL.

> Once this change is made in a given copy, it is irreversible for that copy, so the ordinary GNU General Public License applies to all subsequent copies and derivative works made from that copy.

Of course, as other copies of the library would still be available licensed under the LGPL, this sentence really addresses derivative works.

> This option is useful when you wish to copy part of the code of the Library into a program that is not a library.

This sentence is slightly misleading. Re-licensing a program under the GPL is not just "useful" but necessary if the derivative work is not a library, as explained above.

Section 4 substantially parallels similar provisions of the GPL with regard to providing the source code with the binary code.

> 4. You may copy and distribute the Library (or a portion or derivative of it, under Section 2) in object code or executable form under the terms of Sections 1 and 2 above provided that you accompany it with the complete corresponding machine-readable source code, which must be distributed under the terms of Sections 1 and 2 above on a medium customarily used for software interchange.

As is apparent from the following provisions of the LGPL, the distribution of source code of a library standing alone is more restricted under the LGPL than under the GPL: when the executable or binary code is distributed standing alone, it must be accompanied by the source code.

> If distribution of object code is made by offering access to copy from a designated place, then offering equivalent access to copy the source code from the same place satisfies the requirement to distribute the source code, even though third parties are not compelled to copy the source along with the object code.

The LGPL, like the GPL, does permit the distribution of the source code by offering it on equivalent terms as the executable, such as on an FTP site, if the binary code is so offered.

Section 5 provides the critical definition of the "work that uses the Library." The LGPL was designed to permit open source code to function with code licensed under other models. This section serves that purpose by excluding from the terms of the license "work that uses the Library."

5. A program that contains no derivative of any portion of the Library, but is designed to work with the Library by being compiled or linked with it, is called a "work that uses the Library". Such a work, in isolation, is not a derivative work of the Library, and therefore falls outside the scope of this License.

"[I]n isolation" is the critical phrase of this paragraph, as the rest of the section makes clear.

However, linking a "work that uses the Library" with the Library creates an executable that is a derivative of the Library (because it contains portions of the Library), rather than a "work that uses the library".* The executable is therefore covered by this License. Section 6 states terms for distribution of such executables.

While the "work that uses the Library" remains free to be licensed as the creator wishes, when that work is linked with the Library, the resulting work is considered to be a derivative work (as defined by copyright law) and the LGPL imposes specific terms applicable to the distribution of that program plus library provided in Section 6. This compromise allows creators of "works that use the Library" to retain control over their own works, while imposing some limitation when those works are distributed together with the LGPL-licensed Library.

When a "work that uses the Library" uses material from a header file that is part of the Library, the object code for the work may be a derivative work of the Library even though the source code is not. Whether this is true is especially significant if the work can be linked without the Library, or if the work is itself a library. The threshold for this to be true is not precisely defined by law.

If such an object file uses only numerical parameters, data structure layouts and accessors, and small macros and small inline functions (ten lines or less in length), then the use of the object file is unrestricted, regardless of whether it is legally a derivative work. (Executables containing this object code plus portions of the Library will still fall under Section 6.)

Otherwise, if the work is a derivative of the Library, you may distribute the object code for the work under the terms of Section 6. Any executables containing that work also fall under Section 6, whether or not they are linked directly with the Library itself.

These paragraphs of the LGPL attempt, among other things, to distinguish between different uses of a given Library—what is a "work based on the Library" and what is a "work that uses the Library." These paragraphs attempt to draw a distinction that may be impossible to make, except on a case-by-case basis. The LGPL, however, seems to make three distinctions. First, if the putative "work that uses the Library" includes a header file that is part of the Library, it may well be a "work based on the Library" (and therefore be covered by LGPL), particularly if that work can be linked without the Library or if that work is itself a library. Second, if the putative "work that uses the Library" draws only to a limited extent on the Library, measured by reliance only on the specified categories of functionality—i.e., only "numerical parameters, data structure layouts and accessors, and small macros and small inline functions (ten lines or less in length)"—then it is deemed a "work that uses the

---

* This reference to small-l library should probably be to capital-L Library.

Library" (which falls outside the scope of the LGPL), even if it is otherwise a derivative work, as that term is used in copyright law. While the executable file incorporating the Library must be distributed under Section 6, the "work that uses the Library" itself may be licensed free of any limitation. Third, in a sentence probably included as a savings clause if a work is a "derivative work" of the Library, in the sense that it incorporates any code from the Library (as opposed to the object code "in isolation" described in the first paragraph of this section), it is subject to the distribution requirements of Section 6.

These distinctions are unclear and the impact of this section on creators of potential "work that uses the Library" may be hard to predict. Some interpretations of the LGPL distinguish between the dynamic (compiled together with the underlying program) and the static (not so compiled) linking of programs with libraries. Such distinctions are beyond the scope of this book. However, at least at the time of this writing, FSF-licensed libraries may not be dynamically linked, while libraries affiliated with Linus Torvalds and the Linux project may be. Because of the complexity of such problems, users facing these questions should contact the licensor of the Library in question.

So far, we have seen that the LGPL makes distinctions between essentially three different types of work:

1. The LGPL-licensed Library.
2. The "work that uses the Library."
3. The combined "work that uses the Library" and Library together, which I will refer to here as the "combined work," a term not used in the LGPL.

Putting to one side the problem of linking and the extent to which a "work that uses the Library" and the Library are truly distinct programs, the requirements of the LGPL are fairly clear. The "work that uses the Library," when distributed as a "standalone" may be licensed and distributed however the creator wishes, whether under the GPL, the BSD, a proprietary, or any other license. The "Library" must be distributed under the LGPL: the source code must be available under the same terms as the binary code and licensees of the Library must be given the same rights (and be bound by the same restrictions) as the licensor of the Library. Section 2 of the LGPL also states that when a "combined work" is distributed, it is also subject to distribution under the terms of the LGPL. These terms are spelled out in Section 6.

> 6. As an exception to the Sections above, you may also combine or link a "work that uses the Library" with the Library to produce a work containing portions of the Library, and distribute that work under terms of your choice, provided that the terms permit modification of the work for the customer's own use and reverse engineering for debugging such modifications.

This provision is on its face somewhat unclear. Does this mean that by distributing a combined work, the distributor must distribute the source code for or authorize modifications to the "work that uses the Library"? As is made clear by the following paragraphs, Section 6 requires no such thing.

You must give prominent notice with each copy of the work that the Library is used in it and that the Library and its use are covered by this License. You must supply a copy of this License. If the work during execution displays copyright notices, you must include the copyright notice for the Library among them, as well as a reference directing the user to the copy of this License. Also, you must do one of these things:

After this paragraph follows provisions similar in purpose to those in Section 3 of the GPL. They are designed to give notice of the application of copyright to the Library and the fact that the Library is licensed under the LGPL. They also give licensees access to the source code of the Library and allow them to make modifications to it.

> a) Accompany the work with the complete corresponding machine-readable source code for the Library including whatever changes were used in the work (which must be distributed under Sections 1 and 2 above); and, if the work is an executable linked with the Library, with the complete machine-readable "work that uses the Library", as object code and/or source code, so that the user can modify the Library and then relink to produce a modified executable containing the modified Library. (It is understood that the user who changes the contents of definitions files in the Library will not necessarily be able to recompile the application to use the modified definitions.)

Accordingly, the distributor must distribute the source code to the Library (including any modifications made by the distributor), and the binary code of the "work that uses a Library" provided in such a way so that licensees can modify the Library and relink it to the "work that uses the Library."

> b) Use a suitable shared library mechanism for linking with the Library. A suitable mechanism is one that (1) uses at run time a copy of the library already present on the user's computer system, rather than copying library functions into the executable, and (2) will operate properly with a modified version of the library, if the user installs one, as long as the modified version is interface-compatible with the version that the work was made with.

This provision describes another option for distributing the combined work that may be more user-friendly.

The following provisions are substantially identical to those in Section 3 of the GPL:

> c) Accompany the work with a written offer, valid for at least three years, to give the same user the materials specified in Subsection 6a, above, for a charge no more than the cost of performing this distribution.

> d) If distribution of the work is made by offering access to copy from a designated place, offer equivalent access to copy the above specified materials from the same place.

> e) Verify that the user has already received a copy of these materials or that you have already sent this user a copy.

Section 6(e) of the LPGL offers an option unique to the LGPL, which may be useful when the distibutor is distributing a modified version of the "work that uses the Library" to users who have already received the Library used as part of the combined work.

The form of the executable of the "work that uses the Library" is defined in the following paragraph of Section 6.

> For an executable, the required form of the "work that uses the Library" must include any data and utility programs needed for reproducing the executable from it. However, as a special exception, the materials to be distributed need not include anything that is normally distributed (in either source or binary form) with the major components (compiler, kernel, and so on) of the operating system on which the executable runs, unless that component itself accompanies the executable.

Accordingly, to distribute the combined work in compliance with Section 6, the distributor must include data and utility programs (and any other components) that are necessary to allow the combined work to function as originally intended with the Library, unless those components are already included with the operating system upon which the combined program is intended to run. If the combined work relies on libraries (or other programs) that are intrinsic either to the "work that uses the Library" or the Library itself (or to the operating system), the combined work cannot be distributed without violating the LGPL. This is made explicit in the following paragraph.

> It may happen that this requirement contradicts the license restrictions of other proprietary libraries that do not normally accompany the operating system. Such a contradiction means you cannot use both them and the Library together in an executable that you distribute.

It may be that a distributor would like to distribute a work that consists of the "work that uses the Library" (which the distributor has the power to distribute), the Library, and another program, such as another library, which the distributor does not have the authority to distribute, but that users already own or may be able to purchase. Such a distribution is not permitted under the LGPL. If the distributor cannot distribute all the components of the combined work, the distributor cannot distribute any part of it. End users, of course, are free to combine the combined work with libraries (or other programs) that they may otherwise have access to, as such combinations are outside the scope of the LGPL. However, they may not copy, distribute, or modify such works.

Section 7 addresses the situation in which a distributor has created a work based on the Library and has placed it side by side with another library under a proprietary license (or license other than the LGPL that permits the distributor to distribute it) to make it into what is in effect a single library. The distributor may do so without nullifying any license provisions applicable to the other library, subject to certain conditions.

> 7. You may place library facilities that are a work based on the Library side-by-side in a single library together with other library facilities not covered by this License, and distribute such a combined library, provided that the separate distribution of the work based on the Library and of the other library facilities is otherwise permitted, and provided that you do these two things:
>
> a) Accompany the combined library with a copy of the same work based on the Library, uncombined with any other library facilities. This must be distributed under the terms of the Sections above.

b) Give prominent notice with the combined library of the fact that part of it is a work based on the Library, and explaining where to find the accompanying uncombined form of the same work.

The standalone executable form of the Library must be distributed along with the combined library, subject to the terms otherwise applicable under the LGPL (i.e., with the source code accompanying the Library) and prominent notice must be given as to where the uncombined form of the Library may be found (and presumably accompanied by its source code). This is somewhat confusing because the uncombined form of the work based on the Library must be part of the package. Presumably, identifying the filename would be sufficient.

Section 8 of the LGPL operates much like Section 4 of the GPL.

8. You may not copy, modify, sublicense, link with, or distribute the Library except as expressly provided under this License. Any attempt otherwise to copy, modify, sublicense, link with, or distribute the Library is void, and will automatically terminate your rights under this License. However, parties who have received copies, or rights, from you under this License will not have their licenses terminated so long as such parties remain in full compliance.

Section 9 of the LGPL likewise corresponds to Section 5 of the GPL.

9. You are not required to accept this License, since you have not signed it. However, nothing else grants you permission to modify or distribute the Library or its derivative works. These actions are prohibited by law if you do not accept this License. Therefore, by modifying or distributing the Library (or any work based on the Library), you indicate your acceptance of this License to do so, and all its terms and conditions for copying, distributing or modifying the Library or works based on it.

The remaining sections of the LGPL, 10 through 16, are substantially identical to Sections 6 through 12 of the GPL. They are included here for completeness.

10. Each time you redistribute the Library (or any work based on the Library), the recipient automatically receives a license from the original licensor to copy, distribute, link with or modify the Library subject to these terms and conditions. You may not impose any further restrictions on the recipients' exercise of the rights granted herein. You are not responsible for enforcing compliance by third parties with this License.

11. If, as a consequence of a court judgment or allegation of patent infringement or for any other reason (not limited to patent issues), conditions are imposed on you (whether by court order, agreement or otherwise) that contradict the conditions of this License, they do not excuse you from the conditions of this License. If you cannot distribute so as to satisfy simultaneously your obligations under this License and any other pertinent obligations, then as a consequence you may not distribute the Library at all. For example, if a patent license would not permit royalty-free redistribution of the Library by all those who receive copies directly or indirectly through you, then the only way you could satisfy both it and this License would be to refrain entirely from distribution of the Library.

If any portion of this section is held invalid or unenforceable under any particular circumstance, the balance of the section is intended to apply, and the section as a whole is intended to apply in other circumstances.

It is not the purpose of this section to induce you to infringe any patents or other property right claims or to contest validity of any such claims; this section has the sole purpose of protecting the integrity of the free software distribution system which is implemented by public license practices. Many people have made generous contributions to the wide range of software distributed through that system in reliance on consistent application of that system; it is up to the author/donor to decide if he or she is willing to distribute software through any other system and a licensee cannot impose that choice.

This section is intended to make thoroughly clear what is believed to be a consequence of the rest of this License.

12. If the distribution and/or use of the Library is restricted in certain countries either by patents or by copyrighted interfaces, the original copyright holder who places the Library under this License may add an explicit geographical distribution limitation excluding those countries, so that distribution is permitted only in or among countries not thus excluded. In such case, this License incorporates the limitation as if written in the body of this License.

13. The Free Software Foundation may publish revised and/or new versions of the Lesser General Public License from time to time. Such new versions will be similar in spirit to the present version, but may differ in detail to address new problems or concerns.

Each version is given a distinguishing version number. If the Library specifies a version number of this License which applies to it and "any later version", you have the option of following the terms and conditions either of that version or of any later version published by the Free Software Foundation. If the Library does not specify a license version number, you may choose any version ever published by the Free Software Foundation.

14. If you wish to incorporate parts of the Library into other free programs whose distribution conditions are incompatible with these, write to the author to ask for permission. For software which is copyrighted by the Free Software Foundation, write to the Free Software Foundation; we sometimes make exceptions for this. Our decision will be guided by the two goals of preserving the free status of all derivatives of our free software and of promoting the sharing and reuse of software generally.

NO WARRANTY

15. BECAUSE THE LIBRARY IS LICENSED FREE OF CHARGE, THERE IS NO WARRANTY FOR THE LIBRARY, TO THE EXTENT PERMITTED BY APPLICABLE LAW. EXCEPT WHEN OTHERWISE STATED IN WRITING THE COPYRIGHT HOLDERS AND/OR OTHER PARTIES PROVIDE THE LIBRARY "AS IS" WITHOUT WARRANTY OF ANY KIND, EITHER EXPRESSED OR IMPLIED, INCLUDING, BUT NOT LIMITED TO, THE IMPLIED WARRANTIES OF MERCHANTABILITY AND FITNESS FOR A PARTICULAR PURPOSE. THE ENTIRE RISK AS TO THE QUALITY AND PERFORMANCE OF THE LIBRARY IS WITH YOU. SHOULD THE LIBRARY PROVE DEFECTIVE, YOU ASSUME THE COST OF ALL NECESSARY SERVICING, REPAIR OR CORRECTION.

16. IN NO EVENT UNLESS REQUIRED BY APPLICABLE LAW OR AGREED TO IN WRITING WILL ANY COPYRIGHT HOLDER, OR ANY OTHER PARTY WHO MAY MODIFY AND/OR REDISTRIBUTE THE LIBRARY AS PERMITTED ABOVE, BE LIABLE TO YOU FOR DAMAGES, INCLUDING ANY GENERAL, SPECIAL, INCIDENTAL OR CONSEQUENTIAL DAMAGES ARISING OUT OF THE USE OR

INABILITY TO USE THE LIBRARY (INCLUDING BUT NOT LIMITED TO LOSS OF DATA OR DATA BEING RENDERED INACCURATE OR LOSSES SUSTAINED BY YOU OR THIRD PARTIES OR A FAILURE OF THE LIBRARY TO OPERATE WITH ANY OTHER SOFTWARE), EVEN IF SUCH HOLDER OR OTHER PARTY HAS BEEN ADVISED OF THE POSSIBILITY OF SUCH DAMAGES.

END OF TERMS AND CONDITIONS

Following the end of the LGPL's terms and conditions are instructions on how to implement the LGPL. Again, these mirror the instructions in the GPL.

How to Apply These Terms to Your New Libraries

If you develop a new library, and you want it to be of the greatest possible use to the public, we recommend making it free software that everyone can redistribute and change. You can do so by permitting redistribution under these terms (or, alternatively, under the terms of the ordinary General Public License).

To apply these terms, attach the following notices to the library. It is safest to attach them to the start of each source file to most effectively convey the exclusion of warranty; and each file should have at least the "copyright" line and a pointer to where the full notice is found.

one line to give the library's name and an idea of what it does.
Copyright (C) year name of author

This library is free software; you can redistribute it and/or modify it under the terms of the GNU Lesser General Public License as published by the Free Software Foundation; either version 2.1 of the License, or (at your option) any later version.

This library is distributed in the hope that it will be useful, but WITHOUT ANY WARRANTY; without even the implied warranty of MERCHANTABILITY or FITNESS FOR A PARTICULAR PURPOSE. See the GNU Lesser General Public License for more details.

You should have received a copy of the GNU Lesser General Public License along with this library; if not, write to the Free Software Foundation, Inc., 59 Temple Place, Suite 330, Boston, MA 02111-1307 USA

Also add information on how to contact you by electronic and paper mail.

You should also get your employer (if you work as a programmer) or your school, if any, to sign a "copyright disclaimer" for the library, if necessary. Here is a sample; alter the names:

Yoyodyne, Inc., hereby disclaims all copyright interest in the library 'Frob' (a library for tweaking knobs) written by James Random Hacker.

signature of Ty Coon, 1 April 1990
Ty Coon, President of Vice

That's all there is to it!

The Mozilla Public License 1.1 (MPL 1.1)

In January, 1998, Netscape Communications decided to release the binary code of its Communicator web-brower for free. Less than 24 hours later, it decided to release the Communicator source code as well. As a result, at the same time that Netscape was addressing the many technical problems with transitioning Communicator into open source (including removing substantial amounts of code written by third parties who were unwilling to have their code "open sourced"), Netscape had to address the complex licensing issues involved.*

The Netscape Public License (NPL) and the Mozilla Public License (MPL) were the result of these efforts.† The NPL was substantially similar to the MPL, but it reserved certain rights to Netscape, most importantly, the right on the part of Netscape to relicense code developed by third parties that is derived from Communicator code under a proprietary or other license. Third-party modifiers of NPL-licensed code could thus lose any benefits that might flow from their contributions, without the guarantee, as for instance under the GPL, that their code will remain available to the community of programmers. The MPL does not contain the particular provisions embodying this grant of rights to Netscape.

The MPL constitutes an interesting hybrid of the ideas of the GPL and the BSD licenses already described. While code that falls within the scope of what the license describes as "Covered Code" is subject to many of the restrictions present in the GPL, such as the requirement that it be made available in open source form, the MPL, through its Section 3.7, also permits the use of such "Covered Code" in "Larger Works," meaning that MPL-licensed code can be combined with code licensed under another license. This latter result is expressly prohibited by the GPL and permitted by the BSD License. The MPL establishes something of a middle ground between the two licenses.

Thanks to its heritage as the product of a large American corporation, the MPL reads much more like a standard corporate contract, beginning with a long list of definitions, before going into another long list of numbered paragraphs and sub-paragraphs. Section 1 of the MPL consists entirely of definitions.

> 1. Definitions.
>
> 1.0.1. "Commercial Use" means distribution or otherwise making the Covered Code available to a third party.

Commercial Use is defined in a somewhat counterintuitive way. As defined, it includes any form of distribution, whether in exchange for payment or not.

> 1.1. "Contributor" means each entity that creates or contributes to the creation of Modifications.

---

* For a full description of the considerations that went into the decision to release Navigator as an open source project and the development of the Netscape Public License and the Mozilla Public License, see *Freeing the Source: The Story of Mozilla* in *Open Sources: Voices From the Open Source Revolution*, p. 197 and following. (O'Reilly, 1999).

† The name "Mozilla" is derived from the name for the Navigator code used at Netscape—a combination of "Mosaic," an early web browser, and Godzilla.

The explicit definition of the term "Contributor," and the use of that term throughout the MPL 1.1, distinguishes this license from the others we have previously examined. In the BSD and GPL, for example, no distinction is made between the "Contributor" and "You" the licensee: it is presumed that those persons are one and the same. Such a "Contributor" is also distinguished from the "Initial Developer," which is identified in Appendix A to the license. Obviously, with regard to the Mozilla project itself, the Initial Developer was Netscape.

This idea of "Contributors" to the code reflects the centralized notion behind the MPL and the Mozilla project that it was intended to license. Although it was certainly not mandated by the license itself, the MPL reflects a development model under which "Contributors" would be supplying their work to a continuing project, not one under which licensees would be free to appropriate the code to their own uses, subject to certain restrictions on their distribution of the code.

> 1.2. "Contributor Version" means the combination of the Original Code, prior Modifications used by a Contributor, and the Modifications made by that particular Contributor.

This provision is a natural outgrowth of the use of the idea of Contributor, as that term is used in the license. This has important effects as the Contributor retains a number of important rights over his contribution, as described in more detail later in the license.

> 1.3. "Covered Code" means the Original Code or Modifications or the combination of the Original Code and Modifications, in each case including portions thereof.

This is one of the fundamental terms in the license: Covered Code, Modifications, and Original Code are the three works that are governed by the terms of the license.

> 1.4. "Electronic Distribution Mechanism" means a mechanism generally accepted in the software development community for the electronic transfer of data.

This idea is one that has been described in previous licenses, for example, the GPL's requirement that source code be made available through FTP sites or comparable methods.

> 1.5. "Executable" means Covered Code in any form other than Source Code.

Again, this definition of Executable is somewhat different than the form of binary or executable that has been described previously. Rather than define Executable in terms of its function—i.e., as a program that does work—the MPL defines it by what it is not, as not-Source Code, which is defined later. This provides a broader definition than would be provided by a function driven definition.

> 1.6. "Initial Developer" means the individual or entity identified as the Initial Developer in the Source Code notice required by Exhibit A.

This term has already been addressed, as contrasted to Contributor.

> 1.7. "Larger Work" means a work which combines Covered Code or portions thereof with code not governed by the terms of this License.

Unlike the GPL, as will be seen shortly, the MPL permits the combination of work governed by the license—i.e. the Covered Code—with code not governed by the license as part of a Larger Work. This is subject to certain restrictions relating to the making available of the Covered Code; but if those restrictions are satisfied, a Larger Work may otherwise be distributed as the licensee sees fit, including under a proprietary or other license.

> 1.8. "License" means this document.

This term is self-explanatory.

> 1.8.1. "Licensable" means having the right to grant, to the maximum extent possible, whether at the time of the initial grant or subsequently acquired, any and all of the rights conveyed herein.

This term is probably not strictly necessary, as the term is used in the license in a manner that does not vary from that in common usage. It does preserve, with the clause "whether at the time of the initial grant or subsequently acquired," the licensee from liability if the Initial Developer or Contributor lacks the right to license certain pieces of intellectual property, say, a patent, at the time the licensee exercises rights under the license, but subsequently acquires such a right. One would hope that such situations would be fairly rare, as the licensee (as well as the infringing Initial Developer or Contributor) could probably be held liable for infringement during that interim period.

> 1.9. "Modifications" means any addition to or deletion from the substance or structure of either the Original Code or any previous Modifications. When Covered Code is released as a series of files, a Modification is:
>
> A. Any addition to or deletion from the contents of a file containing Original Code or previous Modifications.
>
> B. Any new file that contains any part of the Original Code or previous Modifications.

This term is also largely self-explanatory, including any works made by modifying the Original Code, which is defined immediately below as that code contributed by the Initial Developer, whether by the licensee (the "You" that is also defined below) or by a Contributor. The "Modifications" definition is important because it marks the extent of Covered Code as distinct from a possible larger work, as described in Section 3.7. The decision about what code constitutes Original Code or a Modification is made on a file-by-file basis.

> 1.10. "Original Code" means Source Code of computer software code which is described in the Source Code notice required by Exhibit A as Original Code, and which, at the time of its release under this License is not already Covered Code governed by this License.

The Original Code, as would be expected, is that source code providing the foundation for the license.

1.10.1. "Patent Claims" means any patent claim(s), now owned or hereafter acquired, including without limitation, method, process, and apparatus claims, in any patent Licensable by grantor.

As described in later clauses, both the Initial Developer and any Contributor grant royalty free licenses to any licensee of the MPL for patents held by them, which are related to the MPL software. The use of the term Patent Claims is a means to grant the broadest rights possible in such patents.

1.11. "Source Code" means the preferred form of the Covered Code for making modifications to it, including all modules it contains, plus any associated interface definition files, scripts used to control compilation and installation of an Executable, or source code differential comparisons against either the Original Code or another well known, available Covered Code of the Contributor's choice. The Source Code can be in a compressed or archival form, provided the appropriate decompression or de-archiving software is widely available for no charge.

As with many of the terms given specific definitions under the MPL, the term Source Code is somewhat different than the term "source code" discussed in connection with previous licenses. There are two principal distinctions. First, Source Code can mean one of two things: either, "the preferred form of the Covered Code for making modifications to it, including all modules it contains, plus any associated interface definition files, scripts used to control compilation and installation of an Executable," which is substantially identical to the use of source code that has been discussed previously; or "source code differential comparisons against either the Original Code or another well known, available Covered Code of the Contributor's choice," i.e., only that part of the source code that is different from the source code in the Original Code or another well-known version of the Covered Code, the source code of which is presumably available. Using this second option may make distribution of Source Code under the MPL logistically simpler and use less bandwidth.

Second, and to the same end of easing distribution, the MPL permits distribution of the Soure Code, defined either way, in the form of compressed or archived files, so long as the file can be decompressed using widely available free (free as in no-charge) software.

1.12. "You" (or "Your") means an individual or a legal entity exercising rights under, and complying with all of the terms of, this License or a future version of this License issued under Section 6.1.

The first part of this definition is similar to the use of "You" as licensee in the GPL and other licenses. One variation is that compliance with the terms of the license is expressly made a condition of the exercise of the rights of the license in the definition of itself.

For legal entities, "You" includes any entity which controls, is controlled by, or is under common control with You. For purposes of this definition, "control" means (a) the power, direct or indirect, to cause the direction or management of such entity, whether by contract or otherwise, or (b) ownership of more than fifty percent (50%) of the outstanding shares or beneficial ownership of such entity.

This second part of the definition is present to include within the scope of the restrictions of the license, with regard to "legal entities," i.e., corporations, partnerships, limited liability companies or other artificial persons recognized by the law, parents, subsidiaries, and sister corporations of the licensee, and is included in similar form in other licenses, as already noted. Any exercise of rights under the license by modification or distribution of the Covered Code or the like would almost certainly bind the related entity to the terms of the license directly, without need for recourse to this provision. Moreover, to the extent such a related entity had not itself exercised any rights under the license, it could argue, perhaps successfully, that it was not bound by the agreement of the licensee.

Nonetheless, this part of the license does narrow the obligation to distribute source code, as required by Section 3.2, at least within the organization. If related entities were deemed to be distinct, they would each have obligation to distribute source code along with executable versions of the code to each other—a result that might be unnecessarily cumbersome, and which is avoided by this definition.

Section 2 of the MPL embodies the first of the two licenses contained in the MPL. As already noted, the MPL distinguishes between the Initial Developer and subsequent Contributors to the program. This distinction is embodied in the two different grants of rights in the MPL, the first of which is the grant of rights by the Initial Developer.

2. Source Code License.

2.1. The Initial Developer Grant.

The Initial Developer hereby grants You a world-wide, royalty-free, non-exclusive license, subject to third party intellectual property claims:

(a) under intellectual property rights (other than patent or trademark) Licensable by Initial Developer to use, reproduce, modify, display, perform, sublicense and distribute the Original Code (or portions thereof) with or without Modifications, and/or as part of a Larger Work; and

(b) under Patents Claims infringed by the making, using or selling of Original Code, to make, have made, use, practice, sell, and offer for sale, and/or otherwise dispose of the Original Code (or portions thereof).

This grant distinguishes between the category of rights applicable to distribution, modifications, and sublicenses of the Original Code when included as part of a Larger Work, as that term is defined earlier or with modifications, and the Original Code when distributed not as part of such a Larger Work. Simply put, the MPL grants a license only of rights excluding patent and trademark rights, i.e., only those rights arising under copyright, when the Original Code is distributed as part of a Larger Work *or* when the Original Code is distributed with Modifications. Rights under any patent applicable to the Original Code are only granted to the distribution (including by sale) of the Original Code (or portions thereof), which stand alone.

This is an important distinction, and any person intending to distribute the Original Code with Modifications or as part of a Larger Work should be wary of it. In the event that such patent or trademark rights do apply to the Original Code, the user should contact the Initial Developer to see if such rights could be obtained separate from the license before proceeding.* In addition, no trademark rights are granted, even for distribution of the unmodified Original Code.†

> (c) the licenses granted in this Section 2.1(a) and (b) are effective on the date Initial Developer first distributes Original Code under the terms of this License.

This provision is largely self-explanatory and is not likely to have much practical effect. If the Original Code has not yet been released under the License, then the Initial Developer retains all intellectual property rights over it and any subsequent user is limited to that very narrow set of rights described in Chapter 1, such as the "fair use" of copyright material. The License would simply not come into effect at all.

> (d) Notwithstanding Section 2.1(b) above, no patent license is granted: 1) for code that You delete from the Original Code; 2) separate from the Original Code; or 3) for infringements caused by: i) the modification of the Original Code or ii) the combination of the Original Code with other software or devices.

This section acts largely as a savings clause to the limitation of patent rights provided in Section 2.1(b). Section 2.1(d)(1) and (2) provide that any patent rights granted by the license are limited to their application in the Original Code. Accordingly, a licensee may not use that patent in another piece of code. Section 2.1(d)(3) appears to reiterate what is already stated by the distinction between Section 2.1(a) and (b): the MPL does not license patent rights for modified versions of the Original Code or Larger Works incorporating the Original Code.

Section 2.2 parallels Section 2.1 but governs contributions to the Covered Code made by Contributors.

> 2.2. Contributor Grant.
>
> Subject to third party intellectual property claims, each Contributor hereby grants You a world-wide, royalty-free, non-exclusive license

This echoes Section 2.1, applying similar terms to grants from Contributors as to the grant from the Initial Developer.

> (a) under intellectual property rights (other than patent or trademark) Licensable by Contributor, to use, reproduce, modify, display, perform, sublicense and distribute the Modifications created by such Contributor (or portions thereof) either on an unmodified basis, with other Modifications, as Covered Code and/or as part of a Larger Work; and

---

* Mitchell Baker, the original drafter of this license, says that "It's possible [this] interpretation is correct, but this was not the intent. The intent was that the patent grant would be for the Original Code whether or not combined with other code, but not for changes to the Original Code." Baker's comment applies to both Section 2.1 and 2.2 of the MPL.

† Assuming that such a user is not seeking to associate such a derivative work with the name or trade dress of the Initial Developer, it is hard to see how a right arising under trademark would effect the use of a piece of functional code. Nonetheless, this is the type of situation in which consultation with an experienced attorney is not only advisable but necessary before proceeding.

Like Section 2.1(a), Section 2.2(a) makes an important distinction between the licensing of patent and trademark rights and the licensing of "other" rights, i.e., rights under copyright. Only the latter rights are granted when the the Contributor's code is used with Modifications or as part of a Larger Work.

> (b) under Patent Claims infringed by the making, using, or selling of Modifications made by that Contributor either alone and/or in combination with its Contributor Version (or portions of such combination), to make, use, sell, offer for sale, have made, and/or otherwise dispose of: 1) Modifications made by that Contributor (or portions thereof); and 2) the combination of Modifications made by that Contributor with its Contributor Version (or portions of such combination).

This provision works much like the equivalent provision governing the Original Code. The one addition is that the patent rights are granted both for the Original Code plus the Contributor's modifications, the "Contributor Version," and for the Modifications made by that Contributor standing alone.

> (c) the licenses granted in Sections 2.2(a) and 2.2(b) are effective on the date Contributor first makes Commercial Use of the Covered Code.

This provision seems to make fairly restrictive the conditions under which the Contributor Version falls within the scope of the license, i.e., not until "Commercial Use." However, as we have already seen in the definitions used in the MPL, Commercial Use simply means any distribution to a third party. Emailing a copy of the Contributor Version to a friend make the license effective on the code, with all that entails. Again, this is something contributors (or potential contributors) need to be wary of.

This distinction becomes important in light of the following section:

> (d) Notwithstanding Section 2.2(b) above, no patent license is granted: 1) for any code that Contributor has deleted from the Contributor Version;

> 2) separate from the Contributor Version;

As with the Original Code, patent rights are granted for use only in the Contributor Version, a point already made clear by Section 2.2(b). The last two numbered subparts of this section state what is essentially a legal truism: the Contributor does not (and, legally, cannot) grant patent rights that he does not hold.

Subpart 3 states that the Contributor does not grant patent licenses for patents infringed by modifications to the Contributor Version by a third party.

> 3) for infringements caused by: i) third party modifications of Contributor Version or ii) the combination of Modifications made by that Contributor with other software (except as part of the Contributor Version) or other devices;

Subpart 4 states that the Contributor does not purport to license parts of the Covered Code (either from the Original Code or modifications made by another contributor) that infringe patent rights that are not the Contributor's own work.

> or 4) under Patent Claims infringed by Covered Code in the absence of Modifications made by that Contributor.

These last two subparts of Section 2.2(d) may seem meaningless because they merely state a legal truism: a person cannot license that which he does not own. However, they are meaningful in that they protect the Contributor from legal liability in that they make clear that the Contributor is not *purporting* to license that which he lacks a right to license.

Much of this license's provisions regarding the fine points of software patents will likely be of little or no importance to most contributors to open source projects: if the contributor's intent is to meaningfully contribute to an open source project without (substantial at least) payment in return, the costs and difficulty of applying for and defending a patent may not be justified.

Section 3 of the MPL imposes the generational limitations of the license, which parallel fairly closely those of the GPL.

> 3. Distribution Obligations.
>
> 3.1. Application of License.
>
> The Modifications which You create or to which You contribute are governed by the terms of this License, including without limitation Section 2.2.

The modifications made by any licensee to the Covered Code must be licensed by the terms applicable to Contributors, as provided for by Section 2.2. Section 3.1 continues:

> The Source Code version of Covered Code may be distributed only under the terms of this License or a future version of this License released under Section 6.1, and You must include a copy of this License with every copy of the Source Code You distribute. You may not offer or impose any terms on any Source Code version that alters or restricts the applicable version of this License or the recipients' rights hereunder. However, You may include an additional document offering the additional rights described in Section 3.5.

The Source Code, the distribution of which on the same terms as the Executable Code is made mandatory by Section 3.2, can only be distributed under this or a future version of the MPL and the License must be distributed with it. "Additional rights," however, may be granted as provided below.

> 3.2. Availability of Source Code.
>
> Any Modification which You create or to which You contribute must be made available in Source Code form under the terms of this License either on the same media as an Executable version or via an accepted Electronic Distribution Mechanism to anyone to whom you made an Executable version available; and if made available via Electronic Distribution Mechanism, must remain available for at least twelve (12) months after the date it initially became available, or at least six (6) months after a subsequent version of that particular Modification has been made available to such recipients. You are responsible for ensuring that the Source Code version remains available even if the Electronic Distribution Mechanism is maintained by a third party.

Section 3.2 makes mandatory the distribution of the Source Code on terms no less favorable than that of the Executable, much like the GPL.

Like the BSD License, the MPL also requires certain attributions of credit for developing the software, albeit only for the Initial Developer and not for any subsequent Contributor.

3.3. Description of Modifications.

You must cause all Covered Code to which You contribute to contain a file documenting the changes You made to create that Covered Code and the date of any change. You must include a prominent statement that the Modification is derived, directly or indirectly, from Original Code provided by the Initial Developer and including the name of the Initial Developer in (a) the Source Code, and (b) in any notice in an Executable version or related documentation in which You describe the origin or ownership of the Covered Code.

This section also requires a "comment" document describing the type and date of any Modifications to the Covered Code. The practical importance of such a requirement is clear. If Contributors scrupulously adhere to this, the decisions by future users (and Contributors) as to which version of a licensed distribution they want to use should be made signficantly easier.

Section 3.4 reflects the MPL's concerns with patent laws and patent infringements.

3.4. Intellectual Property Matters

(a) Third Party Claims.

If Contributor has knowledge that a license under a third party's intellectual property rights is required to exercise the rights granted by such Contributor under Sections 2.1 or 2.2, Contributor must include a text file with the Source Code distribution titled "LEGAL" which describes the claim and the party making the claim in sufficient detail that a recipient will know whom to contact. If Contributor obtains such knowledge after the Modification is made available as described in Section 3.2, Contributor shall promptly modify the LEGAL file in all copies Contributor makes available thereafter and shall take other steps (such as notifying appropriate mailing lists or newsgroups) reasonably calculated to inform those who received the Covered Code that new knowledge has been obtained.

This section says, in so many, words that to the extent a Contributor is aware of third-party patent claims to the Contributor Version, reasonable efforts—i.e., the inclusion of the "LEGAL" file—should be taken to alert future users or contributors that they must secure the appropriate rights from that third party prior to using, distributing, or modifying the Contributor Version. The legal effect of this provision, in terms of protecting the Contributor from claims of infringement, is questionable at best. A holder of a third-party patent certainly could consent to such an arrangement and reach independently negotiated licenses of his patent rights with each of the users or potential contributors that would be interested in licensing his patent. But such a patent holder could probably just as easily object and sue the Contributor for patent infringement for distributing the (admittedly) infringing code, "LEGAL" file or not. Accordingly, to the extent that any Contributor would want to take advantage of this mechanism, it is imperative that such a Contributor reach an understanding with the third-party patent holder before proceeding.

Section 3.4(b) states that the same model (with all the same defects and potential for liability) governs the Contributor Version's use of application programming interfaces. This was included to address issues raised by standards created by participants who later disclose that they have patents on basic mechanisms required to work with those standards.

> (b) Contributor APIs.
>
> If Contributor's Modifications include an application programming interface and Contributor has knowledge of patent licenses which are reasonably necessary to implement that API, Contributor must also include this information in the LEGAL file.

Finally, Section 3.4(c) contains representations implicitly made in Section 2.2, to the effect that the Contributor represents that he believes he has the rights to grant the license he licenses as part of the Contributor Version.

> (c) Representations.
>
> Contributor represents that, except as disclosed pursuant to Section 3.4(a) above, Contributor believes that Contributor's Modifications are Contributor's original creation(s) and/or Contributor has sufficient rights to grant the rights conveyed by this License.

As with many provisions of this license, its legal effects are unclear at best. To the extent the Contributor Version infringes on a third-party patent, the holder of that patent can still sue users, modifiers, or distributors of that version for infringement, representation or not. This subsections is designed to avoid that situation by ensuring that Contributors don't knowingly add patent-infringing code to the project.

Section 3.5 requires that certain notices be attached and provided with the Covered Code with the intention of giving future users of that code notice of the provisions governing it, through inclusion of a notice (attached as Exhibit A) and a copy of the MPL.

> 3.5. Required Notices.
>
> You must duplicate the notice in Exhibit A in each file of the Source Code. If it is not possible to put such notice in a particular Source Code file due to its structure, then You must include such notice in a location (such as a relevant directory) where a user would be likely to look for such a notice. If You created one or more Modification(s) You may add your name as a Contributor to the notice described in Exhibit A. You must also duplicate this License in any documentation for the Source Code where You describe recipients' rights or ownership rights relating to Covered Code.

The second part of Section 3.5, like similar provisions in the GPL, explicitly permits licensees to offer and to charge fees for warranty and support agreements in connection with the Covered Code. Such permission is contingent upon making clear that the licensee is the only person undertaking any such obligation, not the Initial Developer or any Contributor.

You may choose to offer, and to charge a fee for, warranty, support, indemnity or liability obligations to one or more recipients of Covered Code. However, You may do so only on Your own behalf, and not on behalf of the Initial Developer or any Contributor. You must make it absolutely clear than any such warranty, support, indemnity or liability obligation is offered by You alone, and You hereby agree to indemnify the Initial Developer and every Contributor for any liability incurred by the Initial Developer or such Contributor as a result of warranty, support, indemnity or liability terms You offer.

Section 3.6 governs the terms of the distribution of the executable version of Covered Code. It has two principal effects. First, it conditions any distribution of the executable version on compliance with Sections 3.1 through 3.5 already described. Second, it permits distribution of the executable under a different license than the source code, including under a proprietary license.

3.6. Distribution of Executable Versions.

You may distribute Covered Code in Executable form only if the requirements of Section 3.1-3.5 have been met for that Covered Code, and if You include a notice stating that the Source Code version of the Covered Code is available under the terms of this License, including a description of how and where You have fulfilled the obligations of Section 3.2. The notice must be conspicuously included in any notice in an Executable version, related documentation or collateral in which You describe recipients' rights relating to the Covered Code.

The second part governs the terms of distribution of the Executable Code.

You may distribute the Executable version of Covered Code or ownership rights under a license of Your choice, which may contain terms different from this License, provided that You are in compliance with the terms of this License and that the license for the Executable version does not attempt to limit or alter the recipient's rights in the Source Code version from the rights set forth in this License. If You distribute the Executable version under a different license You must make it absolutely clear that any terms which differ from this License are offered by You alone, not by the Initial Developer or any Contributor. You hereby agree to indemnify the Initial Developer and every Contributor for any liability incurred by the Initial Developer or such Contributor as a result of any such terms You offer.

The ability of a licensee or Contributor to "cash in" on the distribution of the Executable Code under a proprietary license is limited by the ability of any licensee to access and compile the source code for himself. Distribution of the executable under different terms also requires indemnifying the Initial Developer and Contributors for any liability that might be incurred—although it is hard to see what, if any, additional liability could possibly accrue to them that would not accrue from the distribution of the source code.

3.7. Larger Works.

You may create a Larger Work by combining Covered Code with other code not governed by the terms of this License and distribute the Larger Work as a single product. In such a case, You must make sure the requirements of this License are fulfilled for the Covered Code.

This provision works hand in hand with the second part of Section 3.6. The Executable Version of the Covered Code can be distributed as part of a Larger Work with code licensed under proprietary or other licenses, subject to the limitations of the MPL, most importantly that the source code of the Covered Code be made available as required by Section 3.2.

This provision is the most important distinction between the MPL and the GPL, which, as already discussed, does not permit integration with non-GPL licensed work, and the LGPL, which permits such integration only on fairly restrictive terms. This is an elegant solution to the problem in its simplicity but is subject to a couple of caveats. First, the other code that is combined with the Covered Code to make the Larger Work must itself be susceptible to such combined distribution: for example, such Larger Work cannot include any GPL-licensed code. It does, however, permit combination with proprietary code, at least to the extent the distributor has the right to distribute such code. Second, and perhaps more importantly, Section 3.7 may provide a substantial incentive for putative or potential Contributors to implement their work where possible as "other code" as opposed to Modifications, which become part of the Covered Code as Contributions upon the first Commercial Distribution of that code, as already described. By adding utility to the Covered Code without falling within its restrictions, such "other code" gives licensees the possibility to profit from the contributions (or Contributions) of others, by selling or otherwise distributing the Larger Work, without sharing the benefits of their own code with that community.

Section 3.7 is the key provision of the license and the permission it gives to Contributors and distributors of Covered Code to incorporate that code into larger works may be seen as a real advantage over the GPL. It avoids the GPL's strict limitations on combining GPL-licensed code with code under other licenses, and it also avoids some of the uncertainties and complexities associated with the LGPL.

The MPL also takes a different approach than the GPL to the situations when statutes, regulations, or judicial decisions invalidate or make impossible the enforcement of terms of the license. As already noted, the GPL and the LGPL forbid exercise of the rights under the license in that situation. The MPL does not.

> 4. Inability to Comply Due to Statute or Regulation.
>
> If it is impossible for You to comply with any of the terms of this License with respect to some or all of the Covered Code due to statute, judicial order, or regulation then You must: (a) comply with the terms of this License to the maximum extent possible; and (b) describe the limitations and the code they affect. Such description must be included in the LEGAL file described in Section 3.4 and must be included with all distributions of the Source Code. Except to the extent prohibited by statute or regulation, such description must be sufficiently detailed for a recipient of ordinary skill to be able to understand it.

The licensee simply must comply with the License to the extent possible and notify other licensees of limitations on the license that result from statute, regulation, or judicial decisions. It is still possible for software to be distributed under the MPL after a hypothetical judicial decision prohibits distribution of some but not all the source code of a given Contributor Version or requires payment of royalties to one or more Contributors but not to others.

5. Application of this License.

This License applies to code to which the Initial Developer has attached the notice in Exhibit A and to related Covered Code.

This provision is self-explanatory. Section 6 substantially provides that Netscape has the right to revise and update the MPL (although they have not done so since issuing MPL 1.1), and have those modified terms govern all code licensed under the MPL. This, obviously, could substantially change the rights or standing of licensees and Contributors to the MPL.

6. Versions of the License.

6.1. New Versions.

Netscape Communications Corporation ("Netscape") may publish revised and/or new versions of the License from time to time. Each version will be given a distinguishing version number.

6.2. Effect of New Versions.

Once Covered Code has been published under a particular version of the License, You may always continue to use it under the terms of that version. You may also choose to use such Covered Code under the terms of any subsequent version of the License published by Netscape. No one other than Netscape has the right to modify the terms applicable to Covered Code created under this License.

Persons exercising rights under the license, such as users of Covered Code, will not lose their rights—they will still be able to use them as defined by previous versions of the license. However, Contributors to the Covered Code might find that the rights they are required to grant have substantially changed or expanded by the new license. Netscape transferred the right to modify the MPL to the Mozilla Foundation when it was founded in July, 2003, and Mitchell Baker reports that there will be a Version 1.2 of the MPL reflecting this at some point.

Developers who are interested in using the MPL, but not in connection with the Mozilla project, are permitted by Section 6.3 to use their own version of the MPL, free of any third party's ability to change its terms.

6.3. Derivative Works.

If You create or use a modified version of this License (which you may only do in order to apply it to code which is not already Covered Code governed by this License), You must (a) rename Your license so that the phrases "Mozilla", "MOZILLAPL", "MOZPL", "Netscape", "MPL", "NPL" or any confusingly similar phrase do not appear in your license (except to note that your license differs from this License) and (b) otherwise make it clear that Your version of the license contains terms which differ from the Mozilla Public License and Netscape Public License. (Filling in the name of the Initial Developer, Original Code or Contributor in the notice described in Exhibit A shall not of themselves be deemed to be modifications of this License.)

Such a license must not be called the MPL and must otherwise be distinct from the MPL and the related NPL. This provision again contrasts with the GPL and the LGPL, which explicitly prohibit the creation of derivative licenses.

Section 7 provides the now-familiar disclaimer of warranties.

> 7. DISCLAIMER OF WARRANTY.
>
> COVERED CODE IS PROVIDED UNDER THIS LICENSE ON AN "AS IS" BASIS, WITHOUT WARRANTY OF ANY KIND, EITHER EXPRESSED OR IMPLIED, INCLUDING, WITHOUT LIMITATION, WARRANTIES THAT THE COVERED CODE IS FREE OF DEFECTS, MERCHANTABLE, FIT FOR A PARTICULAR PURPOSE OR NON-INFRINGING. THE ENTIRE RISK AS TO THE QUALITY AND PERFORMANCE OF THE COVERED CODE IS WITH YOU. SHOULD ANY COVERED CODE PROVE DEFECTIVE IN ANY RESPECT, YOU (NOT THE INITIAL DEVELOPER OR ANY OTHER CONTRIBUTOR) ASSUME THE COST OF ANY NECESSARY SERVICING, REPAIR OR CORRECTION. THIS DISCLAIMER OF WARRANTY CONSTITUTES AN ESSENTIAL PART OF THIS LICENSE. NO USE OF ANY COVERED CODE IS AUTHORIZED HEREUNDER EXCEPT UNDER THIS DISCLAIMER.

Section 7 includes among its disclaimers, in addition to other things, that the Covered Code is "non-infringing." This disclaims all warranties regarding the effect of Sections 2.1, 2.2, and 3.4(c) to the extent that they may be read as representations that the Initial Developer or a Contributor has the right to license a given piece of code under copyright, patent, or trademark law. While the licensee can feel some assurance that he will not be sued by the Initial Developer or Contributor for infringement, provided of course that he complies with the terms of the MPL, he is on his own with regards to third-party intellectual property claims. By using the Covered Code, he undertakes the risk that he may be sued for infringement, without any recourse to the Initial Developer or the Contributors.* (As noted in Chapter 1, this is true of other open source licenses as well, and it is not unique to the MPL.)

Section 8 of the MPL governs the termination of the license. Like much of the rest of MPL, it is similar to, but more forgiving than, parallel provisions of the GPL.

> 8. TERMINATION.
>
> 8.1. This License and the rights granted hereunder will terminate automatically if You fail to comply with terms herein and fail to cure such breach within 30 days of becoming aware of the breach. All sublicenses to the Covered Code which are properly granted shall survive any termination of this License. Provisions which, by their nature, must remain in effect beyond the termination of this License shall survive.

This is more permissive than Section 4 of the GPL, which voids all rights under the license upon its infringement. The MPL, by contrast, provides a 30-day "cure" period following the discovery of such a breach for the licensee to cure. In addition, like the GPL, the breach of the MPL by a distributor does not void sublicenses granted by that distributor to distributees.

---

* To the extent that the Covered Code infringes on third-party intellectual property rights, either the Initial Developer and/or the Contributors are in the same position as the licensee and would have similar liability.

The MPL provides that the license terminates as a consequence of patent litigation brought by a putative licensee with, however, some important limitations. It should be noted that these termination provisions apply only to *patent* claims and not claims alleging infringement of other forms of intellectual property, such as copyright and trademark.

8.2. If You initiate litigation by asserting a patent infringement claim (excluding declaratory judgment actions) against Initial Developer or a Contributor (the Initial Developer or Contributor against whom You file such action is referred to as "Participant") alleging that:

(a) such Participant's Contributor Version directly or indirectly infringes any patent, then any and all rights granted by such Participant to You under Sections 2. 1 and/or 2.2 of this License shall, upon 60 days notice from Participant terminate prospectively, unless if within 60 days after receipt of notice You either: (i) agree in writing to pay Participant a mutually agreeable reasonable royalty for Your past and future use of Modifications made by such Participant, or (ii) withdraw Your litigation claim with respect to the Contributor Version against such Participant. If within 60 days of notice, a reasonable royalty and payment arrangement are not mutually agreed upon in writing by the parties or the litigation claim is not withdrawn, the rights granted by Participant to You under Sections 2.1 and/or 2.2 automatically terminate at the expiration of the 60 day notice period specified above.

If it occurs, the termination of rights under the license is prospective only, i.e., only bars future use of the licensed code, and does not create liability for past uses of the licensed code. The termination is also subject to a 60-day "cooling off period" in which the person alleging infringement can either withdraw the claim or negotiate another resolution with the person against whom the claim is brought, whether the Initial Developer or a Contributor.

Curiously enough, the MPL provides for more punitive termination provisions if the patent infringement alleged against the Initial Developer or a Contributor does not relate to Covered Code but to some other action of such persons.

(b) any software, hardware, or device, other than such Participant's Contributor Version, directly or indirectly infringes any patent, then any rights granted to You by such Participant under Sections 2.1(b) and 2.2(b) are revoked effective as of the date You first made, used, sold, distributed, or had made, Modifications made by that Participant.

Such termination has no "cooling off period" and is, moreover, retroactive. The revocation is "backdated" from the first use of the code under the license by the person suing. The threat of enforcement of this provision creates a strong disincentive for the filing of such patent litigations.

8.3. If You assert a patent infringement claim against Participant alleging that such Participant's Contributor Version directly or indirectly infringes any patent where such claim is resolved (such as by license or settlement) prior to the initiation of patent infringement litigation, then the reasonable value of the licenses granted by such Participant under Sections 2.1 or 2.2 shall be taken into account in determining the amount or value of any payment or license.

This provision has no binding effect and can really be read as exhortatory only. Such a pre-litigation termination would presumably be reached through settlement, which could be done on any terms agreed to by the parties involved, taking into consideration such "reasonable value of the licenses" granted by the MPL.

> 8.4. In the event of termination under Sections 8.1 or 8.2 above, all end user license agreements (excluding distributors and resellers) which have been validly granted by You or any distributor hereunder prior to termination shall survive termination.

This duplicates the effect of Section 8.1.

The following section disclaims liability to the extent permitted by law, like many of the other open source licenses already examined.

> 9. LIMITATION OF LIABILITY.
>
> UNDER NO CIRCUMSTANCES AND UNDER NO LEGAL THEORY, WHETHER TORT (INCLUDING NEGLIGENCE), CONTRACT, OR OTHERWISE, SHALL YOU, THE INITIAL DEVELOPER, ANY OTHER CONTRIBUTOR, OR ANY DISTRIBUTOR OF COVERED CODE, OR ANY SUPPLIER OF ANY OF SUCH PARTIES, BE LIABLE TO ANY PERSON FOR ANY INDIRECT, SPECIAL, INCIDENTAL, OR CONSEQUENTIAL DAMAGES OF ANY CHARACTER INCLUDING, WITHOUT LIMITATION, DAMAGES FOR LOSS OF GOODWILL, WORK STOPPAGE, COMPUTER FAILURE OR MALFUNCTION, OR ANY AND ALL OTHER COMMERCIAL DAMAGES OR LOSSES, EVEN IF SUCH PARTY SHALL HAVE BEEN INFORMED OF THE POSSIBILITY OF SUCH DAMAGES. THIS LIMITATION OF LIABILITY SHALL NOT APPLY TO LIABILITY FOR DEATH OR PERSONAL INJURY RESULTING FROM SUCH PARTY'S NEGLIGENCE TO THE EXTENT APPLICABLE LAW PROHIBITS SUCH LIMITATION. SOME JURISDICTIONS DO NOT ALLOW THE EXCLUSION OR LIMITATION OF INCIDENTAL OR CONSEQUENTIAL DAMAGES, SO THIS EXCLUSION AND LIMITATION MAY NOT APPLY TO YOU.

Except as provided by separate agreement to warranty or otherwise indemnify against loss, as permitted under Section 3.5, any software provided under the MPL is provided "as is," with the user taking responsibility for its use, except to the extent such a disclaimer is prohibited by law.

> 10. U.S. GOVERNMENT END USERS.
>
> The Covered Code is a "commercial item," as that term is defined in 48 C.F.R. 2.101 (Oct. 1995), consisting of "commercial computer software" and "commercial computer software documentation," as such terms are used in 48 C.F.R. 12.212 (Sept. 1995). Consistent with 48 C.F.R. 12.212 and 48 C.F.R. 227.7202-1 through 227.7202-4 (June 1995), all U.S. Government End Users acquire Covered Code with only those rights set forth herein.

These provisions ensure that United States government agencies may be bound by commercial software licensing agreements.

Section 11 contains a bundle of provisions typical in a commercial contract.

> 11. MISCELLANEOUS.
>
> This License represents the complete agreement concerning subject matter hereof. If any provision of this License is held to be unenforceable, such provision shall be

reformed only to the extent necessary to make it enforceable. This License shall be governed by California law provisions (except to the extent applicable law, if any, provides otherwise), excluding its conflict-of-law provisions. With respect to disputes in which at least one party is a citizen of, or an entity chartered or registered to do business in the United States of America, any litigation relating to this License shall be subject to the jurisdiction of the Federal Courts of the Northern District of California, with venue lying in Santa Clara County, California, with the losing party responsible for costs, including without limitation, court costs and reasonable attorneys' fees and expenses. The application of the United Nations Convention on Contracts for the International Sale of Goods is expressly excluded. Any law or regulation which provides that the language of a contract shall be construed against the drafter shall not apply to this License.

This section provides that California law governs interpretation of the contract and provides that the venue for all disputes—in which one of the participants (i.e., either the plaintiff or the defendant) is a citizen or an entity registered to do business in the United States—shall be the federal district court in Santa Clara, California (not coincidentally a venue that was convenient for Netscape when the contract was written, before their acquisition by AOL). It also explicitly provides for shifting of attorneys fees and costs, meaning that whoever loses the lawsuit (if there is a loser) is responsible for paying all the costs associated with the lawsuit, including the other side's "reasonable" attorneys fees.

The next section of the license addresses the situation in which a legal claim is made against the Initial Developer and one or more Contributors and attempts to impose a responsibility on both to jointly address such a claim.

12. RESPONSIBILITY FOR CLAIMS.

As between Initial Developer and the Contributors, each party is responsible for claims and damages arising, directly or indirectly, out of its utilization of rights under this License and You agree to work with Initial Developer and Contributors to distribute such responsibility on an equitable basis. Nothing herein is intended or shall be deemed to constitute any admission of liability.

It is not clear what legal effect this section has, if any. It is certainly possible that both the Initial Developer and a Contributor could be held jointly and severally liable (meaning that each is fully responsible for the violation of the other), say, if the Covered Code was found to infringe on a patent or copyright held by a third party, and both the Initial Developer and the Contributor had distributed the Covered Code. Courts, however, are typically reluctant to enforce such relatively vague obligations. Agreeing to "work with" Initial Developer is exactly such a vague obligation: it may have an exhortative effect, but that is likely to be it.

Section 13 describes a legal arrangement for multiple licensing of the Covered Code.

13. MULTIPLE-LICENSED CODE.

Initial Developer may designate portions of the Covered Code as Multiple-Licensed. Multiple-Licensed means that the Initial Developer permits you to utilize portions of the Covered Code under Your choice of the NPL or the alternative licenses, if any, specified by the Initial Developer in the file described in Exhibit A.

With the MPL, as with any other license, the creator of the work (in this case, the Initial Developer) may issue the work under one or more licenses, and potential licensees are free to choose, *at the beginning*, the license regime under which they will use the work. Once that choice is made regarding the licensee's own contributions to the work or modifications, the licensee is bound to the terms of the license that was chosen and cannot "go back." For example, the Covered Code may be licensed by the Initial Developer both under the MPL and the GPL. A Contributor chooses to work with the Covered Code under the GPL, makes modifications, and distributes those modifications. Having done so, the Contributor then discovers that his Contribution includes a patentable process, which he would much rather license under the more protective MPL. Now, he cannot do this. Having distributed the code under the GPL, with all the terms applicable thereto, the genie cannot be put back in the bottle. The Contributor is, of course, not required to continue to maintain or develop the Covered Code. But he would be prevented from enforcing patent claims to subsequent users or modifiers of that program who adhere to the terms of the GPL. This example is not unique to the MPL, but rather arises under any situation in which a piece of code is multiple-licensed.

Section 13 is the last section of the license. A model "fill-in-the-blanks" Exhibit A follows, for those who choose to become Initial Developers of their programs under the MPL.

EXHIBIT A -Mozilla Public License.

"The contents of this file are subject to the Mozilla Public License Version 1.1 (the "License"); you may not use this file except in compliance with the License. You may obtain a copy of the License at

http://www.mozilla.org/MPL/

Software distributed under the License is distributed on an "AS IS" basis, WITHOUT WARRANTY OF ANY KIND, either express or implied. See the License for the specificlanguage governing rights and limitations under the License.

The Original Code is _____.

The Initial Developer of the Original Code is _____.

Portions created by _____ are Copyright (C) _____ _____. All Rights Reserved.

Contributor(s): _____.

Alternatively, the contents of this file may be used under the terms of the _____ license (the [___] License), in which case the provisions of [_____] License are applicable instead of those above. If you wish to allow use of your version of this file only under the terms of the [____] License and not to allow others to use your version of this file under the MPL, indicate your decision by deleting the provisions above and replace them with the notice and other provisions required by the [___] License. If you do not delete the provisions above, a recipient may use your version of this file under either the MPL or the [___] License."

[NOTE: The text of this Exhibit A may differ slightly from the text of the notices in the Source Code files of the Original Code. You should use the text of this Exhibit A rather than the text found in the Original Code Source Code for Your Modifications.]

The MPL provides a novel solution to the problems faced by Netscape in bringing into open source an already well-established set of code and setting up terms and conditions that would both protect its rights and encourage contributors to modify and improve that work. Its terms and focus reflect its origins: its distinction between the Initial Developer and subsequent Contributors sets it apart from, say, the more freeform development contemplated by the GPL. Its emphasis on patent rights and the limited grant of them provided by the license also reflects its corporate origin and the intent on the part of Netscape to limit, to the extent possible, the grant of rights while still remaining consistent with an open source model. By doing so, the MPL attempts to ensure that both open source volunteers and commercial developers are comfortable cooperating in this legal environment.

Application and Philosophy

The GPL and MPL both have had symbolic as well as practical impacts in the world of software development. Those effects of these licenses, beyond their strict terms, are described next.

The GPL License and the Free Software Philosophy

The impact of the GPL, and its offshoot, the LGPL, on the development of software cannot be overstated. The GPL project that grew up with the license, the GNU/Linux constellation of applications, better known simply as Linux,* has seen its acceptance by users grow steadily from the early 1990s to the point where it now poses the only significant competitor to the Windows operating system.

This success, depending on your point of view, arises either because of, or despite, the fact that the GPL bars any development of software from GPL-licensed software that is not itself GPL licensed. The GPL seems to embody the maxim that "Freedom in a commons brings ruin to all."† By requiring that all contributions to GPL projects be themselves GPL licensed, the GPL ensures not only that these contributions are available to other programmers (or at least those programmers willing to work within the GPL framework) but also encourages contributions from those programmers to whom it is important that their contributions be made, and remain, "free," as that term is used in the GPL.

---

* For a discussion of this nomenclature, see the essay "What's in a Name?" contained in Richard M. Stallman, *Free Software: Free Society* (Free Software Foundation, 2002) (p. 51 and following).

† Quotation from Garett Hardin is taken from William Vollman, *Rising Up and Rising Down* (McSweeneys 2003) (Vol. III, p. 219). "Freedom," as the term is used in the quotation, is the absence of rules: the GPL itself is an embodiment of the principle that certain types of freedom require rules in order to be preserved.

The existence of such programmers is by now beyond dispute. Based on the success of the GNU/Linux project alone, the free software project has succeeded. Part of this success is due to the fact that the GPL has as important a symbolic purpose as a practical one. The restrictions of the GPL (and the LGPL) have greatly shaped the nature of development of software that is GPL-licensed. Programmers, by and large, respect the GPL and conform their behavior accordingly. The development of projects under the GPL depends on each participant adhering to the terms of the license by making his or her own contribution available to the community of developers. This adherence has resulted in the great success enjoyed by GPL-licensed projects.

But the GPL has an equally important aspirational purpose. Given that the GPL is often viewed as the "purest" form of licensing in nurturing and encouraging open development of software, development under this license has drawn programmers who take seriously the larger concept of open software development. This has had results beyond those caused by the terms of the license itself.

Contrary to the beliefs of some, the GPL does not require that software running on a GPL-licensed operating system be licensed under the GPL. Similarly, the GPL does not require that only GPL-licensed programs be distributed as part of a distribution containing GPL-licensed code. For example, many of the GNU/Linux distributions, including those of Caldera, a significant early GNU/Linux distributor, included both the GPL-licensed Linux operating system and proprietary licensed code. Caldera paid royalties (as required by the terms of the proprietary software) on proprietary software that was distributed on the same CD-ROM as the operating system. Because the proprietary software did not compile with the operating system, this was perfectly consistent with the terms of the GPL. Purchasers of the Caldera distribution were free to install the GNU/Linux operating system and to install the proprietary software from the same CD-ROM on the same computer.

Despite the fact that such distributions are completely consistent with the GPL, some programmers and distributors have disfavored such distributions, on the grounds that such distribution is inconsistent with the spirit of free software development. A well-known distributor of GNU/Linux software, the Debian project, for example, has taken the position that every piece of software distributed as part of a GNU/Linux distribution should be licensed under a free software license.* This view, held by many members of the free software community, has significantly influenced the development of software under the GPL.

Taking just one example, a substantial movement arose to counter the K Desktop Environment (or KDE), a graphic user interface (GUI) frontend on the GNU/Linux operating system, which some perceived as an encroachment on the free software philosophy.† Beginning in 1996, a programmer named Mattias Ettrich started to

---

* See *http://www.debian.org/social_contract* for more details.

† For a more thorough description of this episode, see Chapter 15, "Trolls Versus Gnomes" in *rebel code: inside linux and the open source revolution*, Glyn Moody (Perseus Publishing, 2001).

develop KDE based on the Qt Toolkit, a non-GPL licensed program written and owned by Trolltech.* While the Qt Toolkit was available without cost, and while its source code did eventually become available,† there was a strong counterreaction to the development of such a potentially critical piece of software under a non-GPL license. As a result, a separate team of programmers began to develop the GNU Network Object Model Environment or GNOME, announced in August, 1997. As a result, both the KDE and the GNOME programs, both well-supported by developers and applications, are growing and thriving today.

Conversely, the development of free software projects is not determined, or even necessarily shaped, by the terms of the GPL. While the GPL encourages a certain type of development, it does not mandate any particular type of development structure. Indeed, it invites many different approaches to development. As described in Chapter 7, the initial components of the GNU/Linux operating system—the GNU C Compiler and Emacs, among others—were developed under a very different model of software development than the Linux kernel. Moreover, as also described in Chapter 7, even for projects licensed under non-GPL licenses, there are significant advantages to maintaining an "open development" model in which code is kept available to the open source community and not developed (as is permitted) under proprietary licenses.

While its terms may provide the foundation for free software development, the GPL is also a potent symbol of a much larger, and more important, idea of how software (or any other work) should be made and maintained. The success of this license has been driven as much by the ideals that it represents as by strict application of its legal terms.

The Mozilla Public License: Circumstances and Opportunities

As already described, the MPL was the result of a decision by Netscape Communications—one of the first Internet companies—to open source license the code to its Netscape Communicator software in January, 1998. At that time, Netscape was in an intense competition with Microsoft, whose rival web browser, Internet Explorer, had the advantage of its close association with Microsoft's dominant Windows operating system. The MPL was an attempt to get some of the benefit of open source development into a program developed under a proprietary license.

The initial announcement of the "opening" of the Communicator code was greeted with great enthusiasm (and certainly boosted public perception of open source software), although Netscape's own economic condition—and its eventual absorption

---

* The Q Public License is discussed in Chapter 4.

† As noted in Chapter 4, Trolltech eventually cross-licensed the Qt Toolkit under the GPL after receiving substantial pressure to do so from the free software community.

into America Online—caused problems for the project. A thorough rewriting and a focus on standards-compliance have created a strong Mozilla culture, in many ways independent of its roots in Netscape. Open sourcing the project by itself didn't reverse Netscape's fortunes, but it has been a key source of continued innovation in the web browser market. The continued vitality of this project was demonstrated on June 27, 2004, with the release of the FireFox web browser by the Mozilla Foundation.

The MPL itself has thrived as an open source license. The well-constructed, well-written MPL has certainly found a niche: only the BSD, GPL, and LGPL Licenses are associated with substantially more projects than the MPL. The MPL has also been used as the base for a number of other Open Source Initiative-certified licenses, including the Apple Public License, the Nokia Open Source License, and the Sun Public License.

As can be seen from the examples of the GPL and the MPL, the success of licenses is a factor less of the terms or the wording of those licenses than of the ideas that they represent. Powerful, meaningful ideas draw minds, and the success of open source and free software licensing is the result of the minds that such ideas can draw.

CHAPTER 4

Qt, Artistic, and Creative Commons Licenses

This chapter addresses two licenses closely associated with particular programs: the Q Public License (the Qt Toolkit) and the Artistic License (Perl). Each of these licenses has unique features, reflecting the specific terms that their creators wished to impose on users or modifiers of their work. Unlike the GPL or BSD licenses, these licenses are not frequently applied to programs other than those for which they were originally developed, and they tend to be adapted only for the code originally licensed under them and derivative works. Nonetheless, because these licenses are still in frequent use and because they provide some interesting contrasts to the licenses already discussed, they are described at some length in this chapter.

Also discussed is the Creative Commons license—the fruit of an effort to expand the open source model of development beyond software to literature and the arts. While its creators state that it is not applicable to software, it is a well-written license and has begun what will be an interesting experiment at the very least.

The Q Public License

The Q Public License (QPL) was designed by the Norwegian firm Trolltech to govern the distribution of its software, the Qt Toolkit. The Qt Toolkit is a crossplatform toolkit for the development of graphical user interface (GUI) applications. It is used in KDE, a graphical user interface frequently used as a desktop environment for UNIX and UNIX-like operating systems, including many varieties of Linux. As KDE became more popular for use in Linux operating systems, concerns developed in the open source and free software community about the limitations imposed by the QPL. In reaction to this pressure, Trolltech agreed to cross-license the Qt Toolkit under the GPL as well as the QPL, after which the developers of KDE immediately shifted their license to GPL. Distribution of the Qt Toolkit and KDE has since been predominantly under the GPL.

The QPL provides a novel approach to a number of open source licensing issues. Among other things, the QPL permits distributions of modifications to covered software in the form of patches under less restrictive terms than modifications compiled with the original code, and provides certain rights applicable only to the initial developer of the licensed code.

The QPL is presented in numbered sections following the first (unlabeled) section that is the introduction. This introduction includes the copyright notice for the license itself, permits distribution and copying of the license explicitly, and provides that the license applies to all software containing the appropriate copyright notice.

> Copyright © 1999 Trolltech AS, Norway.
>
> Everyone is permitted to copy and distribute this license document.
>
> The intent of this license is to establish freedom to share and change the software regulated by this license under the open source model.
>
> This license applies to any software containing a notice placed by the copyright holder saying that it may be distributed under the terms of the Q Public License version 1.0. Such software is herein referred to as the Software. This license covers modification and distribution of the Software, use of third-party application programs based on the Software, and development of free software which uses the Software.

This is standard form for an open source license. The section's last sentence makes clear that the license is intended to apply to all programs "based on the Software" and "which uses the Software." As was the case with the GPL, any software that is based on or uses the Software must itself comply with the terms of the QPL or otherwise violate the terms of the original grant of rights under the QPL.

Sections 1 through 6 of the QPL appear under the section heading "Grant of Rights." Section 1 reiterates and further articulates the generational limitations applicable to QPL-licensed software

> 1. You are granted the non-exclusive rights set forth in this license provided you agree to and comply with any and all conditions in this license. Whole or partial distribution of the Software, or software items that link with the Software, in any form signifies acceptance of this license.

Any work that incorporates, relies on, or links to the Software must be governed by its terms.* Distinctions concerning the effect of linking and libraries† are described later in Sections 5 and 6.

Section 2 articulates the right to distribute unmodified versions of the software.

---

* A QPL-licensed piece of software can still operate on the same system as software licensed under another license. For exampe, the KDE program may run on a GPL-licensed system: as already noted, the simple operation of a program is outside the scope of the GPL. Similarly, the operation of the GPL software, assuming it does not link with the QPL licensed software, does not violate the QPL.

† The importance of libraries and linking are described in detail in connection with the LGPL in Chapter 3.

2. You may copy and distribute the Software in unmodified form provided that the entire package, including—but not restricted to—copyright, trademark notices and disclaimers, as released by the initial developer of the Software, is distributed.

The only apparent limitation on the exercise of this right is that the copyright and trademark notices and the disclaimers applicable to the Software (described at the end of the license) are distributed with the Software. However, Section 4 also requires compliance with certain provisions as a prerequisite to distribution of the unmodified Software, beyond those in Section 1. Any person distributing the Software should comply with both sections.

Section 3 permits the distribution of modifications to the Software, in the form of patches.

3. You may make modifications to the Software and distribute your modifications, in a form that is separate from the Software, such as patches.

The QPL provides substantially different restrictions on distributions of modifications as patches than it does on distributions of modifications in executable code. The distribution of modifications as patches has significant benefits to the original developer, some benefits and drawbacks to users of the modified software, and some substantial drawbacks for contributors. Distributing modifications as patches clearly delineates, in a way that no set of notices ever could, what part of the software is the work of the initial developer and what part of it is a result of the work of contributors. This has the effect of protecting the reputation of the initial developers and of making clear the primacy of the developer's work.

From a user's point of view, there is the benefit, presuming that the initial work is good, that the end user will always have access to the functionality embedded in the original work. The user does not have to compile the patches, after all. On the other hand, to the extent that such a user wants to access functions or improvements made by contributors, she is put to the task of recompiling the source code to include the patches, which is not an insurmountable obstacle.

Another product that allows free distribution but prohibits changes is the qmail mail server. For details on its distribution rules, see *http://cr.yp.to/qmail/dist.html*. As a result, developers extending qmail also use patching methods, although there aren't any explicit rules on the nature of those patches.

From the point of view of the contributors, the distribution of modifications in the form of patches presents a serious drawback. Because of the additional effort required by the end user, users are less likely to use the contributor's version of the software than the initial developer's. Why then would a contributor choose to distribute software as a patch? The reason is because the QPL requires contributors to surrender much fewer rights to their work when that work is distributed only as a patch. The last sentence of Section 3 with the section's two subparts follow.

The following restrictions apply to modifications:

a. Modifications must not alter or remove any copyright notices in the Software.

b. When modifications to the Software are released under this license, a non-exclusive royalty-free right is granted to the initial developer of the Software to distribute your modification in future versions of the Software provided such versions remain available under these terms in addition to any other license(s) of the initial developer.

These restrictions are quite limited. The first, Section 3(a), requires only that the patch not contain modifications that would have the effect of altering or removing copyright notices. Section 3(b) requires that the contributor permit the initial developer (Trolltech in the case of the Qt Toolkit) to gain a royalty-free license to the patch. The initial developer's exercise of rights under this license is contingent on the developer itself releasing the code containing the modification in future versions of the Software under the QPL. Other than these restrictions, a contributor releasing a patch need not surrender any other rights. He can license the patch under any license, including a proprietary license, that does not prohibit compliance with Section 3(a) and (b).* Moreover, the QPL does not require that the creator of such a patch make available the source code for that patch.

Section 4 governs the distributions of executable code both with and without modifications, which is in deliberate contrast to the distribution of executable code and patches provided by Section 3. The distribution of unmodified versions of the code is already permitted by Section 2; nonetheless, the restrictions imposed by Section 4—including the requirements that source code be made available and that a copy of the license be provided with the code—should be considered to be in addition to, not in place of, the restrictions imposed by Section 2.

With regards to modified versions of the Software, Section 4 provides an alternate licensing scheme to the provision of modifications in the form of patches, as described in Section 3. Section 4 permits the distribution of modifications into machine executable code (including the code in the original Software) thereby avoiding the burdens placed on end users by distributing modifications as patches. However, by distributing modified executable code, the contributor is obligated to make the source code readily available and to license the modifications under the QPL.

4. You may distribute machine-executable forms of the Software or machine-executable forms of modified versions of the Software, provided that you meet these restrictions:

a. You must include this license document in the distribution.

b. You must ensure that all recipients of the machine-executable forms are also able to receive the complete machine-readable source code to the distributed Software, including all modifications, without any charge beyond the costs of data transfer, and place prominent notices in the distribution explaining this.

---

* For example, because of the GPL's bar on any deviations from its terms, the contributor could not license a patch under the GPL and distribute it for use with a QPL-licensed piece of software.

    c. You must ensure that all modifications included in the machine-executable forms are available under the terms of this license.

This license also permits multiple licensing; i.e., the contributor can make his modifications available under another license, such as the GPL or a proprietary license, so long as they are also available under the QPL. As already noted, all of these restrictions, including the inclusion of the license document, apply equally to distributions of the unmodified Software as well.

Section 5 permits the user to combine the Software with other products, including libraries.

    5. You may use the original or modified versions of the Software to compile, link and run application programs legally developed by you or by others.

This section does *not* address the distribution of such Software with other application programs, but only addresses actions by end users using the Software. Distribution of a QPL-licensed program linked with a library (under a non-QPL license) is not permitted except as described in Section 6.

Section 6 describes the restrictions applicable to distributions of the Software as linked to other software. While they do not require that such "other software" be licensed under the QPL, these restrictions require both that the source code for the other software be made available and that the "other software" be subject to a license that permits distribution and modification of that software without a fee.

    6. You may develop application programs, reusable components and other software items that link with the original or modified versions of the Software. These items, when distributed, are subject to the following requirements:

        a. You must ensure that all recipients of machine-executable forms of these items are also able to receive and use the complete machine-readable source code to the items without any charge beyond the costs of data transfer.

        b. You must explicitly license all recipients of your items to use and re-distribute original and modified versions of the items in both machine-executable and source code forms. The recipients must be able to do so without any charges whatsoever, and they must be able to re-distribute to anyone they choose.

        c. If the items are not available to the general public, and the initial developer of the Software requests a copy of the items, then you must supply one.

There is no provision for distribution of the Software as part of a larger work, as there is, for example, with the LGPL. Subsections 6(a) and (b) thus essentially require that "other software" itself be licensed under an open source license, although not necessarily the QPL. In addition, consistent with its emphasis on the rights of the initial developer, subsection 6(c) of the QPL provides that the initial developer can request a copy of the "other software" in the event the distribution is non-public or the initial developer is otherwise unable to obtain a copy.

The next section of the QPL is the "Limitation of Liability" section.

In no event shall the initial developers or copyright holders be liable for any damages whatsoever, including—but not restricted to—lost revenue or profits or other direct, indirect, special, incidental or consequential damages, even if they have been advised of the possibility of such damages, except to the extent invariable law, if any, provides otherwise.

Pairing with the "Limitation of Liability" is the "No Warranty" section.

The Software and this license document are provided AS IS with NO WARRANTY OF ANY KIND, INCLUDING THE WARRANTY OF DESIGN, MERCHANTABILITY AND FITNESS FOR A PARTICULAR PURPOSE.

As with the open source licenses examined previously, these provisions seek to limit the liability of the initial developer, contributors, and distributors to the maximum possible extent.

The final section, "Choice of Law," actually contains a choice of law provision and a choice of forum provision.

This license is governed by the Laws of Norway. Disputes shall be settled by Oslo City Court.

Non-Norwegians considering adopting the QPL to license their own software would be well-advised to revise at least this part of the license.

The QPL has some interesting features. The distinction between requirements placed on modifications distributed in patches and the requirements placed on modifications distributed incorporated into executable code is meaningful and may prove useful at least in some contexts. However, with the cross-licensing of the Qt Toolkit under the GPL, and the GPL's adoption by the KDE developers, the QPL may become less important as a license.

Artistic License (Perl)

The Artistic (or Perl Artistic) License is named because of its stated intention to allow the initial developer to maintain "artistic" control over the licensed software and derivative works created from it. The Perl License is substantially identical to the Artistic License, but it includes an additional paragraph, which provides another option for commercial distribution.

Developed by Larry Wall in the late 1980s, Perl is a ubiquitous programming language, based on C (among other languages) and is found frequently in UNIX and UNIX-based systems. It is omnipresent on the World Wide Web, with thousands, if not millions, of web sites running combinations of Perl scripts over Apache web servers. Part of Perl's strength as a language is its ability to tie together different programs and languages that were not initially intended to work together.

Because of Perl's ubiquity and because Perl is licensed under both the Artistic License and the GPL, programmers and users are as likely to come across the Perl License as any other open source or free software license except the GPL, BSD, or

LGPL. The core, the standard Perl libraries, the optional modules, and the documentation that make up Perl were initiated by Larry Wall but have involved the contributions of thousands of people, making Perl one of the most successful open source projects to date.

Unfortunately, the Artistic License is notoriously vague and confusing. This description and commentary will, hopefully, dispel at least some of that confusion.

Like the MPL and the QPL already discussed, the Artistic License was designed for use in connection with a particular program—Perl—and not as a generally applicable license, like the BSD or MIT Licenses, or the GPL, although it certainly could be used apart from Perl. (The Artistic License is frequently used for Perl modules, including many of those on the Comprehensive Perl Archive Network at *http://cpan.org*.)

The first section of the Artistic License is its preamble.

> The Artistic License
>
> August 15, 1997
>
> Preamble
>
> The intent of this document is to state the conditions under which a Package may be copied, such that the Copyright Holder maintains some semblance of artistic control over the development of the package, while giving the users of the package the right to use and distribute the Package in a more-or-less customary fashion, plus the right to make reasonable modifications.

The Artistic License was designed in substantial part to allow Larry Wall and his group to maintain control over the Perl project, while encouraging both participation in the project and innovation outside the project.

Like the MPL, the Artistic License begins with a list of definitions.

> Definitions
>
> • "Package" refers to the collection of files distributed by the Copyright Holder, and derivatives of that collection of files created through textual modification.

"Package" is used in place of "Software" or "Covered Code" or "Program," but it means the same thing: the code originally issued under the applicable license and its modifications and derivative works.

> • "Standard Version" refers to such a Package if it has not been modified, or has been modified in accordance with the wishes of the Copyright Holder as specified below.

This refers to the unmodified, original version of the code *and* to the versions modified following certain restrictions identified by the Copyright Holder. Like the initial developer in the MPL and QPL, the Copyright Holder retains certain additional rights above those of other contributors or users of the code.

> • "Copyright Holder" is whoever is named in the copyright or copyrights for the package.

As already noted, the Copyright Holder retains certain additional privileges with regards to the Package.

- "You" is you, if you're thinking about copying or distributing this Package.

"You" is everybody other than the Copyright Holder.

- "Reasonable copying fee" is whatever you can justify on the basis of media cost, duplication charges, time of people involved, and so on. (You will not be required to justify it to the Copyright Holder, but only to the computing community at large as a market that must bear the fee.)

This term adds nothing to the license. As the definition itself notes, the licensee is permitted to charge only "market price"—i.e., whatever the market will bear. As noted in Chapter 1, however, the fact that any distributee can freely distribute source and executable code tends to keep such fees low, at least for software in which the market has some interest.

- "Freely Available" means that no fee is charged for the item itself, though there may be fees involved in handling the item. It also means that recipients of the item may redistribute it under the same conditions they received it.

As used in the license, this definition embodies the generational limitation of the Artistic License. Code that is "freely available" can be distributed under the same terms that the unmodified code was received—i.e., under the terms of the Artistic License.

Section 1 of the license provides for distribution of the source code of the Standard Version of the Package, as long as the license is distributed with it.

1. You may make and give away verbatim copies of the source form of the Standard Version of this Package without restriction, provided that you duplicate all of the original copyright notices and associated disclaimers.

Section 2 in substance permits the user to "update" a given version of the Package so as to incorporate code that is part of the Standard Version.

2. You may apply bug fixes, portability fixes and other modifications derived from the Public Domain or from the Copyright Holder. A Package modified in such a way shall still be considered the Standard Version.

The question of modifications from the "Public Domain" is somewhat unclear. As written, it means that any bug fixes, portability fixes, or other modifications to the Package—as to which copyright and other intellectual property rights either have been expressly disavowed or have lapsed through the passage of time—may be incorporated and the code will still be considered the Standard Version. This introduces a substantial element of uncertainty into what "Standard Version" means. Any one of many different programs (depending on what fixes or modifications have been applied) can equally be described as the Standard Version.

Section 2 does protect the Standard Version against the encroachment of copyright claims of persons other than the Copyright Holder; the Copyright Holder at least can feel confident that the Standard Version (assuming that all users and contributors adhere to the terms of the license) does not contain any code that the Copyright Holder does not have the power to modify, relicense, or distribute.

Section 3 addresses modifications that are not part of the Standard Version. Such modifications must be clearly marked, and, in addition, the modifier must take additional steps if the modifications are distributed outside the modifier's own use or that of his organization.

> 3. You may otherwise modify your copy of this Package in any way, provided that you insert a prominent notice in each changed file stating how and when you changed that file, and provided that you do at least ONE of the following:

Clear notification of the fact that this version has changed is a precondition for any modification of the licensed work. In addition, the modifier must conform to one of the following options:

> a. place your modifications in the Public Domain or otherwise make them Freely Available, such as by posting said modifications to Usenet or an equivalent medium, or placing the modifications on a major archive site such as ftp.uu.net, or by allowing the Copyright Holder to include your modifications in the Standard Version of the Package.

This is somewhat confusing. The first "sub-option," placing the modifications in the public domain, should not be difficult. The modifier would simply be required to make the modifications publicly available and to place a notice on them that no copyright or other forms of intellectual property rights will be enforced with regards to that work.[*]

The second "sub-option" presents substantially more difficulties. "[O]therwise making [the modifications] Freely Available" would seem to require complying with the definition of "Freely Available" given earlier, requiring that the item itself be given without charge and that the persons receiving it have the right both to use the modifications and to redistribute them on terms no more restrictive than those under which they themselves received the work. Complying with these requirements would not be particularly difficult: a contributor could license the modifications under, for example, the BSD or MIT Licenses described earlier, and put them in a publicly available place for download without charge, other than for the costs of transmission or copying. In such an event, the original work, the Standard Version, would still be licensed under the Artistic License, even though the modifications would be under another license that fell within the definition of "Freely Available."

---

[*] The public domain is discussed in more detail later. A sample Public Domain Dedication can be found at *http://creativecommons.org/licenses/publicdomain/*. There is some uncertainty about the effectiveness of such public domain dedication, however.

While this course of action would be in compliance with the requirement of this "sub-option," it is not clear that this is in fact what is required by the terms of the license. This is because the illustrative examples given after the expression of this requirement actually undermine it. "[P]osting said modifications to Usenet or an equivalent medium, or placing the modifications on a major archive site such as *ftp.uu.net*" by themselves will not permit any person to copy, distribute, or modify those modifications, except as permitted by the doctrine of fair use, as described in Chapter 1. Simply placing a work in a public place does not waive any protections of copyright that might otherwise be attached. As already noted, a work need not even carry a copyright notice to be protected by copyright. Without an explicit disclaimer of copyright protection (such as a public domain dedication) or a licensing agreement, prudent users will assume that such work is still protected by copyright and substantially unavailable for use. Accordingly, this part of the license could create a potentially awkward situation where a modifier, who does in fact want these modifications to be publicly available as the Artistic License seems to require, publicly posts those modifications but does not provide a license that would allow for their free use.*

The third "sub-option" permits a modifier to comply with the license by entering into a separate arrangement with the Copyright Holder. The purpose of this is to permit the Copyright Holder to include the modifications in the Standard Version. While having the same immediate effect as placing the modifications in the public domain, by using this "sub-option," the modifier may be able to retain additional rights, such as the right to license exclusively the modifications for use in another application. Obviously, this depends on the arrangement with the Copyright Holder.

The second of the options prevents public distribution of the modifications but may be appropriate for many situations in which the modifier wants to have the benefit of the modified code for his own (or his own organization's) use but does not want to surrender intellectual property rights that are associated with the modifications.

> b. use the modified Package only within your corporation or organization.

The third option allows for technical modifications that will likely limit the compatibility of the modified code with the Standard Version.

> c. rename any non-standard executables so the names do not conflict with standard executables, which must also be provided, and provide a separate manual page for each non-standard executable that clearly documents how it differs from the Standard Version.

---

* The fact that this happens all the time in open source development does not eliminate the possibility of a misunderstanding that could lead to a legal dispute. A contributor may actually not know that he is "licensing" work that he submits to an open source or free software project, or he may think better of it after having done so, and take some action to claw his submission back. This situation seems to rarely, if ever, arise. Nonetheless, those considering taking leadership positions in such projects should take reasonable efforts to make sure that contributors are aware of the licensing terms applicable to the project.

This variation reflects the Artistic License's association with Perl, with its use of programming language–specific terms, such as "standard and non-standard executables" and "manual pages." Using this variation permits a "fork" in the development of the underlying software, with the modified version developing separate and apart from the Standard Version. In essence, modifiers are free to "take their ball and go home" but at the cost of splitting off from what is likely to be the most popular version of the underlying code, the Standard Version.

The fourth and final option is one inherent in any license: negotiating separately with the original licensor.

> d. make other distribution arrangements with the Copyright Holder.

Section 4 governs the distribution of both the Standard Version and any modified versions of the Package in executable form or object code. The rights to distribution it grants are in addition to the rights granted by Section 1 to distribute the *source* code of the Package.

> 4. You may distribute the programs of this Package in object code or executable form, provided that you do at least ONE of the following:

These requirements apply any time any part of the Package is distributed in executable form, whether modified or not.

> a. distribute a Standard Version of the executables and library files, together with instructions (in the manual page or equivalent) on where to get the Standard Version.

The license appears to allow each of the forms of distribution to be used no matter whether the Standard Version itself is being distributed—a Standard Version with user modifications (for example, with modifications the user has issued into the public domain)—or a modified version under Section 3(c). Accordingly, a distributor could lawfully distribute a modified version and remain in technical compliance with the license by providing only the executables and libraries of the Standard Version together with instructions on where to get the (source code presumably of the) Standard Version. This is so, even though it seems clear that distribution of a modified, nonstandard version of the code should be made under Section 4(c). This is another of the ambiguities of the license.

> b. accompany the distribution with the machine-readable source of the Package with your modifications.

This option seems intended for distributions of the Standard Version where the code has been modified under the first "sub-option" described in Section 3(a)—i.e., where the modifier has placed his modifications in the public domain. This would be the most sensible way for such a distribution to be done, although, as already noted, the distributor may exercise any of the options in distributing the executable form of the Package.

c. accompany any non-standard executables with their corresponding Standard Version executables, giving the non-standard executables non-standard names, and clearly documenting the differences in manual pages (or equivalent), together with instructions on where to get the Standard Version.

The third option clearly mirrors Section 3(c) governing the creation of modified, nonstandard versions of the program. While not required, modifications of the Package created under Section 3(c) should be distributed under the terms of Section 4(c) to best support the purposes of the license.

Finally, as was the case with the licensing of modifications, a distributor can always negotiate a separate, permissible manner of distribution with the Copyright Holder.

d. make other distribution arrangements with the Copyright Holder.

Section 5 governs the charges that may be imposed by a distributor in connection with the distribution of the Package, whether in the Standard Version or a modified version.

5. You may charge a reasonable copying fee for any distribution of this Package. You may charge any fee you choose for support of this Package. You may not charge a fee for this Package itself. However, you may distribute this Package in aggregate with other (possibly commercial) programs as part of a larger (possibly commercial) software distribution provided that you do not advertise this Package as a product of your own.

As already noted, "reasonable copying fee" has no enforceable meaning, as the way it is defined makes reference only to the price that the market will bear. Because the license permits anyone to distribute the source code and the executable form of the Package, competition will likely impose its own limits on any fees charged by distributors, as is typically the case for open source and free software licensed programs. As is the case with the GPL and all of the other licenses already examined, this license does not prohibit agreements to support the use of the Package, which presumably would include warranties or other comparable guarantees of functionality. Finally, this section also permits distribution of the Package as part of a distribution unit with commercial (or non-commercial) software, so long as the distributor does not claim to be the author of the Package and, implicitly, so long as the other requirements of Section 4 are complied with. This last permission is subject to an important limitation in several variations of the Artistic license, including the Perl Artistic License. This limitation is described in more detail later.

Section 6 also reflects the Artistic License's connection to Perl, a programming language, and makes explicit that programs in Perl do not fall within the scope of the license but belong to whoever generated them.

6. The scripts and library files supplied as input to or produced as output from the programs of this Package do not automatically fall under the copyright of this Package, but belong to whomever generated them, and may be sold commercially, and may be aggregated with this Package.

Section 6 further permits the distribution of libraries or scripts with the code that is so generated. Obviously, such libraries or scripts may be necessary for the code to function. This is described in the optional Section 8.

Section 7 excludes from the scope of the license C or Perl subroutines linked by the user with the Package.

> 7. C or perl subroutines supplied by you and linked into this Package shall not be considered part of this Package.

Section 8 of the Artistic License contains the non-endorsement clauses typical in open source and free software licenses and prevents the use of the Copyright Holder's name in connection with the sale or distribution of modified versions of the Package or code developed from the Package under Section 6.

> 8. The name of the Copyright Holder may not be used to endorse or promote products derived from this software without specific prior written permission.

There is another optional Section 8 that also appears in variations of the Artistic License, most importantly, the Perl Artistic License.

> 8. Aggregation of this Package with a commercial distribution is always permitted provided that the use of this Package is embedded; that is, when no overt attempt is made to make this Package's interfaces visible to the end user of the commercial distribution. Such use shall not be construed as a distribution of this Package.

Although not stated explicitly, this section is meant to address the same situation as governed by Section 6: where what is at issue is not the Package itself (i.e., the Perl scripts and libraries) being modified and distributed, but code that relies on the Package in order to properly function (i.e., software written in Perl). This Section 8 accordingly limits the generally free distribution of the source and executable codes under Section 1 and 4 respectively when that distribution is part of a commercial aggregate with the Package. In those situations, the Package may be utilized as part of the commercial program, but its interfaces (and, correspondingly, the ability to write new scripts in Perl) must be blocked from the end user. This section is presumably included to prevent commercial distributions of programs written in Perl from competing with the parallel open source distributions of Perl that are intended to encourage innovation and contributions to Perl itself. While commercial distributors are free to employ Perl's functionality in their commercial programs, such commercial programs are shut out from Perl's own development cycle.

Finally, Section 9 of the Artistic License contains the standard disclaimers of warranty found in most open source and free software licenses.

> 9. THIS PACKAGE IS PROVIDED "AS IS" AND WITHOUT ANY EXPRESS OR IMPLIED WARRANTIES, INCLUDING, WITHOUT LIMITATION, THE IMPLIED WARRANTIES OF MERCHANTIBILITY AND FITNESS FOR A PARTICULAR PURPOSE.

The Artistic License is designed for centralized projects, much like the QPL and the MPL. Because of this and the license's emphasis on the rights of the Copyright Holder, it is probably not suited for freeform software development projects. In addition, it has ambiguities in key terms governing modification and distribution of the licensed code. Nonetheless, it is worth taking the time to understand because of Perl's ubiquity. Moreover, as discussed, it is not difficult for contributors to Perl (or other projects licensed under the Artistic License), despite the license's ambiguities, to comply with both the letter and the spirit of the license.

Creative Commons Licenses

The Creative Commons series of licenses are the product of the Creative Commons Corporation, a not-for-profit organization founded in 2001 and currently based at Stanford University Law School. In December, 2002, inspired by the GPL, the Creative Commons Corporation issued a series of licenses designed to encourage creators of works to make their work available for public use. While not written for use in connection with software, the Creative Commons Licenses provide a solid basis for licensing the "open source" use of other expressions, including texts, music, web sites, and film. One of their licenses is described here to reflect that the ideas behind open source and free software licensing are applicable to more than just software. Additionally, the Creative Commons Licenses are solidly constructed and well-written: as such, they provide a good model for those who are considering drafting their own open source licenses.

In addition to the licenses, the Creative Commons Corporation provides two other services worth noting, at least briefly. First, Creative Commons offers a "Public Domain Dedication," a sort of ultra-permissive license that denotes the creator's surrender of all rights under copyright.* As noted in connection with the Artistic License, the dedication of a work to the public domain is a simple and straightforward way to permit unrestricted use of a work. Second, Creative Commons offers the "Founder's Copyright," a contractual undertaking between the creator and Creative Commons that mimics the effect of the original copyright laws: copyright is granted for 14 years and is renewable for one additional 14-year period.

All the Creative Commons Licenses permit the free copying and distribution of the licensed work. Some variations also permit the distribution of derivative works, some on terms that require the creator of the derivative work to license that work under

---

* There is some question as to whether the Creative Commons Public Domain Dedication is legally effective as a contract because there is no exchange of consideration. The importance of mutual consideration is discussed in more detail in Chapter 6. Although the Public Domain Dedication may not be of binding legal effect as a license, there may be other legal methods by which it could be enforced, including the theory of reliance. Before making a Public Domain Dedication, a creator of a work may want to consider using instead a relatively unrestrictive license such as the BSD or MIT licenses described in Chapter 2. In any event, before relying on a work falling within the scope of such a dedication, a user should contact a knowledgeable lawyer to address its enforceability in the particular circumstances presented.

the same license, in the same manner as the GPL. The full variety of Creative Commons Licenses are available at *creativecommons.org*. The one described here is the "Attribution–ShareAlike" license that permits free distribution of the original work and creation and distribution of derivative works subject to the limitation that such works themselves be subject to the terms of the Creative Commons License. The license also requires that distributions of both original and derivative works contain attributions crediting the original author of the work. This license does not distinguish between commercial and non-commercial uses of a work: one of the more common limitations in Creative Commons Licenses is a bar on commercial use of works and derivative works. By contrast to the other licenses described in this book, this Creative Commons License governs the use of a written text, not a software program.

 Creative Commons released a new set of licenses on May 25, 2004. A description of the revised license follows the discussion of the original license.

Paired with each Creative Commons License is the so-called "Commons Deed," a document which expresses in short form the privileges granted and restrictions imposed by the license. The Commons Deed for the Attribution–ShareAlike License, Version 1.0, is shown in Figure 4-1.

The license begins with a disclaimer of warranties by Creative Commons itself as the provider of the license.

> CREATIVE COMMONS CORPORATION IS NOT A LAW FIRM AND DOES NOT PROVIDE LEGAL SERVICES. DISTRIBUTION OF THIS DRAFT LICENSE DOES NOT CREATE AN ATTORNEY-CLIENT RELATIONSHIP. CREATIVE COMMONS PROVIDES THIS INFORMATION ON AN "AS-IS" BASIS. CREATIVE COMMONS MAKES NO WARRANTIES REGARDING THE INFORMATION PROVIDED, AND DISCLAIMS LIABILITY FOR DAMAGES RESULTING FROM ITS USE.

This warranty disclaims any liability for use of the license and disclaims any implication that an attorney-client relationship has been created by the license.

The license proper begins with an introduction that states that by exercising any rights under the license, the user accepts the terms of the license, a provision modeled on the substantially similar provision in the GPL.

> License
>
> THE WORK (AS DEFINED BELOW) IS PROVIDED UNDER THE TERMS OF THIS CREATIVE COMMONS PUBLIC LICENSE ("CCPL" OR "LICENSE"). THE WORK IS PROTECTED BY COPYRIGHT AND/OR OTHER APPLICABLE LAW. ANY USE OF THE WORK OTHER THAN AS AUTHORIZED UNDER THIS LICENSE IS PROHIBITED.
>
> BY EXERCISING ANY RIGHTS TO THE WORK PROVIDED HERE, YOU ACCEPT AND AGREE TO BE BOUND BY THE TERMS OF THIS LICENSE. THE LICENSOR GRANTS YOU THE RIGHTS CONTAINED HERE IN CONSIDERATION OF YOUR ACCEPTANCE OF SUCH TERMS AND CONDITIONS.

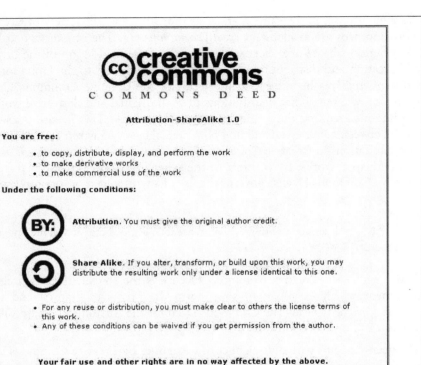

Figure 4-1. The Commons Deed for the Attribution–ShareAlike License, Version 1.0

As discussed in Chapter 6, the absence of a signed agreement between the licensor and licensee may not bar the creation of an enforceable contract. Moreover, as noted in connection with the discussion of the GPL license, a user has no real interest in asserting that a license is unenforceable. After all, without the privileges granted by the license, the user has no right to use the work except in the very limited manner permitted by fair use.

Like the QPL, the MPL, and the Artistic License, the Creative Commons License begins with a list of definitions.

1. **Definitions**

    a. **"Collective Work"** means a work, such as a periodical issue, anthology or encyclopedia, in which the Work in its entirety in unmodified form, along with a number of other contributions, constituting separate and independent works in themselves, are assembled into a collective whole. A work that constitutes a Collective Work will not be considered a Derivative Work (as defined below) for the purposes of this License.

The license explicitly permits distributions of the licensed work both on its own and as part of a collective work. This provision has a similar effect to the "mere aggregation" language of the GPL, although it is somewhat more explicit.*

> b. **"Derivative Work"** means a work based upon the Work or upon the Work and other pre-existing works, such as a translation, musical arrangement, dramatization, fictionalization, motion picture version, sound recording, art reproduction, abridgment, condensation, or any other form in which the Work may be recast, transformed, or adapted, except that a work that constitutes a Collective Work will not be considered a Derivative Work for the purpose of this License.

Unlike a Collective Work, a Derivative Work must be distributed only under the same terms that apply to the original work.

> c. **"Licensor"** means the individual or entity that offers the Work under the terms of this License.

> d. **"Original Author"** means the individual or entity who created the Work.

As noted in Chapter 1, while the author or creator of a work is the person in whom copyright initially vests (except in the case of work for hire), the person enjoying rights under copyright frequently will not be the same person who originally created the work because of contractual assignment or otherwise. This license distinguishes between the original author and the holder of the copyright, and it gives rights to the Original Author.

> e. **"Work"** means the copyrightable work of authorship offered under the terms of this License.

This term is self-explanatory.

> f. **"You"** means an individual or entity exercising rights under this License who has not previously violated the terms of this License with respect to the Work, or who has received express permission from the Licensor to exercise rights under this License despite a previous violation.

As provided by Section 7, the license terminates upon breach of any provision by the licensee.

The next section reiterates what is already the case: that the license does not prohibit or limit any rights that could be exercised under the doctrine of fair use or first sale doctrines.†

> 2. **Fair Use Rights.** Nothing in this license is intended to reduce, limit, or restrict any rights arising from fair use, first sale or other limitations on the exclusive rights of the copyright owner under copyright law or other applicable laws.

---

* Section 2(c) of the GPL reads, in part, "mere aggregation of another work not based on the Program with the Program (or with a work based on the Program) on a volume of a storage or distribution medium does not bring the other work under the scope of this License."

† The first sale doctrine guarantees certain rights to purchasers of physical expressions of copyrighted work, including the right to loan that copy to others, to resell it, and to make personal use of it.

Section 3 of the license provides the critical operating language of the license.

> 3. **License Grant.** Subject to the terms and conditions of this License, Licensor hereby grants You a worldwide, royalty-free, non-exclusive, perpetual (for the duration of the applicable copyright) license to exercise the rights in the Work as stated below:
>
> > a. to reproduce the Work, to incorporate the Work into one or more Collective Works, and to reproduce the Work as incorporated in the Collective Works;

This permits free distribution of the original work, whether as part of a Collective Work or otherwise.

> > b. to create and reproduce Derivative Works;

The creation and distribution of derivative works is subject to the important limitation, as described in Section 4(b), that such derivative works must be distributed under the same license that governs the distribution of the original work, which is this Creative Commons License.

> > c. to distribute copies or phonorecords of, display publicly, perform publicly, and perform publicly by means of a digital audio transmission the Work including as incorporated in Collective Works;

The rights to perform a given work are generally governed separate and apart from the rights to copy and distribute a work. For example, the purchase of a hardcopy of the text of a play does not convey the right to publicly perform that play. This subsection includes the grant of such performance rights in the scope of the license.

> > d. to distribute copies or phonorecords of, display publicly, perform publicly, and perform publicly by means of a digital audio transmission Derivative Works;

This provision conveys performance rights for derivative works.

> > The above rights may be exercised in all media and formats whether now known or hereafter devised. The above rights include the right to make such modifications as are technically necessary to exercise the rights in other media and formats. All rights not expressly granted by Licensor are hereby reserved.

This grants rights to use or distribute the work in all media, including those not yet invented.

The next section identifies the restrictions applicable to exercise rights under the license.

> 4. **Restrictions.** The license granted in Section 3 above is expressly made subject to and limited by the following restrictions:
>
> > a. You may distribute, publicly display, publicly perform, or publicly digitally perform the Work only under the terms of this License, and You must include a copy of, or the Uniform Resource Identifier for, this License with every copy or phonorecord of the Work You distribute, publicly display, publicly perform, or publicly digitally perform.

Like the other licenses already described, this provision requires that the terms of the license be provided along with the licensed work. As an alternative, however, this license also provides that the distributor may include a "Uniform Resource Identifier," a URL that points to the text of the license.

> You may not offer or impose any terms on the Work that alter or restrict the terms of this License or the recipients' exercise of the rights granted hereunder. You may not sublicense the Work. You must keep intact all notices that refer to this License and to the disclaimer of warranties.

Like the GPL, the Creative Commons License bars the inclusion of any condition that "alters or restricts" the terms of the license. Accordingly, work licensed under the Creative Commons cannot include work licensed under other licenses that impose any restrictions, such as the GPL or the MPL License already discussed.

> You may not distribute, publicly display, publicly perform, or publicly digitally perform the Work with any technological measures that control access or use of the Work in a manner inconsistent with the terms of this License Agreement.

This prohibits any distributor from distributing the work in a manner intended to prevent copying—such distributions frustrate the purpose of the license. This could prevent, for example, distribution of the work or derivative in some electronic book formats that contain copy protection, or in CD or DVD formats that are designed to frustrate digital copying.

> The above applies to the Work as incorporated in a Collective Work, but this does not require the Collective Work apart from the Work itself to be made subject to the terms of this License.

This reiterates the exclusion from the effect of the license on other works contained in a Collective Work.

> If You create a Collective Work, upon notice from any Licensor You must, to the extent practicable, remove from the Collective Work any reference to such Licensor or the Original Author, as requested. If You create a Derivative Work, upon notice from any Licensor You must, to the extent practicable, remove from the Derivative Work any reference to such Licensor or the Original Author, as requested.

This right permits a Licensor to disassociate either herself and/or the Original Author from association with a Collective Work or a Derivative Work, if so desired. Note that the right belongs to the Licensor, not the Original Author. A subsequent restriction requires attribution to be given to the Licensor of the Original Work, unless the Licensor notifies the Licensee of a contrary desire.

Section 4(b) imposes the same restrictions on the distribution or performance of Derivative Works that Section 4(a) imposes on the Original Work. Moreover, by imposing these obligations on all potential creators of Derivative Works, the license requires that Derivative Works be distributed only under the terms of this license, with all the grants of rights and restrictions that this entails. This generational limitation is substantially similar to the copyleft imposed by the GPL.

b. You may distribute, publicly display, publicly perform, or publicly digitally perform a Derivative Work only under the terms of this License, and You must include a copy of, or the Uniform Resource Identifier for, this License with every copy or phonorecord of each Derivative Work You distribute, publicly display, publicly perform, or publicly digitally perform. You may not offer or impose any terms on the Derivative Works that alter or restrict the terms of this License or the recipients' exercise of the rights granted hereunder, and You must keep intact all notices that refer to this License and to the disclaimer of warranties. You may not distribute, publicly display, publicly perform, or publicly digitally perform the Derivative Work with any technological measures that control access or use of the Work in a manner inconsistent with the terms of this License Agreement. The above applies to the Derivative Work as incorporated in a Collective Work, but this does not require the Collective Work apart from the Derivative Work itself to be made subject to the terms of this License.

The "right of disassociation" described in Section 4(b) already includes the right to disassociate from Derivative Works as well as Original Works.

Section 4(c) contains a requirement of attribution that distinguishes this license from other Creative Commons Licenses. In both the original and Derivative Works, the Original Author of the work (not necessarily the Licensor) must be given credit appropriate to the format of the distribution, unless, under Section 4(b), the Licensor requests otherwise.

c. If you distribute, publicly display, publicly perform, or publicly digitally perform the Work or any Derivative Works or Collective Works, You must keep intact all copyright notices for the Work and give the Original Author credit reasonable to the medium or means You are utilizing by conveying the name (or pseudonym if applicable) of the Original Author if supplied; the title of the Work if supplied; in the case of a Derivative Work, a credit identifying the use of the Work in the Derivative Work (e.g., "French translation of the Work by Original Author," or "Screenplay based on original Work by Original Author"). Such credit may be implemented in any reasonable manner; provided, however, that in the case of a Derivative Work or Collective Work, at a minimum such credit will appear where any other comparable authorship credit appears and in a manner at least as prominent as such other comparable authorship credit.

Section 5 contains the representations and warranties provisions applicable to the license. Unlike every other license examined so far, the Creative Commons License contains a warranty of non-infringement, albeit one limited by the representation that the original Licensor has undertaken only "reasonable inquiry" to ensure that the Work does not contain infringing material or anything that could be considered defamatory or damaging to the privacy rights of any person.

5. **Representations, Warranties and Disclaimer**

a. By offering the Work for public release under this License, Licensor represents and warrants that, to the best of Licensor's knowledge after reasonable inquiry:

i. Licensor has secured all rights in the Work necessary to grant the license rights hereunder and to permit the lawful exercise of the rights granted hereunder without You having any obligation to pay any royalties, compulsory license fees, residuals or any other payments;

ii. The Work does not infringe the copyright, trademark, publicity rights, common law rights or any other right of any third party or constitute defamation, invasion of privacy or other tortious injury to any third party.

The obligation imposed by this provision is substantial. *No potential Licensor should use this version of the Creative Commons license without seriously considering the obligations imposed by this section.* If the work to be licensed is entirely the creation of the Licensor, and the Licensor can fairly satisfy himself that he did not infringe on other copyrights and that the work is not defamatory or otherwise injurious to third parties, then this provision may provide no difficulty. In the case of an aesthetic work (a play, short story, or poem), that would be a sufficient inquiry and the Licensor could proceed to use the Creative Commons License with confidence. In the case of software or a similar work, however, because of the vague and potentially broad application of software patent rights, no Licensor—without exhaustive review and consultation with an experienced attorney—could possibly feel confident that a particular piece of code does not infringe on any valid patent. Accordingly, the inclusion of such representations in licenses applicable to software is not recommended. While the Licensor need only to undertake "reasonable inquiry" to ensure that the work is non-infringing, the licensor is still making an affirmative representation upon which others may reasonably rely. Version 2.0 of the Creative Commons License does not contain these representations and is almost certainly a better license to use under such circumstances.

Moreover, this representation presents substantial hazards for the licensing of any work under this license if that work includes anything created by another person, including work putatively in the public domain. In the event such work turns out to infringe on the copyright of any third party, the Licensor would be liable not only to that third party whose rights have been infringed (as is the case with every open source and free software license, regardless of the language of that license) but to all the licensees. This could result in the Licensor becoming responsible for a potentially enormous amount of damages—for example, if a licensee relied on the rights granted under the license in entering into a business opportunity, which it can no longer pursue after discovery of the violation.

In sum, in making contractual representations, one must exercise significant caution. Given the potential exposure to liability, Licensors should approach this section with care.

Section 5(b) contains a standard disclaimer of warranties, excepting only the warranty of non-infringement just discussed.

b. EXCEPT AS EXPRESSLY STATED IN THIS LICENSE OR OTHERWISE AGREED IN WRITING OR REQUIRED BY APPLICABLE LAW, THE WORK IS LICENSED ON AN "AS IS" BASIS, WITHOUT WARRANTIES OF ANY KIND, EITHER EXPRESS OR IMPLIED INCLUDING, WITHOUT LIMITATION, ANY WARRANTIES REGARDING THE CONTENTS OR ACCURACY OF THE WORK.

Section 6 contains the disclaimer of liability, again, subject to the exception for the warranty of non-infringement.

6. **Limitation on Liability.** EXCEPT TO THE EXTENT REQUIRED BY APPLICABLE LAW, AND EXCEPT FOR DAMAGES ARISING FROM LIABILITY TO A THIRD PARTY RESULTING FROM BREACH OF THE WARRANTIES IN SECTION 5, IN NO EVENT WILL LICENSOR BE LIABLE TO YOU ON ANY LEGAL THEORY FOR ANY SPECIAL, INCIDENTAL, CONSEQUENTIAL, PUNITIVE OR EXEMPLARY DAMAGES ARISING OUT OF THIS LICENSE OR THE USE OF THE WORK, EVEN IF LICENSOR HAS BEEN ADVISED OF THE POSSIBILITY OF SUCH DAMAGES.

Section 7 governs termination of the license, which essentially occurs upon any breach by the licensee. As is the case with the GPL, the breach by one licensee does not result in the termination of the license to those persons to whom the licensee has distributed the Original Work, a Derivative Work, or a Collective Work, so long as those licensees themselves remain in compliance with the license.

7. **Termination**

   a. This License and the rights granted hereunder will terminate automatically upon any breach by You of the terms of this License. Individuals or entities who have received Derivative Works or Collective Works from You under this License, however, will not have their licenses terminated provided such individuals or entities remain in full compliance with those licenses. Sections 1, 2, 5, 6, 7, and 8 will survive any termination of this License.

Section 7(b) explicates what is implicit in every license, which is that the licensor can license the work to others under different terms than those contained in the license.

   b. Subject to the above terms and conditions, the license granted here is perpetual (for the duration of the applicable copyright in the Work). Notwithstanding the above, Licensor reserves the right to release the Work under different license terms or to stop distributing the Work at any time; provided, however that any such election will not serve to withdraw this License (or any other license that has been, or is required to be, granted under the terms of this License), and this License will continue in full force and effect unless terminated as stated above.

This ability to "cross-license" or "relicense" the work does not affect any license previously granted, and this provision should be of little comfort to potential licensors with cold feet.

Section 8, appropriately labeled Miscellaneous, contains a number of provisions that are redundant of provisions already discussed or irrelevant in all but a very small number of possible scenarios involving the license.

8. **Miscellaneous**

   a. Each time You distribute or publicly digitally perform the Work or a Collective Work, the Licensor offers to the recipient a license to the Work on the same terms and conditions as the license granted to You under this License.

   b. Each time You distribute or publicly digitally perform a Derivative Work, Licensor offers to the recipient a license to the original Work on the same terms and conditions as the license granted to You under this License.

This is entirely redundant to Section 3. Any "You" under the license is someone with access both to the Work (or a Derivative or Collective Work) and the license itself—i.e., everyone who would fall into the descriptions Section 8(a) and (b).

Section 8(c) is a savings clause typical in commercial contracts.

> c. If any provision of this License is invalid or unenforceable under applicable law, it shall not affect the validity or enforceability of the remainder of the terms of this License, and without further action by the parties to this agreement, such provision shall be reformed to the minimum extent necessary to make such provision valid and enforceable.

Section 8(d), in phrasing again typical of commercial contracts, prevents oral modifications to the license and requires any waivers or amendments to be written.

> d. No term or provision of this License shall be deemed waived and no breach consented to unless such waiver or consent shall be in writing and signed by the party to be charged with such waiver or consent.

Finally, Section 8(e) provides a "merger clause" indicating that the license is the entire agreement between the parties, superseding any prior agreement, whether oral or written.

> e. This License constitutes the entire agreement between the parties with respect to the Work licensed here. There are no understandings, agreements or representations with respect to the Work not specified here. Licensor shall not be bound by any additional provisions that may appear in any communication from You. This License may not be modified without the mutual written agreement of the Licensor and You.

Following the last of the license's sections is another set of disclaimers and limitations by Creative Commons itself, restating and expanding the restrictions announced at the beginning of the license.

> Creative Commons is not a party to this License, and makes no warranty whatsoever in connection with the Work. Creative Commons will not be liable to You or any party on any legal theory for any damages whatsoever, including without limitation any general, special, incidental or consequential damages arising in connection to this license. Notwithstanding the foregoing two (2) sentences, if Creative Commons has expressly identified itself as the Licensor hereunder, it shall have all rights and obligations of Licensor.

> Except for the limited purpose of indicating to the public that the Work is licensed under the CCPL, neither party will use the trademark "Creative Commons" or any related trademark or logo of Creative Commons without the prior written consent of Creative Commons. Any permitted use will be in compliance with Creative Commons' then-current trademark usage guidelines, as may be published on its website or otherwise made available upon request from time to time.

> Creative Commons may be contacted at *http://creativecommons.org/*.

Creative Commons issued a new series of licenses on May 25, 2004. The Attribution–ShareAlike Version 2.0 is described here and shown in Figure 4-2. Because most of the license remains unchanged, the subsequent commentary only addresses the new features of the license. For purposes of completeness, however, the license is provided in its entirety. The first change to the license is one that arises under the choose-your-own-license menu on the Creative Commons web site. Because the overwhelming preference among its users for licenses is to require attribution, attribution of the work to its original author is now a standard feature of the license.

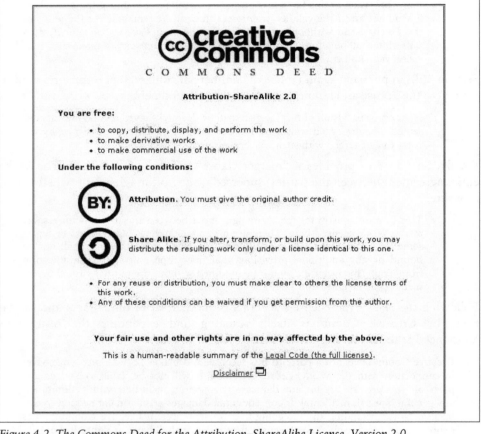

Figure 4-2. The Commons Deed for the Attribution–ShareAlike License, Version 2.0

CREATIVE COMMONS CORPORATION IS NOT A LAW FIRM AND DOES NOT PROVIDE LEGAL SERVICES. DISTRIBUTION OF THIS LICENSE DOES NOT CREATE AN ATTORNEY-CLIENT RELATIONSHIP. CREATIVE COMMONS PROVIDES THIS INFORMATION ON AN "AS-IS" BASIS. CREATIVE COMMONS MAKES NO WARRANTIES REGARDING THE INFORMATION PROVIDED, AND DISCLAIMS LIABILITY FOR DAMAGES RESULTING FROM ITS USE.

License

THE WORK (AS DEFINED BELOW) IS PROVIDED UNDER THE TERMS OF THIS CREATIVE COMMONS PUBLIC LICENSE ("CCPL" OR "LICENSE"). THE WORK IS PROTECTED BY COPYRIGHT AND/OR OTHER APPLICABLE LAW. ANY USE OF THE WORK OTHER THAN AS AUTHORIZED UNDER THIS LICENSE OR COPYRIGHT LAW IS PROHIBITED.

BY EXERCISING ANY RIGHTS TO THE WORK PROVIDED HERE, YOU ACCEPT AND AGREE TO BE BOUND BY THE TERMS OF THIS LICENSE. THE LICENSOR GRANTS YOU THE RIGHTS CONTAINED HERE IN CONSIDERATION OF YOUR ACCEPTANCE OF SUCH TERMS AND CONDITIONS.

1. **Definitions**

    a. **"Collective Work"** means a work, such as a periodical issue, anthology or encyclopedia, in which the Work in its entirety in unmodified form, along with a number of other contributions, constituting separate and independent works in themselves, are assembled into a collective whole. A work that constitutes a Collective Work will not be considered a Derivative Work (as defined below) for the purposes of this License.

    b. **"Derivative Work"** means a work based upon the Work or upon the Work and other pre-existing works, such as a translation, musical arrangement, dramatization, fictionalization, motion picture version, sound recording, art reproduction, abridgment, condensation, or any other form in which the Work may be recast, transformed, or adapted, except that a work that constitutes a Collective Work will not be considered a Derivative Work for the purpose of this License. For the avoidance of doubt, where the Work is a musical composition or sound recording, the synchronization of the Work in timed-relation with a moving image ("synching") will be considered a Derivative Work for the purpose of this License.

In order to use music in combination with a moving image under United States copyright law, the user must generally arrange to acquire "synchronization rights" from the author of the musical work and to pay synchronization royalties for such use. The last sentence of this definition, not present in Version 1.0 of the license, makes clear that such a use of the licensed work is included in the rights granted by the license.

    c. **"Licensor"** means the individual or entity that offers the Work under the terms of this License.

    d. **"Original Author"** means the individual or entity who created the Work.

    e. **"Work"** means the copyrightable work of authorship offered under the terms of this License.

    f. **"You"** means an individual or entity exercising rights under this License who has not previously violated the terms of this License with respect to the Work, or who has received express permission from the Licensor to exercise rights under this License despite a previous violation.

    g. **"License Elements"** means the following high-level license attributes as selected by Licensor and indicated in the title of this License: Attribution, ShareAlike.

2. **Fair Use Rights.** Nothing in this license is intended to reduce, limit, or restrict any rights arising from fair use, first sale or other limitations on the exclusive rights of the copyright owner under copyright law or other applicable laws.

3. **License Grant.** Subject to the terms and conditions of this License, Licensor hereby grants You a worldwide, royalty-free, non-exclusive, perpetual (for the duration of the applicable copyright) license to exercise the rights in the Work as stated below:

    a. to reproduce the Work, to incorporate the Work into one or more Collective Works, and to reproduce the Work as incorporated in the Collective Works;

b. to create and reproduce Derivative Works;

c. to distribute copies or phonorecords of, display publicly, perform publicly, and perform publicly by means of a digital audio transmission the Work including as incorporated in Collective Works;

d. to distribute copies or phonorecords of, display publicly, perform publicly, and perform publicly by means of a digital audio transmission Derivative Works.

The following subsection, 3(e), was added to Version 2.0 to address specific applications of copyright to musical compositions.

e. For the avoidance of doubt, where the work is a musical composition:

i. **Performance Royalties Under Blanket Licenses**. Licensor waives the exclusive right to collect, whether individually or via a performance rights society (e.g. ASCAP, BMI, SESAC), royalties for the public performance or public digital performance (e.g. web-cast) of the Work.

Most publishers of musical works are members of one of the three major performing rights societies, ASCAP, BMI, and SESAC. These organizations collect royalties from the performance of musical works in situations in which it would be administratively difficult for an individual publisher to collect, such as from radio stations and jukeboxes. These organizations then distribute those funds according to complex formulas among their members. This subsection makes clear that the licensor does not intend to enforce such rights against its licensees or to authorize one of the performing rights societies to do so on its behalf.

ii. **Mechanical Rights and Statutory Royalties**. Licensor waives the exclusive right to collect, whether individually or via a music rights society or designated agent (e.g. Harry Fox Agency), royalties for any phonorecord You create from the Work ("cover version") and distribute, subject to the compulsory license created by 17 USC Section 115 of the US Copyright Act (or the equivalent in other jurisdictions).

United States copyright law also provides authors of musical composition the right to collect royalties from artists who perform those works and distribute copies on fixed media, such as phonograph records or compact discs. As is the case with synchronization rights and performance rights, Version 2.0 of the license makes clear that the Licensor intends to grant those rights without payment of royalties to its licensees.

f. **Webcasting Rights and Statutory Royalties**. For the avoidance of doubt, where the Work is a sound recording, Licensor waives the exclusive right to collect, whether individually or via a performance-rights society (e.g. SoundExchange), royalties for the public digital performance (e.g. webcast) of the Work, subject to the compulsory license created by 17 USC Section 114 of the US Copyright Act (or the equivalent in other jurisdictions).

This extends the waiver of the right to collect royalties for performance rights for Web broadcasts of the Work.

The above rights may be exercised in all media and formats whether now known or hereafter devised. The above rights include the right to make such modifications as are technically necessary to exercise the rights in other media and formats. All rights not expressly granted by Licensor are hereby reserved.

4. **Restrictions.** The license granted in Section 3 above is expressly made subject to and limited by the following restrictions:

a. You may distribute, publicly display, publicly perform, or publicly digitally perform the Work only under the terms of this License, and You must include a copy of, or the Uniform Resource Identifier for, this License with every copy or phonorecord of the Work You distribute, publicly display, publicly perform, or publicly digitally perform. You may not offer or impose any terms on the Work that alter or restrict the terms of this License or the recipients' exercise of the rights granted hereunder. You may not sublicense the Work. You must keep intact all notices that refer to this License and to the disclaimer of warranties. You may not distribute, publicly display, publicly perform, or publicly digitally perform the Work with any technological measures that control access or use of the Work in a manner inconsistent with the terms of this License Agreement. The above applies to the Work as incorporated in a Collective Work, but this does not require the Collective Work apart from the Work itself to be made subject to the terms of this License. If You create a Collective Work, upon notice from any Licensor You must, to the extent practicable, remove from the Collective Work any reference to such Licensor or the Original Author, as requested. If You create a Derivative Work, upon notice from any Licensor You must, to the extent practicable, remove from the Derivative Work any reference to such Licensor or the Original Author, as requested.

b. You may distribute, publicly display, publicly perform, or publicly digitally perform a Derivative Work only under the terms of this License, a later version of this License with the same License Elements as this License, or a Creative Commons iCommons license that contains the same License Elements as this License (e.g. Attribution-ShareAlike 2.0 Japan). You must include a copy of, or the Uniform Resource Identifier for, this License or other license specified in the previous sentence with every copy or phonorecord of each Derivative Work You distribute, publicly display, publicly perform, or publicly digitally perform. You may not offer or impose any terms on the Derivative Works that alter or restrict the terms of this License or the recipients' exercise of the rights granted hereunder, and You must keep intact all notices that refer to this License and to the disclaimer of warranties. You may not distribute, publicly display, publicly perform, or publicly digitally perform the Derivative Work with any technological measures that control access or use of the Work in a manner inconsistent with the terms of this License Agreement. The above applies to the Derivative Work as incorporated in a Collective Work, but this does not require the Collective Work apart from the Derivative Work itself to be made subject to the terms of this License.

Section 4(b) of Version 2.0 explicitly permits the transnational licensing of works, so long as each of the License Elements in the "new" license are contained in the original license. This permits, however, essentially only the "relicensing" of the Work under other, substantially identical, Creative Commons Licenses. Section 4(b) also permits such "relicensing" under later versions of the same Creative Commons license, a feature not present in Version 1.0.

c. If you distribute, publicly display, publicly perform, or publicly digitally perform the Work or any Derivative Works or Collective Works, You must keep intact all copyright notices for the Work and give the Original Author credit reasonable to the medium or means You are utilizing by conveying the name (or pseudonym if applicable) of the Original Author if supplied; the title of the Work if supplied; to the extent reasonably practicable, the Uniform Resource Identifier, if any, that Licensor specifies to be associated with the Work, unless such URI does not refer to the copyright notice or licensing information for the Work; and in the case of a Derivative Work, a credit identifying the use of the Work in the Derivative Work (e.g., "French translation of the Work by Original Author," or "Screenplay based on original Work by Original Author"). Such credit may be implemented in any reasonable manner; provided, however, that in the case of a Derivative Work or Collective Work, at a minimum such credit will appear where any other comparable authorship credit appears and in a manner at least as prominent as such other comparable authorship credit.

Section 4(c) of Version 2.0 adds a new requirement in providing attribution to the Author by requiring that the Licensee include a URI or hyperlink directing a future user to the Original Work. This requirement is subject to some limitations. First, the link must be provided by the Author. Licensees have no obligation to track down the correct URI if none is provided. Second, such linking must be "reasonably practicable," that is, the hyperlink should function and should direct the user to that Original Work. Third, that hyperlinked reference must contain the copyright and licensing information associated with the Original Work.

In what is likely the most substantial departure from Version 1.0, Version 2.0 of the license provides for no warranty of non-infringment as part of the license. Version 2.0 also specifically disclaims warranties of merchantability, fitness for a particular purpose, accuracy, and the absence of defects. The license otherwise contains similar disclaimers as to representations and warranties and limitations on liability.

5. **Representations, Warranties and Disclaimer**

   UNLESS OTHERWISE AGREED TO BY THE PARTIES IN WRITING, LICENSOR OFFERS THE WORK AS-IS AND MAKES NO REPRESENTATIONS OR WARRANTIES OF ANY KIND CONCERNING THE MATERIALS, EXPRESS, IMPLIED, STATUTORY OR OTHERWISE, INCLUDING, WITHOUT LIMITATION, WARRANTIES OF TITLE, MERCHANTIBILITY, FITNESS FOR A PARTICULAR PURPOSE, NONINFRINGEMENT, OR THE ABSENCE OF LATENT OR OTHER DEFECTS, ACCURACY, OR THE PRESENCE OF ABSENCE OF ERRORS, WHETHER OR NOT DISCOVERABLE. SOME JURISDICTIONS DO NOT ALLOW THE EXCLUSION OF IMPLIED WARRANTIES, SO SUCH EXCLUSION MAY NOT APPLY TO YOU.

6. **Limitation on Liability.** EXCEPT TO THE EXTENT REQUIRED BY APPLICABLE LAW, IN NO EVENT WILL LICENSOR BE LIABLE TO YOU ON ANY LEGAL THEORY FOR ANY SPECIAL, INCIDENTAL, CONSEQUENTIAL, PUNITIVE OR EXEMPLARY DAMAGES ARISING OUT OF THIS LICENSE OR THE USE OF THE WORK, EVEN IF LICENSOR HAS BEEN ADVISED OF THE POSSIBILITY OF SUCH DAMAGES.

7. **Termination**

   a. This License and the rights granted hereunder will terminate automatically upon any breach by You of the terms of this License. Individuals or entities who have received Derivative Works or Collective Works from You under this License, however, will not have their licenses terminated provided such individuals or entities remain in full compliance with those licenses. Sections 1, 2, 5, 6, 7, and 8 will survive any termination of this License.

b. Subject to the above terms and conditions, the license granted here is perpetual (for the duration of the applicable copyright in the Work). Notwithstanding the above, Licensor reserves the right to release the Work under different license terms or to stop distributing the Work at any time; provided, however that any such election will not serve to withdraw this License (or any other license that has been, or is required to be, granted under the terms of this License), and this License will continue in full force and effect unless terminated as stated above.

8. **Miscellaneous**

a. Each time You distribute or publicly digitally perform the Work or a Collective Work, the Licensor offers to the recipient a license to the Work on the same terms and conditions as the license granted to You under this License.

b. Each time You distribute or publicly digitally perform a Derivative Work, Licensor offers to the recipient a license to the original Work on the same terms and conditions as the license granted to You under this License.

c. If any provision of this License is invalid or unenforceable under applicable law, it shall not affect the validity or enforceability of the remainder of the terms of this License, and without further action by the parties to this agreement, such provision shall be reformed to the minimum extent necessary to make such provision valid and enforceable.

d. No term or provision of this License shall be deemed waived and no breach consented to unless such waiver or consent shall be in writing and signed by the party to be charged with such waiver or consent.

e. This License constitutes the entire agreement between the parties with respect to the Work licensed here. There are no understandings, agreements or representations with respect to the Work not specified here. Licensor shall not be bound by any additional provisions that may appear in any communication from You. This License may not be modified without the mutual written agreement of the Licensor and You.

Sections 7 and 8 of Version 2.0 of the license are identical to those same provisions in Version 1.0.

The Creative Commons project is just getting started. It remains an open question whether the ideas behind the open source and free software licensing movement will have the same impact on aesthetic works that they had on software. Nonetheless, the Creative Commons Licenses provide a good foundation for the attempt.

There are also a few licenses meant for documentation, notably the GNU Free Documentation License (GFDL), available at *http://www.gnu.org/copyleft/fdl.html*, and the Open Publication License (OPL), available at *http://www.opencontent.org/openpub/*. These are more tightly focused on technical documentation and publishing, but offer free and open source analogs to this aspect of the software development world.

CHAPTER 5
Non-Open Source Licenses

In the previous chapters, we have examined open source and free software licenses, all of which permit, to varying extents, substantial inroads on the protections otherwise available under copyright or patent law. In this chapter, by contrast, we examine one variety of a classic proprietary license, as well as the Sun Community Source licenses and the Microsoft Shared Source Initiative.

Classic Proprietary License

The classic proprietary license needs relatively little explanation. The license does not need to distinguish, for example, between source and binary code: the source code is simply not made available. The license need not distinguish between distribution of derivative and original works: with one very narrow exception, neither is permitted. Proprietary licenses, like the one described below, may contain "open source" licensed software (under the more permissive licenses, like the MIT and BSD Licenses), but the code they license may not be included in any open source project, unless the code is licensed under a parallel non-proprietary license that permits such use.

The following license is the creation of the author. It licenses the hypothetical software of the Mildew Corporation, using terms found in virtually all proprietary licenses.

> 1. General. The software, documentation and any fonts accompanying this License whether on disk, in read only memory, on any other media or in any other form (collectively the "Software") are licensed, not sold, to you by Mildew Computer, Inc. ("Mildew") for use only under the terms of this License, and Mildew reserves all rights not expressly granted to you. The rights granted herein are limited to Mildew's intellectual property rights in the Mildew Software and do not include any other patents or intellectual property rights. You own the media on which the Mildew Software is recorded but Mildew and/or Mildew's licensor(s) retain ownership of the Software itself.

This provision provides that the software and associated documentation provided by Mildew are only licensed, not sold, to the consumer. This provision is substantially similar in effect to language used in the open source and free software licenses already described. The only rights granted are those specifically described in the license; all other rights are reserved.

The sentence stating that Mildew does not license any property rights other than those that it owns is likely meaningless. By licensing the Software, Mildew is implicitly representing that it has the authority to license all of its components, whether those components are its own work or not. It seems unlikely that a court would hold that Mildew was not responsible for damages to a consumer arising from infringement if the Software turned out to infringe the intellectual property rights of a third party. After all, given the closed nature of the licensed software, consumers are not allowed to determine for themselves whether the software was infringing, even if they have the inclination or the resources to do so.

The second section of the license makes clear the very strict limitations on the use of the software: not only may the end user not distribute the software, he cannot even install more than one copy of it at a time.

> 2. Permitted License Uses and Restrictions. This License allows you to install and use one (1) copy of the Software on a single device or computer at a time. This License does not allow the Software to exist on more than one such device or computer at a time, and you may not make the Software available over a network where it could be used by multiple devices or multiple computers at the same time.

Because of these limitations, every user of the software, whether on a network or otherwise, must be individually licensed. This type of restriction is contained in almost every proprietary license and is universally enforced by the courts. The second paragraph continues with a narrow exception to this restriction.

> You may make one copy of the Software in machine-readable form for backup purposes only; provided that the backup copy must include all copyright or other proprietary notices contained on the original.

The next part of this sentence expressly bars any attempt to derive any of the utility of the code for use other than in the licensed Software.

> Except as and only to the extent expressly permitted in this License or by applicable law, you may not copy, decompile, reverse engineer, disassemble, attempt to derive the source code of, modify, or create derivative works of the Software or any part thereof. Any attempt to do so is a violation of the rights of Mildew and its licensors of the Software. If you breach this restriction, you may be subject to prosecution and damages.

Breaching this provision would certainly terminate the license and would render the user liable for damages for further use. Although it is hard to see what damages, if any, Mildew would suffer from such unauthorized use beyond the sales price of another unit of the Software, such use could obviously lead to more substantial forms of infringement through the creation and distribution of derivative works. In addition, reverse engineering or otherwise trying to derive the source code from software could violate U.S. copyright law or the Digital Millennium Copyright Act. Such source code certainly could not be used or distributed in any event, without violating the civil and criminal laws of the United States.

The final provision is a special disclaimer of liability, noting that the Software is not intended for use in high-risk applications.

> THE SOFTWARE IS NOT INTENDED FOR USE IN WHICH THE FAILURE OF THE SOFTWARE COULD LEAD TO DEATH, PERSONAL INJURY, OR SEVERE PHYSICAL OR ENVIRONMENTAL DAMAGE.

The third section bars transfers or sales of the licensed software, except for the exception provided under law by the first-sale doctrine, which permits users to sell the rights acquired by license along with the physical medium, regardless of the terms under which the work was originally acquired.

> 3. Transfer. You may not rent, lease, lend or sublicense the Software. You may, however, make a one-time permanent transfer of all of your license rights to the Software to another party, provided that: (a) the transfer must include all of the Software, including all its component parts, original media, printed materials and this License; (b) you do not retain any copies of the Software, full or partial, including copies stored on a computer or other storage device; and (c) the party receiving the Software reads and agrees to accept the terms and conditions of this License.

This paragraph does not grant any rights to the licensee that he or she would not otherwise have by operation of law.

Like most of the open source and free software licenses already examined, the license provides for automatic termination upon any breach of the license.

> 4. Termination. This License is effective until terminated. Your rights under this License will terminate automatically without notice from Mildew if you fail to comply with any term(s) of this License. Upon the termination of this License, you shall cease all use of the Mildew Software and destroy all copies, full or partial, of the Mildew Software.

However, because the rights granted by the license are so limited in the first place, the effects of the termination are not likely to be severe, at least for programs purchased by individual consumers. As already noted, the measure of damages for continuing use of the licensed program is not likely to be greater than the sales price of the Software. It should be noted, however, that U.S. copyright laws provide for potentially severe penalties for unlawful distribution of copyrighted material, including punitive damages.

The fifth section provides a limited warranty for the medium on which the code of the Software is carried. Commercial software usually carries at least this minimal a warranty.

> 5. Limited Warranty on Media. Mildew warrants the media on which the Software is recorded and delivered by Mildew to be free from defects in materials and workmanship under normal use for a period of ninety (90) days from the date of original retail

purchase. Your exclusive remedy under this Section shall be, at Mildew's option, either a refund of the purchase price of the product containing the Software or replacement of the Software which is returned to Mildew. THIS LIMITED WARRANTY AND ANY IMPLIED WARRANTIES ON THE MEDIA INCLUDING, BUT NOT LIMITED TO, THE IMPLIED WARRANTIES OF MERCHANTABILITY AND OF FITNESS FOR A PARTICULAR PURPOSE, ARE LIMITED IN DURATION TO NINETY (90) DAYS FROM THE DATE OF ORIGINAL RETAIL PURCHASE. SOME JURISDICTIONS DO NOT ALLOW LIMITATIONS ON HOW LONG AN IMPLIED WARRANTY LASTS, SO THE ABOVE LIMITATION MAY NOT APPLY TO YOU. THE LIMITED WARRANTY SET FORTH HEREIN IS THE ONLY WARRANTY MADE TO YOU AND IS PROVIDED IN LIEU OF ANY OTHER WARRANTIES (IF ANY) CREATED BY ANY DOCUMENTATION OR PACKAGING. THIS LIMITED WARRANTY GIVES YOU SPECIFIC LEGAL RIGHTS, AND YOU MAY ALSO HAVE OTHER RIGHTS WHICH VARY BY JURISDICTION.

The following provisions restate the same limitations articulated by the second to last sentence of the fifth paragraph: Mildew disclaims all responsibility for any damages caused by the Software, except to the extent it is prohibited from doing so by law.

6. Disclaimer of Warranties. YOU EXPRESSLY ACKNOWLEDGE AND AGREE THAT USE OF THE SOFTWARE IS AT YOUR SOLE RISK AND THAT THE ENTIRE RISK AS TO SATISFACTORY QUALITY, PERFORMANCE, ACCURACY AND EFFORT IS WITH YOU. EXCEPT FOR THE LIMITED WARRANTY ON MEDIA SET FORTH ABOVE AND TO THE MAXIMUM EXTENT PERMITTED BY APPLICABLE LAW, THE SOFTWARE IS PROVIDED "AS IS", WITH ALL FAULTS AND WITHOUT WARRANTY OF ANY KIND, AND DANGER AND DANGER'S LICENSORS (COLLECTIVELY REFERRED TO AS "DANGER" FOR THE PURPOSES OF SECTIONS 6 AND 7) HEREBY DISCLAIM ALL WARRANTIES AND CONDITIONS WITH RESPECT TO THE SOFTWARE, EITHER EXPRESS, IMPLIED OR STATUTORY, INCLUDING, BUT NOT LIMITED TO, THE IMPLIED WARRANTIES AND/OR CONDITIONS OF MERCHANTABILITY, OF SATISFACTORY QUALITY, OF FITNESS FOR A PARTICULAR PURPOSE, OF ACCURACY, OF QUIET ENJOYMENT, AND NON-INFRINGEMENT OF THIRD PARTY RIGHTS. DANGER DOES NOT WARRANT AGAINST INTERFERENCE WITH YOUR ENJOYMENT OF THE SOFTWARE, THAT THE FUNCTIONS CONTAINED IN THE SOFTWARE WILL MEET YOUR REQUIREMENTS, THAT THE OPERATION OF THE SOFTWARE WILL BE UNINTERRUPTED OR ERROR-FREE, OR THAT DEFECTS IN THE SOFTWARE WILL BE CORRECTED. NO ORAL OR WRITTEN INFORMATION OR ADVICE GIVEN BY DANGER SHALL CREATE A WARRANTY. SHOULD THE SOFTWARE PROVE DEFECTIVE, YOU ASSUME THE ENTIRE COST OF ALL NECESSARY SERVICING, REPAIR OR CORRECTION. SOME JURISDICTIONS DO NOT ALLOW THE EXCLUSION OF IMPLIED WARRANTIES OR LIMITATIONS ON APPLICABLE STATUTORY RIGHTS OF A CONSUMER, SO THE ABOVE EXCLUSION AND LIMITATIONS MAY NOT APPLY TO YOU.

7. Limitation of Liability. TO THE EXTENT NOT PROHIBITED BY LAW, IN NO EVENT SHALL DANGER BE LIABLE FOR PERSONAL INJURY, OR ANY INCIDENTAL, SPECIAL, INDIRECT OR CONSEQUENTIAL DAMAGES WHATSOEVER, INCLUDING, WITHOUT LIMITATION, DAMAGES FOR LOSS OF PROFITS, LOSS OF DATA, BUSINESS INTERRUPTION OR ANY OTHER COMMERCIAL DAMAGES OR LOSSES, ARISING OUT OF OR RELATED TO YOUR

USE OR INABILITY TO USE THE SOFTWARE, HOWEVER CAUSED, REGARD-
LESS OF THE THEORY OF LIABILITY (CONTRACT, TORT OR OTHERWISE)
AND EVEN IF DANGER HAS BEEN ADVISED OF THE POSSIBILITY OF SUCH
DAMAGES. SOME JURISDICTIONS DO NOT ALLOW THE LIMITATION OF
LIABILITY FOR PERSONAL INJURY, OR OF INCIDENTAL OR CONSEQUEN-
TIAL DAMAGES, SO THIS LIMITATION MAY NOT APPLY TO YOU. In no event
shall Mildew's total liability to you for all damages (other than as may be required by
applicable law in cases involving personal injury) exceed the amount of fifty dollars
($50.00). The foregoing limitations will apply even if the above stated remedy fails of
its essential purpose.

For a more thorough discussion of the meaning and effect of such provisions, see the
discussion of warranties in Chapter 1. The last sentence of the seventh paragraph
provides a fallback position for Mildew. In the event that use of the Software results
in damages to the user, the most the user can collect is $50. It seems unlikely that
this provision would ever be enforced: to the extent that a court determines that Mildew is liable in spite of all the previous disclaimers, it seems unlikely to limit the
injured party to $50 in recovery.

8. Export Law Assurances. You may not use or otherwise export or reexport the Software except as authorized by United States law and the laws of the jurisdiction in
which the Software was obtained. In particular, but without limitation, the Software
may not be exported or re-exported (a) into (or to a national or resident of) any U.S.
embargoed countries (currently Cuba, Iran, Iraq, Libya, North Korea, Sudan and
Syria) or (b) to anyone on the U.S. Treasury Department's list of Specially Designated
Nationals or the U.S. Department of Commerce Denied Person's List or Entity List. By
using the Software, you represent and warrant that you are not located in, under control of, or a national or resident of any such country or on any such list.

The eighth section of Mildew's license does not impose additional restrictions on
users so much as inform them on the limitations on their ability to transfer the software, even in the limited manner described in the third section.

The ninth section provides that U.S. government users are bound by the same terms
of the license as are other users, provisions typical in commercial software licenses.

9. Government End Users. The Software and related documentation are "Commercial
Items", as that term is defined at 48 C.F.R. §2.101, consisting of "Commercial Computer Software" and "Commercial Computer Software Documentation", as such terms
are used in 48 C.F.R. §12.212 or 48 C.F.R. §227.7202, as applicable. Consistent with
48 C.F.R. §12.212 or 48 C.F.R. §227.7202-1 through 227.7202-4, as applicable, the
Commercial Computer Software and Commercial Computer Software Documentation are being licensed to U.S. Government end users (a) only as Commercial Items
and (b) with only those rights as are granted to all other end users pursuant to the
terms and conditions herein. Unpublished-rights reserved under the copyright laws of
the United States.

The tenth section provides choice of law and forum selection clauses as previously
discussed in connection with the Mozilla Public License in Chapter 3.

10. Controlling Law and Severability and Choice of Forum. This License will be governed by and construed in accordance with the laws of the State of Colorado, as
applied to agreements entered into and to be performed entirely within Colorado

between Colorado residents, that is, without giving any effect to the choice of laws provisions of the State of Colorado. This License shall not be governed by the United Nations Convention on Contracts for the International Sale of Goods, the application of which is expressly excluded. If for any reason a court of competent jurisdiction finds any provision, or portion thereof, to be unenforceable, the remainder of this License shall continue in full force and effect. You agree that the only courts in which You will bring lawsuits concerning the application or enforcement of this License are courts of competent jurisdiction located in the State of Colorado and you consent to the exercise of jurisdiction by any such court. This paragraph shall survive in full force and effect regardless of any termination of this License.

This paragraph works one minor variation on the typical forum selection clause, in that it imposes a limitation only on "You"—i.e., the licensee. The Licensor presumably could bring an action in any court having jurisdiction over the licensee, not just the courts of Colorado.

The eleventh section reflects that the Software contains code originally licensed under an open source license, in this case, code licensed under an MIT License.

11. Third Party Notices and Conditions. The Software may include or utilize certain software which is owned by Mongrel Mix, the source code of which is available under the MIT License (the "Mongrel Mix Code"). Mildew may make modifications to this Mongrel Mix Code. The license for the Mongrel Mix Code is included here as Exhibit A. Those terms are fully applicable to the use of those portions of the Software that consist of or are derived from the Mongrel Mix Code.

The conditions imposed by the MIT license are described in Chapter 2. Mildew, as a licensee of Mongrel Mix, has complied with its license obligations by noting that Mongrel Mix originated part of the code contained in the Software and by attaching the license applicable to that Code as an exhibit. As described in Chapter 2, Mildew is under no obligation to make available the source code for its modifications to the Mongrel Mix code or the original, unmodified source code. Enterprising end users, of course, can track down the original source code for themselves.

The final provision contains a merger provision and a bar on oral modifications, as previously described.

12. Complete Agreement; Governing Language. This License constitutes the entire agreement between the parties with respect to the Software licensed hereunder and supersedes all prior or contemporaneous understandings regarding such subject matter. No amendment to or modification of this License will be binding unless in writing and signed by Mildew.

A proprietary license, because it authorizes so few actions beyond the use of the program for the purpose for which it was intended, is usually simple to describe and to understand, despite the legal language. As described in Chapter 1, because the underlying code is kept closed, these licenses tend to create evolutionary dead ends. Every year, as software companies like Mildew go out of business, all of the utility of their code dies with them. Even after the rights under copyright or patent have expired, that code is essentially buried (assuming anyone, at that point, is still interested in it), because the source code for the program is unlikely to be available.

The proprietary license described here is a "shrinkwrap" license typical to single license sales of programs to individual members of the public. Like any other license, however, proprietary licenses are subject to significant variation. For example, it would not be impossible for a proprietary license to make available the source code for the licensed program but prohibit any use of that source code for some defined period of time, such as five years. This would preserve much of the benefit of the proprietary license model—the ability to make income off of a monopoly—while avoiding at least one negative outcome of the proprietary model.

As in everything else, negotiating power has considerable effect on the terms of the license in question. This license presumes highly asymmetric bargaining power. The seller of the software in question has the better bargaining position: the incremental profit increase associated with the additional sale of a single license, from its point of view, is far too little to justify individual negotiation. The buyer of the software is left essentially in a take-it-or-leave-it position and the result is a license highly favorable to the seller.

This is not always the case. In a situation in which the poles of power are reversed, such as when the seller is a small software cooperative and the buyer is a Fortune 500 company, the buyer will probably demand a number of benefits not included in this license, such as express warranties that the software will work as described, access to the source code, and perhaps the right to make changes to the source code, or even to distribute modified versions of the program.

Thus, while the Mildew proprietary license is not an atypical license for the class of licenses it represents—that is, "shrinkwrap" licenses for sales of individual licenses to the public—it is not intended to describe all proprietary licenses. Individually negotiated licenses, particularly between parties with more equal bargaining power, may contain substantially different terms and avoid some of the negative consequences of proprietary licensing.

Sun Community Source License

In addition to the varieties of open source and free software licenses already discussed, there are licenses that do not fall within the Open Source definition but incorporate some elements of open source principles. The Sun Community Source License (SCSL) is one such license, developed by Sun to incorporate some of the benefits of open source development into two proprietary Sun products, Jini and the programming language Java. Sun has been very careful not to characterize this license as an open source license; the license clearly is not such a license. The most important distinction between this license and open source licenses is the Sun-imposed compatibility requirement. While users are free to modify the licensed work, they may not deploy modified versions of that work without compatibility compliance being certified by the licensor, i.e., Sun. This puts substantial limits on the applicability of the open source model to Sun's project. Such restrictions may, however, be justified by Sun's desire to ensure that Java maintains its cross-platform portability, which incremental tweaks in individual versions could quickly undermine. In addition, commercial use of the SCSL-licensed code may require the payment of a royalty, which is, again, inconsistent with the open source model.

Despite the fact that the SCSL is not an open source license, it embodies an innovative licensing principle—lying somewhere between the classic proprietary and the open source models already described—and is a natural development of the developer-centric licenses already described, such as the Mozilla Public License and the Artistic License.

Like these last two licenses, the SCSL begins with a long list of definitions that contain the most important terms in the license.

> I. DEFINITIONS.
>
> "Community Code" means Reference Code, Contributed Code, and any combination thereof.

This definition consists of two terms defined later in the license. "Community Code" is all the code governed by the license.

> "Community Member" means You and any other party that has entered into and has in effect a version of this License (or who is similarly authorized and obligated by Original Contributor) for the Technology with Original Contributor.

In conformity with its emphasis on community and community development, the SCSL does not refer to "users" or the familiar "you" of other licenses but to Community Members. As is made clear, becoming a Community Member is as simple as agreeing to be bound by the license, which is a consequence of any use of the Community Code.

> "Contributed Code" means (a) Error Corrections, (b) Shared Modifications and (c) any other code other than Reference Code made available by Community Members in accordance with this License.

This definition again relies on terms defined later in the license. Such references are not necessary for this definition, which is sufficiently accompanied by subsection (c)—i.e., that any code subject to the license that is not "Reference Code" is maintained by Sun, the "Original Contributor."

> "Contributed Code Specifications" means the functional, interface and operational specifications and documentation for Contributed Code.

One of the conditions of making Contributed Code is the provision of specifications to the Original Developer. This requirement is described in Section III. With this requirement, the SCSL separates itself from the more free-flowing open source and free software licenses already described: a potential contributor might, quite reasonably, ask herself whether it is worthwhile to contribute to a project that not only requires compatibility testing, but drafting of specifications, in addition to creating the code.

"Covered Code" means Community Code and Modifications.

"Error Corrections" mean Modifications which correct any failure of Covered Code to conform to any aspect of the Technology Specifications.

Covered Code includes Community Code, which has already been defined, and Modifications, which are defined separately, with a definition not substantially different than that inherent in the language. Error Corrections are a subspecies of modifications, to which special conditions attach, which are improvements made to one or another person's code in order that they better comply with relevant specifications.

"Interfaces" means classes or other programming code or specifications designed for use with the Technology comprising a means or link for invoking functionality, operations or protocols and which are additional to or extend the interfaces designated in the Technology Specifications.

This definition encompasses any interface or portal that accesses the functionality of the Covered Code.

"Modifications" means any (a) change or addition to Covered Code, or (b) new source or object code implementing any portion of the Technology Specifications, but (c) excluding any incorporated Reference Code.

This definition brings within the definition of Covered Code not only derivative works made from the Reference Code or Covered Code, but "gap-filling" code designed to implement the Technology Specifications, which, again, is separately defined. Any part of the Reference Code, whether incorporated into a subsequent modification (even, presumably, as part of a "new" process or routine) is excluded from the definition of Modifications.

"Original Contributor" means Sun Microsystems, Inc. and its successors and assigns.

This is self-explanatory.

"Reference Code" means source code for the Technology designated by Original Contributor at the Technology Site from time to time.

This is the original code on which the project is initially based. The maintenance of the "official version" at the Technology Site allows Sun to update the Reference Code periodically.

"Research Use" means research, evaluation, development, educational or personal and individual use, excluding use or distribution for direct or indirect commercial (including strategic) gain or advantage.

This is one of the key terms of the SCSL. All the rights granted by this version of the license are only for such "Research Use"—i.e., the development of improvements for personal or individual use, excluding any commercial use. Commercial use of the Covered Code requires a separate license, which is described later in this chapter. Distribution to others is permitted, but only if they agree to similarly limited use of the Covered Code. This is a major restriction, and one that should be carefully considered before any contribution is made under the license. While a given contributor's addition to the license may be cross-licensed (i.e., licensed under another license as well as the SCSL), so that he may take commercial advantage of his own work or simply distribute it to others for their free use of it, including commercial use. However, given the fact that the contribution is likely to be tied closely (perhaps irremovably) to Covered Code, such a contribution may simply be of no use apart from the environment it was originally designed for. Thus, unlike all of the open source and free software licenses examined so far, the SCSL does not permit the full functional use of the original code plus modifications even by contributors to the project.

"Shared Modifications" means those Modifications which Community Members elect to share with other Community Members pursuant to Section III.B.

Modifications that are shared with other Community Members are granted with all the intellectual property rights associated with them, as described in Section III.B, which includes the right to distribute, use, and modify the contributed work. "Modifications," except for "Error Corrections," do not have to be shared, and the SCSL is careful in distinguishing between "Contributed Code" and "Modifications."

"Technology Specifications" means the functional, interface and operational specifications and documentation for the Technology designated by Original Contributor at the Technology Site from time to time.

The Technology Specifications are the fundamentals of the design provided by the Original Contributor, and which operate as the foundation both for the original work—i.e., the Reference Code—and all subsequent modifications or derivative works created therefrom.

"Technology" means the technology described in and contemplated by the Technology Specifications and which You have received pursuant to this License.

This provision really adds nothing to the license as the term Technology has no meaning apart from the specifications. It is not the Technology that is being licensed, but the Reference Code and the Covered Code: the Community Code built up upon the Technology Specifications.

"Technology Site" means the website designated by Original Contributor for accessing Community Code and Technology Specifications.

This is the web site created and operated by the Original Contributor as the launching pad for the development project.

"You" means the individual executing this License or the legal entity or entities represented by the individual executing this License. "Your" is the possessive of "You."

"You" is the licensee, the contributor, and modifier of code under the license.

II. PURPOSE.

Original Contributor is licensing the Reference Code and Technology Specifications and is permitting implementation of Technology under and subject to this Sun Community Source License (the "License") to promote research, education, innovation and product development using the Technology.

COMMERCIAL USE AND DISTRIBUTION OF TECHNOLOGY IS PERMITTED ONLY UNDER OPTIONAL SUPPLEMENTS/ ATTACHMENTS TO THIS LICENSE.

The purpose of this section is to make clear that the rights granted by this license do not include the right to distribute commercially or otherwise profit from the licensed work. The "research use" limitation of this license, as already described, reserves those rights to the Original Contributor. The commercial use supplement to the license, described below, provides some such rights, subject, however, to restrictions and conditions described therein.

The rights granted by this research form of the license are described in Section III.

III. RESEARCH USE RIGHTS.

A. From Original Contributor. Subject to and conditioned upon Your full compliance with the terms and conditions of this License, including Sections IV (Restrictions and Community Responsibilities) and V.E.7 (International Use), Original Contributor:

So long as the terms of the license are complied with, the licensee is granted the following, limited, rights from the Original Contributor.

1. grants to You a non-exclusive, worldwide and royalty-free license to the extent of Original Contributor's intellectual property rights in and covering the Reference Code and Technology Specifications to do the following for Your Research Use only:

The original form of the work being licensed is embodied in the Reference Code and the Technology Specifications, and the Original Contributor is granting rights with respect to those works only.

a) reproduce, prepare derivative works of, display and perform the Reference Code, in whole or in part, alone or as part of Covered Code;

This provision permits the duplication of the Reference Code, presumably only for the licensee's own individual use, as is made clear later, and to make derivative works (i.e., modifications) from the Reference Code.

b) reproduce, prepare derivative works of and display the Technology Specifications;

This grants identical rights as III(A)(1)(a), but with respect to the Technology Specifications. The licensee, however, may not "perform" the Technology Specifications. (It's difficult to imagine staging such a performance.)

c) distribute source or object code copies of Reference Code, in whole or in part, alone or as part Covered Code, to other Community Members or to students;

This is part of the non-commercial restrictions of the license. Distribution of the Reference Code in source code form, with or without Community Code, may be made only to other Community Members (similarly restricted against its commercial use) or to students. Section IV(A) provides an additional restriction on the exercise of this right by requiring that the distributor of the source code obtain verification (on the part of Community Members) of their status or acknowledgment (on the part of students) of the restrictions applicable to the source code. This limitation on the availability of source code is a marked distinction between this license and the open source licenses previously examined.

> d) distribute object code copies of Reference Code, in whole or in part, alone or as part of object code copies of Covered Code, to third parties;

Object code may be distributed freely to third parties, including third parties not bound by the license, an important distinction under the SCSL. Improved versions of the original program may be distributed to third parties, at least in the form of object code.

> e) use Original Contributor's class, interface and package names only insofar as necessary to accurately reference or invoke Your Modifications for Research Use; and

This provision refers to programming elements unique to the licensed program. The intent of this provision is to limit as much as possible unnecessary duplication or editing of the Reference Code and is intended to preserve uniformity.

> f) use any associated software tools (excluding Compliance Materials), documents and information provided by Original Contributor at the Technology Site for use in exercising the above license rights.

To the extent the Original Contributor makes such tools available (as Sun, in fact, has), the licensee has the right to use them in connection with the licensed code.

> B. Contributed Code. Subject to and conditioned upon compliance with the terms and conditions of this License, including Sections IV (Restrictions and Community Responsibilities) and V.E.7 (International Use), each Community Member:

This section addresses those rights that are granted by Community Members (anyone who makes a derivative work from or modifies the Reference Code) to other Community Members. The grant of such rights is a necessary condition of the license.

> 1. grants to each Community Member a non-exclusive, perpetual, irrevocable, worldwide and royalty-free license to the extent of such Community Member's intellectual property rights in and covering its Contributed Code, to reproduce, modify, display and distribute its Contributed Code, in whole or in part, in source code and object code form, to the same extent as permitted under such Community Member's License with Original Contributor (including all supplements/ attachments thereto).

This is an unfortunately ambiguous provision because of two separate drafting choices. The first drafting choice is the double use of the term Community Member. Each Community Member is granting the defined rights to every other Community Member. The section should be read so that the Community Member granting the rights (the "granting Community Member") grants the defined rights to his or her Contributed Code to every other Community Member (the "receiving Commmunity Member") to the same extent that the granting Community Member grants those rights to the Original Contributor.

The second drafting choice that makes this provision somewhat ambiguous is the fact that the grant of rights to receiving Community Members is not actually defined in this section. It is defined by reference to the grant of rights in the following section, which describes those rights granted to the Original Contributor by granting community members.

The use of the term "License" further confuses matters, as the principal effect of the SCSL is the licensing of the code made available by the Original Contributor to Community Members. While the SCSL also, unambiguously, includes a license of each Community Member's work to the Original Contributor, as described in the following section, this is not the first interpretation that an ordinary person is going to put to the term "License," as used in this section. Nonetheless, that is the right way to read that term.

The incorporation by reference to the following section was probably done to make it easier for Sun to issue modified versions of the license (which it is entitled to do as described later) by linking the grant of rights here to the grant of rights to the Original Contributor described in the following paragraph. This does, however, somewhat obscure the meaning of this section.

The next section provides a broad grant of rights by each Community Member to the Original Contributor—Sun—and by reference to every other Community Member.

> 2. grants to Original Contributor a non-exclusive, perpetual, irrevocable, worldwide and royalty-free license to the extent of such Community Member's intellectual property rights in and covering its Contributed Code and Contributed Code Specifications, to (a) use, reproduce, modify, display, prepare derivative works of and distribute Contributed Code and modifications and derivative works thereof, in whole or in part, in source code and object code form, as part of Reference Code or other technologies based in whole or in part on Reference Code or Technology; (b) prepare, use, reproduce, modify, display, prepare derivative works of and distribute Contributed Code Specifications, and modifications and derivative works thereof, in whole or in part, in connection with the exercise of such rights; and (c) sublicense any of the foregoing through multiple tiers of distribution.

This is a very broad grant of rights. The Original Contributor may use any of the work contributed by the Community Member, without any meaningful limitation, whether in the Covered Code or otherwise, including the right to license this code to others. The Original Contributor is not limited by the Research Use limitations applicable to Community Members. Again, however, the SCSL does not require that Modifications become Contributed Code.

> C. Subcontracting. You may provide Covered Code to a contractor for the sole purpose of providing development services exclusively to You consistent with Your rights under this License. Such Contractor must be a Community Member or have executed an agreement with You that is consistent with Your rights and obligations under this License. Such subcontractor must assign exclusive rights in all work product to You. You agree that such work product is to be treated as Covered Code.

This provision does not provide the Community Member with any meaningful new rights. Community Members already have the right under Section III(1)(c) and (d) to distribute source code and object code to Community Members. So long as the putative subcontractor is a Community Member and has executed the acknowledgment required by the license, the participation of that person would be consistent with the license without any further action by the Community Member or the putative subcontractor.

> D. No Implied Licenses. Neither party is granted any right or license other than the licenses and covenants expressly set out herein. Other than the licenses and covenants expressly set out herein, Original Contributor retains all right, title and interest in Reference Code and Technology Specifications and You retain all right, title and interest in Your Modifications and associated specifications. Except as expressly permitted herein, You must not otherwise use any package, class or interface naming conventions that appear to originate from Original Contributor.

This provision is the equivalent of the merger clauses described in connection with licenses previously described in this book. It establishes that there is no agreement or grant of rights provided by any party other than those described in the SCSL. It is not clear what effect, if any, flows from the language that no other license is granted to use "any package, class or interface naming convention that *appear to originate* from Original Contributor" (emphasis added). As is the case with any piece of intellectual property, and as repeatedly stressed throughout this book, in the absence of a specific license (or other form of legal protection, such as fair use), the user undertakes a substantial risk by using, modifying, or distributing any work.

In addition to complying with the terms of use already described, each Community Member has certain affirmative obligations under the SCSL that are described in the following section.

> IV. RESTRICTIONS AND COMMUNITY RESPONSIBILITIES.
>
> As a condition to Your license and other rights, You must comply with the restrictions and responsibilities set forth below, as modified or supplemented, if at all, in Attachment B, Additional Requirements and Responsibilities.

Attachment B is a rider that Sun may use to impose additional restrictions or obligations in negotiations with individual users. The form of the license for the Jini package, for example, contains such additional limitations and restrictions. They are, however, not described in this book.

> A. Source Code Availability. You must provide source code and any specifications for Your Error Corrections to Original Contributor as soon as practicable.

This provision imposes an affirmative obligation on the Community Member not only to provide one category of modifications to the work, Error Corrections (defined above), but to do so "as soon as practicable." The enforcement of this provision is obviously somewhat problematic. More importantly, however, "Error Corrections" are the one category of Modifications that must be shared and that a Contribution cannot maintain a proprietary interest in.

You may provide other Contributed Code to Original Contributor at any time, in Your discretion. Original Contributor may, in its discretion, post Your Contributed Code and Contributed Code Specifications on the Technology Site.

The intent of the SCSL is to maintain modifications and improvements to the Covered Code in a centralized location available to all Community Members, i.e., the Technology Site, to maximize participation.

Additionally, You may post Your Contributed Code and/or Contributed Code Specifications for Research Use on another website of Your choice; provided, however that You may distribute or display source code of Covered Code and the Technology Specifications only for Research Use and only to: (i) Community Members from whom You have first obtained a certification of status in the form set forth in Attachment A-1, and (ii) students from whom You have first obtained an executed acknowledgment in the form set forth in Attachment A-2. You must keep a copy of each such certificate and acknowledgment You obtain and provide a copy to Original Contributor, if requested.

The SCSL also permits the posting of Covered Code on Community Members' own sites. However, this grant of rights is limited in that the source code may only be made available, consistent with the other terms of the license, to those persons who have agreed to be bound by the SCSL: students and Community Members.

B. Notices. You must reproduce without alteration copyright and other proprietary notices in any Covered Code that You distribute. The statement, "Use and Distribution is subject to the Sun Community Source License available at http://www.sun. com/software/communitysource" must appear prominently in Your Modifications and, in all cases, in the same file as all Your copyright and other proprietary notices.

This is a standard term in open source and free software licenses.

C. Modifications. You must include a "diff" file with Your Contributed Code that identifies and details the changes or additions You made, the version of Reference Code or Contributed Code You used and the date of such changes or additions. In addition, You must provide any Contributed Code Specifications for Your Contributed Code. Your Modifications, whenever created, are Covered Code and You expressly agree that use and distribution, in whole or in part, of Your Modifications shall only be done in accordance with and subject to this License.

As was the case with the MPL and some of the other open source licenses, the licensee has the obligation to provide to other licensees and to the Original Contributor a file identifying those changes that he has made to the Covered Code. In addition, under the SCSL, he must provide any applicable Contributed Code Specifications. The last sentence makes explicit what is implicit throughout the license, i.e., that the creation, use, and distribution of Covered Code is governed by the license.

D. Distribution Requirements. You may distribute object code of Covered Code to third parties for Research Use only pursuant to a license of Your choice which is consistent with this License.

This is a difficult provision. The only license that a Community Member can feel is comfortably "consistent" with the SCSL is the SCSL itself. While it might be possible to add or modify provisions of the SCSL, without very careful drafting, such a license would very likely limit a right the SCSL requires the grant of or appear to grant rights the Community Member does not have the power to grant. In any event, because such distribution is for "Research Use" only, the license of that distribution is not likely to be of much value to anyone. Those who agree to be bound by the SCSL should intend to work in its framework.

E. Extensions.

1. You may create and add Interfaces but, unless expressly permitted at the Technology Site, You must not incorporate any Reference Code in Your Interfaces. If You choose to disclose or permit disclosure of Your Interfaces to even a single third party for the purposes of enabling such third party to independently develop and distribute (directly or indirectly) technology which invokes such Interfaces, You must then make the Interfaces open by (a) promptly following completion thereof, publishing to the industry, on a non-confidential basis and free of all copyright restrictions, a reasonably detailed, current and accurate specification for the Interfaces, and (b) as soon as reasonably possible, but in no event more than thirty (30) days following publication of Your specification, making available on reasonable terms and without discrimination, a reasonably complete and practicable test suite and methodology adequate to create and test implementations of the Interfaces by a reasonably skilled technologist.

As described in the definitions section, Interfaces refers to any code or protocol that makes available the functionality of the Referenced Code but is not part of the Technology as supported by the Original Contributor. Because of the substantial risk that the development of such interfaces pose to the control of the Original Contributor,* strict provisions apply to such development. The distribution of even one copy to one other person (even presumably for "Research Use," although the language in this provision is not exactly clear on this point) triggers the requirement to make the specifications for the interface available free of all copyright restrictions (i.e., in the public domain). The developer must make available for testing (by the Original Contributor) the code implementing the interface. But the developer does not surrender his intellectual property to the interface. Assuming that the interface does not itself contain Referenced Code, it falls outside the scope of the SCSL. Moreover, as the following provision makes clear, while the specifications must be freely available for others to attempt to implement, the interface itself remains the developer's work.

2. You shall not assert any intellectual property rights You may have covering Your Interfaces which would necessarily be infringed by the creation, use or distribution of all reasonable independent implementations of Your specification of such Interfaces by Original Contributor or a Community Member. Nothing herein is intended to prevent You from enforcing any of Your intellectual property rights covering Your specific implementation of Your Interfaces, or functionality using such Interfaces, other than as specifically set forth in this Section IV.E.2.

---

* Such an interface, for example, could permit the Referenced Code to be incorporated into other programs by calls or routines, permitting a potentially different and broader use of the Referenced Code than originally envisioned. Assuming that the Referenced Code is itself readily available commercially, the commercial development of such an interface could have a profound effect on the distribution and development of the Referenced Code itself. Compare the relatively slight restrictions of the LGPL for contrast.

The surrender of the intellectual property embodied in the specifications is substantial, as it presents a roadmap to developing a "reasonable independent implementation." The SCSL strikes a balance between encouraging independent innovation and making sure that innovation remains in the community of developers under the license.

Section V of the license contains the "General Terms," all provisions common to commercial licenses described in other variations covered earlier in this book.

> V. GENERAL TERMS.
>
> A. License Versions.
>
> Only Original Contributor may promulgate new versions of this License. New code and specifications which You may subsequently choose to accept will be subject to any new License in effect at the time of Your acceptance of such code and specifications. Once You have accepted Reference Code, Technology Specifications, Contributed Code and/or Contributed Code Specifications under a version of this License, You may continue to use such version of Reference Code, Technology Specifications, Contributed Code and/or Contributed Code Specifications under that version of the License.

As with the GPL, the Original Contributor retains to itself the right to develop new versions of the license. Users are not bound by such licenses (but rather only by the previous version or versions that they have agreed to) until such time as they "accept"—that is, use, modify, or distribute—work licensed under that new license.

> B. Disclaimer Of Warranties.
>
> 1. COVERED CODE, ALL TECHNOLOGY SPECIFICATIONS AND CONTRIBUTED CODE SPECIFICATIONS ARE PROVIDED "AS IS", WITHOUT WARRANTIES OF ANY KIND, EITHER EXPRESS OR IMPLIED INCLUDING, WITHOUT LIMITATION, WARRANTIES THAT ANY SUCH COVERED CODE, TECHNOLOGY SPECIFICATIONS AND CONTRIBUTED CODE SPECIFICATIONS ARE FREE OF DEFECTS, MERCHANTABLE, FIT FOR A PARTICULAR PURPOSE OR NON-INFRINGING OF THIRD PARTY RIGHTS. YOU AGREE THAT YOU BEAR THE ENTIRE RISK IN CONNECTION WITH YOUR USE AND DISTRIBUTION OF ANY AND ALL COVERED CODE, TECHNOLOGY SPECIFICATIONS AND CONTRIBUTED CODE SPECIFICATIONS UNDER THIS LICENSE. NO USE OF ANY COVERED CODE, TECHNOLOGY SPECIFICATIONS OR CONTRIBUTED CODE SPECIFICATIONS IS AUTHORIZED EXCEPT SUBJECT TO AND IN CONSIDERATION FOR THIS DISCLAIMER.

This disclaimer of warranties disclaims any warranty implied or otherwise from the Technology Specifications and the Contributed Code specifications, but not from the code itself. Given that the SCSL essentially prohibits use of the code other than for "Research Use" excluding any commercial uses, at most a very limited liability could attach in any event.

> 2. You understand that, although Original Contributor and each Community Member grant the licenses set forth in the License and any supplements/attachments hereto, no assurances are provided by Original Contributor or any Community Member that Covered Code or any specifications do not infringe the intellectual property rights of any third party.

This provision disclaims any warranty of non-infringement as to any other person's intellectual property rights. As is the case with all the licenses (except the Creative Commons license to the extent already discussed) described so far, the user is on his own with regard to third-party intellectual property claims that may be made in connection with rights granted under the license, without recourse to the Original Contributor or any Community Member.

> 3. You acknowledge that Reference Code and Technology Specifications are neither designed nor intended for use in the design, construction, operation or maintenance of any nuclear facility.

This provision speaks for itself.

> C. Infringement; Limitation Of Liability.

> 1. Original Contributor and each Community Member disclaim any liability to all Community Members for claims brought by any third party based on infringement of intellectual property rights.

This provision generally disclaims any liability above and beyond disclaiming any particular warranty.

In addition, in the event of any third-party claim, the Original Contributor reserves the right to suspend the grant of rights effected by the license.

> 2. If any portion of, or functionality implemented by, the Community Code, Technology or Technology Specifications becomes the subject of a claim or threatened claim of infringement ("Affected Materials"), Original Contributor may, in its unrestricted discretion, suspend Your rights to use and distribute the Affected Materials under this License. Such suspension of rights will be effective immediately upon Original Contributor's posting of notice of suspension on the Technology Site. Original Contributor has no obligation to lift the suspension of rights relative to the Affected Materials until a final, non-appealable determination is made by a court or governmental agency of competent jurisdiction that Original Contributor is legally able, without the payment of a fee or royalty, to reinstate Your rights to the Affected Materials to the full extent contemplated hereunder. Upon such determination, Original Contributor will lift the suspension by posting a notice to such effect on the Technology Site. Nothing herein shall be construed to prevent You, at Your option and expense, and subject to applicable law and the restrictions and responsibilities set forth in this License and any supplements/attachments, from replacing Community Code in Affected Materials with non-infringing code or independently negotiating, without compromising or prejudicing Original Contributor's position, to obtain the rights necessary to use Affected Materials as herein permitted.

The Original Contributor is required to reinstate those rights, but only upon securing a final non-appealable judgment of non-infringement. This would come only after what would likely be a very lengthy legal process, which the Original Contributor has no obligation to undertake. Users are, however, free to negotiate with the complaining party directly and to obtain a separate license from that person to continue to use the work alleged to be infringing. Whether this is a realistic possibility will depend on the circumstances.

3. ORIGINAL CONTRIBUTOR'S LIABILITY TO YOU FOR ALL CLAIMS RELATING TO THIS LICENSE OR ANY SUPPLEMENT/ATTACHMENT HERETO, WHETHER FOR BREACH OR TORT, IS LIMITED TO THE GREATER OF ONE THOUSAND DOLLARS (US$1000.00) OR THE FULL AMOUNT PAID BY YOU FOR THE MATERIALS GIVING RISE TO THE CLAIM, IF ANY. IN NO EVENT WILL ORIGINAL CONTRIBUTOR BE LIABLE FOR ANY INDIRECT, PUNITIVE, SPECIAL, INCIDENTAL OR CONSEQUENTIAL DAMAGES IN CONNECTION WITH OR ARISING OUT OF THIS LICENSE (INCLUDING, WITHOUT LIMITATION, LOSS OF PROFITS, USE, DATA OR ECONOMIC ADVANTAGE OF ANY SORT), HOWEVER IT ARISES AND ON ANY THEORY OF LIABILITY (including negligence), WHETHER OR NOT ORIGINAL CONTRIBUTOR HAS BEEN ADVISED OF THE POSSIBILITY OF SUCH DAMAGE. LIABILITY UNDER THIS SECTION V.C.3 SHALL BE SO LIMITED AND EXCLUDED, NOTWITHSTANDING FAILURE OF THE ESSENTIAL PURPOSE OF ANY REMEDY.

As a fallback to the previous disclaimers, the SCSL further limits any remedy to the payment of $1,000 or the return of whatever the purchase price may have been for the materials licensed. This provision protects only the Original Contributor.

D. Termination.

1. You may terminate this License at any time by notifying Original Contributor in writing.

This provision, while apparently simple, is complicated in practice. The following subsections addressing termination only provide for the end of the withdrawing Community Member's rights under the SCSL. Read alone, Section D might seem to indicate that the withdrawing Community Member loses his rights to the licensed work, the Original Contributor loses any rights granted by the withdrawing Community Member, but other Community Members do not lose any rights that may have been granted by the withdrawing members. However, as described below, this interpretation is almost certainly wrong.

2. All Your rights will terminate under this License (including any supplements/ attachments hereto) if You fail to comply with any of the material terms or conditions of this License (including any supplements/attachments hereto) and do not cure such failure within thirty (30) days after becoming aware of such noncompliance.

This provision is largely self-explanatory. The most frequent failure to comply with the license is likely to be the unlicensed commercial use of property granted only for "Research Use." This termination provision also governs the Commercial Use supplement described in more detail later. Unlike the GPL, termination is not immediate upon violation, but upon failure to cure within 30 days after the licensee learns of the non-compliance.

3. If You institute patent litigation against any Community Member with respect to a patent applicable to Community Code, then any patent licenses granted by such Community Member to You under this License shall terminate as of the date such litigation is filed. If You institute patent litigation against Original Contributor or any Community Member alleging that Covered Code, Technology or Technology

Specifications infringe Your patent(s), then Original Contributor may in its sole discretion terminate all rights granted to You under this License (including any supplements/attachments hereto) immediately upon written notice.

Like the GPL, the SCSL also withdraws certain rights upon the institution of patent litigation proceedings. If the patent litigation is against another Community Member, any patent rights held by that Community Member are withdrawn: depending on the circumstances, this may have no effect at all on the suing Community Member's use of the licensed property. However, if the suit is against the Original Contributor, the Original Contributor may terminate all rights under the license (including, presumably, rights granted by other Community Members) upon written notice.

4. Upon termination, You must discontinue all uses and distribution of Covered Code, except that You may continue to use, reproduce, prepare derivative works of, display and perform Your Modifications, so long as the license grants of this license are not required to do so, for purposes other than to implement functionality designated in any portion of the Technology Specifications. Properly granted sublicenses to third parties will survive termination. Provisions which, by their nature, should remain in effect following termination survive.

The withdrawing Community Member, as noted above, loses all rights granted under the license. His ownership of whatever intellectual property was contributed to the project are unaffected and he may relicense that property or otherwise act in connection with it as he sees fit. The important language in this section is the limitation of the effect of withdrawal: "Properly granted sublicenses to third parties will survive termination." Thus, properly granted sublicenses (i.e., to other Community Members) are unaffected.

If read by itself, Section D might support the inference that termination results in the withdrawl of rights previously granted by each Contributor to the Original Contributor. This inference is almost certainly wrong. Section III(B)(2) provides for a "perpetual" and "irrevocable" grant of rights by each Contributor to the Original Contributor with regard to "Contributed Code." Termination, whatever the cause, would not reverse that grant of rights.

The last sentence of this section provides that sections of the license should survive, presumably such as the limitations of liability and the choice of law and forum provisions.

E. Miscellaneous.

1. Trademark. You agree to comply with Original Contributor's Trademark & Logo Usage Requirements, as modified from time to time, available at the Technology Site. Except as expressly provided in this License, You are granted no rights in or to any Sun, Jini, Jiro or Java trademarks now or hereafter used or licensed by Original Contributor (the "Sun Trademarks"). You agree not to (a) challenge Original Contributor's ownership or use of Sun Trademarks; (b) attempt to register any Sun Trademarks, or any mark or logo substantially similar thereto; or (c) incorporate any Sun Trademarks into Your own trademarks, product names, service marks, company names or domain names.

This provision incorporates by reference the limitation on use of Sun's trademarks provided at the Technology Site. These bar any infringing use of Sun's trademarks.

> 2. Integration and Assignment. Original Contributor may assign this License (and any supplements/attachments) to another by written notification to You. This License (and executed supplements/attachments) represents the complete agreement of the parties concerning the subject matter hereof.

This provision serves two purposes. First, it provides that the Original Contributor can assign the license—sell or transfer its rights under the license—simply on written notice. Second, this provision indicates that the SCSL is the only agreement between the parties, superseding any previous agreements, oral or written, to the extent such existed, which they probably didn't.

> 3. Severability. If any provision of this License is held unenforceable, such provision shall be reformed to the extent necessary to make it enforceable unless to do so would defeat the intent of the parties, in which case, this License shall terminate.

> 4. Governing Law. This License is governed by the laws of the United States and the State of California, as applied to contracts entered into and performed in California between California residents. The choice of law rules of any jurisdiction and the United Nations Convention on Contracts for the International Sale of Goods shall not apply, nor shall any law or regulation which provides that a contract be construed against the drafter.

> 5. Dispute Resolution.

> a) Any dispute arising out of or relating to this License shall be finally settled by arbitration as set forth in this Section V.E.5, except that either party may bring an action in a court of competent jurisdiction (which jurisdiction shall be exclusive), relative to any dispute relating to such party's intellectual property rights or Your compliance with Original Contributor's compatibility requirements. Arbitration will be administered (i) by the American Arbitration Association (AAA), (ii) in accordance with the rules of the United Nations Commission on International Trade Law (UNCITRAL) (the "Rules") in effect at the time of arbitration, modified as set forth herein, and (iii) by an arbitrator described in Section V.E.5.b who shall apply the governing laws required under Section V.E.4 above. Judgment upon the award rendered by the arbitrator may be entered in any court having jurisdiction to enforce such award. The arbitrator must not award damages in excess of or of a different type than those permitted by this License and any such award is void.

> b) All proceedings will be in English and conducted by a single arbitrator selected in accordance with the Rules who is fluent in English, familiar with technology matters pertinent in the dispute and is either a retired judge or practicing attorney having at least ten (10) years litigation experience. Venue for arbitration will be in San Francisco, California, unless the parties agree otherwise. Each party will be required to produce documents relied upon in the arbitration and to respond to no more than twenty-five single question interrogatories. All awards are payable in US dollars and may include for the prevailing party (i) pre-judgment interest, (ii) reasonable attorneys' fees incurred in connection with the arbitration, and (iii) reasonable costs and expenses incurred in enforcing the award.

c) Nothing herein shall limit either party's right to seek injunctive or other provisional or equitable relief at any time.

These are all provisions standard in commercial contracts. The first preserves the remainder of the agreement in the event that one or more provisions are invalidated. The second provides that California law governs the interpretation of the SCSL. The third provides for arbitration of disputes, meaning that instead of a court, a single arbitrator, familiar with the matters in dispute, would determine the result of any dispute. Arbitration proceedings may be faster and less expensive to the parties than formal court proceedings. However, the relative merits of arbitration, as opposed to ordinary civil litigation, are well beyond the scope of this book.

6. U.S. Government. If this Software is being acquired by or on behalf of the U.S. Government or by a U.S. Government prime contractor or subcontractor (at any tier), the Government's rights in this Software and accompanying documentation shall be only as set forth in this license, in accordance with 48 CFR 227.7201 through 227.7202-4 (for Department of Defense acquisitions) and with 48 CFR 2. 101 and 12.212 (for non-DoD acquisitions).

This provision provides that U.S. government users have the same rights under the agreements as any other person.

7. International Use.

a) Covered Code is subject to US export control laws and may be subject to export or import regulations in other countries. Each party shall comply fully with all such laws and regulations and acknowledges its responsibility to obtain such licenses to export, re-export or import as may be required. You must pass through these obligations to all Your licensees.

b) You must not distribute Reference Code or Technology Specifications into countries other than those listed on the Technology Site by Original Contributor, from time to time.

This provision puts Community Members on notice that U.S. law may limit the rights of foreign users to Covered Code. Users located outside the United States, or who intend to distribute Covered Code to such persons, should consult with an attorney before doing so.

The remaining parts of the license consist of forms indicating acceptance of the license and are included here for purposes of completeness.

READ ALL THE TERMS OF THIS LICENSE CAREFULLY BEFORE ACCEPTING.

BY CLICKING ON THE ACCEPT BUTTON BELOW, YOU ARE ACCEPTING AND AGREEING TO ABIDE BY THE TERMS AND CONDITIONS OF THIS LICENSE.

YOU REPRESENT THAT YOU ARE legally entitled to grant the licenses set forth herein and that you have sufficient copyrights to allow each Community Member and Original Contributor to use and distribute Your Shared Modifications and Error Corrections as herein permitted (including as permitted in any supplements/attachments to this License).

IF YOU ARE AGREEING TO THIS LICENSE IN AN EMPLOYEE OR AGENT CAPACITY, YOU REPRESENT THAT YOU ARE AUTHORIZED TO BIND YOUR EMPLOYER OR PRINCIPAL TO THE LICENSE.

WHETHER YOU ARE ACTING ON YOUR OWN BEHALF OR THAT OF YOUR EMPLOYER OR PRINCIPAL, YOU MUST BE OF MAJORITY AGE AND OTHERWISE COMPETENT TO ENTER INTO CONTRACTS.

IF YOU DO NOT MEET THESE CRITERIA, OR YOU DO NOT AGREE TO ANY OF THE TERMS OF THIS LICENSE, CLICK ON THE REJECT BUTTON AND EXIT NOW.

ACCEPT LICENSE REJECT LICENSE AND EXIT

The following two attachments are certifications of status as a Community Member or as a Student. As previously described, the license requires that Community Members obtain such certifications prior to distributing Covered Code.

ATTACHMENT A-1

COMMUNITY MEMBER CERTIFICATE

"You certify that You are a Licensee in good standing under the Sun Community Source License for the _____ Technology (fill in applicable Technology and Version) (the "License") and that You agree to use and distribute code, documentation and information You may obtain pursuant to this certification only in accordance with the terms and subject to the conditions of the License."

Add to the end of the foregoing, as appropriate:

For written documents:

"Signature:_____

Printed Name

and Title:_____

Company _____ "

For web downloads add buttons with the following:

"Agreed and AcceptedReject and Exit"

ATTACHMENT A-2

STUDENT ACKNOWLEDGMENT

"You acknowledge that this software and related documentation has been obtained by your educational institution subject to the Sun Community Source License (the "License"). You have been provided with access to the software and documentation for use only in connection with your course work as a matriculated student of your educational institution. Commercial use of the software and documentation is expressly prohibited.

THIS SOFTWARE AND RELATED DOCUMENTATION CONTAINS PROPRIETARY MATERIALS OF SUN MICROSYSTEMS, INC. PROTECTED BY VARIOUS INTELLECTUAL PROPERTY RIGHTS. YOUR USE OF THE SOFTWARE AND DOCUMENTATION IS LIMITED."

Add to the end of the foregoing, as appropriate:

For written documents:

"Signature:_____

Printed Name :_____ "

For web downloads add buttons with the following:

"Agreed and Accepted Reject and Exit"

Those persons who undertake such distributions should be sure to collect and retain such certifications from all persons whose work is governed by the SCSL.

The Commercial Use Supplement

As described, the SCSL does not permit commercial use of the licensed code: the only uses permitted are for "Research Use," defined as "research, evaluation, development, educational or personal and individual use, excluding use or distribution for direct or indirect commercial (including strategic) gain or advantage." Not only may the licensee not distribute the licensed code for commercial use, he may not even "use" it to that end, for example, as part of an application for use in a business.

Commercial use is permitted, however, under the SCSL's Commercial Use Supplement, described below. This supplement, however, is an entirely different license, and it licenses an entirely different category of code. The SCSL research use license permits testing and development of unfinished code; the SCSL Commercial Use Supplement permits use (including commercial use) of code that, having passed through the period of research and development contemplated by the research use license, has been tested and deemed compliant with the standards governing the code.

COMMERCIAL USE SUPPLEMENT TO SUN COMMUNITY SOURCE LICENSE

I. PURPOSE AND EFFECT.

This Commercial Use Supplement General Terms ("CUSupp") is required for Commercial Use of Covered Code and shall be made effective as to any Technology specified in a Technology Specific Attachment once such Technology Specific Attachment is signed by You and Original Contributor. The rights and responsibilities set forth in this CUSupp are additional to those in Your License. You have agreed to the terms of the License by selecting the "Accept" button at the end of the License or by executing a hardcopy License with Original Contributor. You acknowledge that the License is binding on You.

The Commercial Use Supplement or CUSupp is technology-specific and requires the execution of the research use license applicable to that technology.

II. DEFINITIONS. Capitalized terms used but not defined in this CUSupp shall have the same meaning as the identical capitalized terms in Section I of the License. Additional terms are defined as follows:

The CUSupp incorporates by reference all the definitions previously given in the research use license.

"Commercial Use" means uses and distributions of Covered Code for any direct or indirect commercial or strategic gain or advantage.

This covers every use not permitted by the research use license.

"Compliant Implementation" means Covered Code that fully implements and conforms to the Technology Specifications and complies with the Compliance Materials, the License, this CUSupp and applicable Technology Specific Attachment(s).

This is a critical term of the CUSupp, as it applies only to code that is a "Compliant Implemention."

"Compliance Materials" means the test programs, guides, documentation and other materials identified in the Technology Specific Attachment(s) for use in establishing that Covered Code is a Compliant Implementation, as may be revised by Original Contributor from time to time.

These materials are the benchmarks for determining compliance and are provided by the Original Contributor. They may be modified from time to time, which could result in an implementation, once determined to be compliant, to fall out of compliance upon the revision of the Compliance Materials.

"Technology Specific Attachment(s)" means an attachment or attachments to the License and this CUSupp which contains terms and conditions specific to the Technology therein identified as well as the specifics of the Compliance Materials and requirements for such Technology.

Variations of the CUSupp unique to different Technologies may have additional terms attached to the supplement. The Sun Jini technology has such additional terms. (They are not described in this book.)

III. COMMERCIAL USE RIGHTS.

A. Commercial Use. Subject to and conditioned upon Your compliance with the terms and conditions of Your Research Use license and the additional terms and conditions set forth in this CUSupp and associated Technology Specific Attachment(s), including the provisions of Section IV, below, Original Contributor hereby adds to those rights enumerated under Section III.A.1 of the Research Use license the non-exclusive, worldwide, royalty-bearing right to, within the specified Field of Use denoted in the Technology Specific Attachment:

There are two provisions in this section that immediately stand out. The first is the "royalty-bearing" language: use of the Covered Code for commercial purposes may be subject to payment of a royalty, at a rate to be specified in the Technology Specific Attachment. The second is the "specified Field of Use": while the licensee may be permitted to use the Covered Code for commercial purposes, the scope of that right could be very narrowly circumscribed—and, again, the critical language will be contained in the Technology Specific Attachment. Subject to these very important limitations, the licensee has the rights to:

1. use the Compliance Materials to determine whether Covered Code constitutes a Compliant Implementation;

The CUSupp permits, indeed requires, that the licensee test the Covered Code himself to determine if it is a Compliant Implementation.

2. use, reproduce, display, perform and distribute internally source and object code copies of Compliant Implementations for Commercial Use;

This permits distribution of Compliant Implementations internally in the form of both source and object code. Distribution of non-compliant implementations within an organization is allowed under the Research Use permissions granted by the SCSL is allowed, presuming that all distributees have agreed to be bound by the terms of the SCSL.

3. reproduce and distribute to third parties and Community Members through multiple tiers of distribution object code copies of Compliant Implementations for Commercial Use;

Only object (or executable) code of the Compliant Implementations may be distributed to third parties, or even to Community Members, for Commercial Use. However, this provision does not limit the rights granted to distribute code to Community Members for non-Commercial Use or Research Use.

4. reproduce and distribute the source code of Compliant Implementations to Community Members licensed for Commercial Use of the same Technology; and

Community Members who have the same Technology license for Commercial Use can distribute both object and source code among themselves.

5. reproduce and distribute a copy of the Technology Specifications (which may be reformatted, but must remain substantively unchanged) with Compliant Implementations for Commercial Use.

This provision is self-explanatory. The Commercial Use of the code governed by CUSupp is further limited by certain additional restrictions.

IV. ADDITIONAL RESTRICTIONS AND COMMUNITY RESPONSIBILITIES.

As a condition to the Commercial Use rights granted above, You must comply with the following restrictions and community responsibilities (in addition to those in the License)

F. Certification. You may distribute source code of Compliant Implementations for Commercial Use only to Original Contributor or to Community Members from whom You have first obtained a certification of status in the form set forth in Attachment A-1. You must keep a copy of each such certificate and acknowledgment You obtain and provide a copy to Original Contributor, if requested.

As is the case with the SCSL, distributors of code under the CUSupp must take affirmative action to ensure the recipients of code are permitted to receive that code, by requesting and maintaining certifications from the recipients.

G. Compliance Materials. Depending on the Technology licensed, Your access to and use of the Compliance Materials may be subject to additional requirements such as entering into a support agreement and trademark license. Such additional requirements, if any, are as set out in the Technology Specific Attachment. You agree to comply fully with all such applicable requirements.

This notifies potential licensees that the Original Contributor may attach additional conditions and restrictions that would be contained in the Technology Specific Attachment.

> H. Compatibility. Only Compliant Implementations may be used and distributed for Commercial Use.

This restates a condition already made clear in the SCSL and the CUSupp.

> I. Commercial Distribution Requirement.
>
> 1. You may distribute object code copies for Commercial Use as herein contemplated under a license agreement of Your choice which is consistent with Your rights and obligations under the License and this CUSupp. You may provide warranties, indemnities and/or other additional terms and conditions in Your license agreements, provided that it is clear that such additional terms and conditions are offered by You only. You hereby agree to hold Original Contributor and each Community Member harmless and indemnify against any liability arising in connection with such terms and conditions. You will pay all damages, costs and fees awarded by a court or arbitrator having jurisdiction over the matter or any settlement amount negotiated by You and attributable to such claim.

As noted, in connection with the SCSL, the only license guaranteed to comply with the SCSL and the CUSupp is the SCSL/CUSupp itself. The CUSupp, however, like the GPL and some other licenses already described, explicitly permits the licensee to provide warranties, indemnifications, or similar additional terms. Such warranties and guaranties do not bind the Original Contributor or any other Community Member, and the grantor of such warranties or guaranties agrees not only not to bind such persons but to "hold them harmless," meaning that the grantor agrees to pay any legal judgment againt the Original Contributor or other Community Members, as well as any legal fees associated with their defense, that might arise from the issuance of such a warranty or guaranty.

> 2. You may distribute or display the Technology Specifications only pursuant to the specification license agreement applicable to the Technology Specifications in question in the exact form provided by Original Contributor on the Technology Site, and provided that You require, as a pre-condition of any third party's access to Technology Specifications distributed or displayed by You, acceptance by such third party of the terms of such specification license.

This is more a form of notice than a specific provision. In addition to the terms of the SCSL and the CUSupp, the licensee may also be bound by the terms of the Technology Specific Attachment and also by the terms of the "specification license agreement applicable to the Technology Specifications." Depending on the Technology being licensed, the licensee may be bound by (and accordingly should read carefully) not one but four distinct documents: the SCSL, the CUSupp, the Technology Specific Attachments, and the license agreement governing the Technology Specifications; the last two of which are separate from the licenses described here.

> J. End User License Terms. You must include the following terms and conditions in end user license agreements accompanying copies of Compliant Implementations distributed for Commercial User hereunder:

If the licensee distributes the code under a license other than the SCSL/CUSupp, such a license must include the following terms.

1. Software contains copyrighted information of Sun Microsystems, Inc. and title is retained by Sun.

2. Use, duplication or disclosure by the United States government is subject to the restrictions set forth in the Rights in Technical Data and Computer Software clauses in DFARS 252.227-701(c)(1)(ii) and FAR 52.227-19(c)(2) as applicable.

The following section, governing the right (or the option) to defend claims, is really more a part of insurance contracts than software licensing.

K. Defense of Claims.

1. By Original Contributor.

a) Notwithstanding Section V.C.1 of the License, Original Contributor will defend, at its expense, any legal proceeding brought against You to the extent based on a claim that Your authorized Commercial Use of Reference Code is an infringement of a third party trade secret or copyright in a country that is a signatory to the Berne Convention, and will pay all damages, costs and fees awarded by a court of competent jurisdiction, or such settlement amount negotiated by Original Contributor, attributable to such claim. The foregoing shall not apply to any claims of intellectual property infringement based upon the combination of code or documentation supplied by Original Contributor with code, technology, or documentation from other sources.

With regards to the rights granted by the CUSupp only, the Original Contributor (i.e., Sun) will undertake the legal defense of specified claims—including presumably the costs of hiring legal counsel—and will indemnify, paying all legal damages that may result from the specified claims. This defense applies only to a narrow range of claims, including only those claims of copyright or trade secret that arise out of the licensee's use of the Reference Code distributed by the Original Contributor. This excludes patent claims and any claims arising from code not put forward as being developed by the Original Contributor.

The Original Contributor has the right, but not the obligation, to defend patent claims arising from the Reference Code.

b) Original Contributor will have the right, but not the obligation, to defend You, at Original Contributor's expense, in connection with a claim that Your Commercial Use of Reference Code is an infringement of a third party patent, and, if Original Contributor elects in its sole discretion to defend You, will pay all damages, costs and fees awarded by a court or tribunal of competent jurisdiction, or such settlement amount negotiated by Original Contributor and attributable to such claim.

The duty to defend is complex in nature, and again, more the subject of insurance law than software licensing. In essence, the party undertaking the defense (here, the Original Contributor) has the obligation to defend the licensee and to act solely in the interest of the licensee in the course of that defense. However, insofar as the Original Contributor (in legal terms, the indemnitor) is paying for and directing the defense, the tendency for such an indemnitor is to protect its own interests (whether they are consistent with the interests of the licensee or not) in the course of such a defense. The Original Contributor has an interest in not having a judgment entered against anyone, including its licensees, that could limit its own ability to exercise the rights to the Reference Code. These provisions are the result of that interest, not necessarily any generosity on the part of Sun.

The CUSupp applies a mirror provision requiring that licensees undertake a similar duty to defend both the Original Contributor and other Community Members from arising from any code contributed by the licensee; from any warranty or guarantee granted by the licensee and from any claim arising from any commercial use of the Covered Code, excepting only patent claims that arise from the Reference Code, which fall under the previous section.

> 2. By You. Notwithstanding Section V.C.1 of the License, You will defend, at Your expense, any legal proceeding brought against any Original Contributor and any Community Member to the extent based on a claim: (a) that the use, reproduction or distribution of any of Your Contributed Code or Contributed Code Specifications is an infringement of a third party trade secret or copyright in a country that is a signatory to the Berne Convention; (b) arising in connection with any representation, warranty, support, indemnity, liability or other license terms that you may offer in connection with any Covered Code; or (c) arising from Your Commercial Use of Covered Code, other than a claim covered by Section IV.K.1 above, and other than a patent claim based solely on Reference Code. You will pay all damages, costs and fees awarded by a court of competent jurisdiction, or such settlement amount negotiated by Original Contributor, attributable to such claim.

This is a significant obligation. It should give pause to any licensee considering offering as Contributed Code any code that could even arguably be considered a violation of applicable copyright or patent law.

> 3. Prerequisites. Under Sections IV.K.1.a and IV.K.1.b, You must, and under Section IV.K.2, Original Contributor or a Community Member must: (a) provide notice of the claim promptly to the indemnifying party; (b) give the indemnifying party sole control of the defense and settlement of the claim; (c) provide to indemnifying party, at the indemnifying party's expense, all available information, assistance and authority to defend and settle; and (d) have not compromised or settled such claim or proceeding with the indemnifying party's prior written consent.

As a prerequisite to such indemnification, the party seeking indemnification must provide prompt notice, cooperate with the indemnitor, and surrender its own right to defend (including the right to settle) the given claim. As noted above, there may certainly be occasions in which a party is better off defending a claim on its own than in seeking indemnification. The resolution of such issues is, however, beyond the scope of this book.

> 4. Entire Liability. Section IV.K.1 states Original Contributor's entire liability and Your sole and exclusive remedy with respect to claims of infringement of any intellectual property rights brought by any third party or any Community Member. Section IV.K.2 states Your entire liability and Original Contributor's sole and exclusive remedy with respect to claims of infringement of any intellectual property rights brought by any third party or any Community Member.

This section merely provides that indemnification provisions just described provide the sole remedy and that no other protection is available under the CUSupp.

> L. Notice of Breach or Infringement. You agree to notify Original Contributor should You become aware of any potential or actual breach or violation of the License or infringement of the Technology or any of Original Contributor's intellectual property rights in the Technology, Reference Code or Technology Specifications.

This is an interesting provision. Licensees are required to inform the Original Contributor if they become aware of any potential infringment of the Original Contributor's property.

> M. Proprietary Rights Notices. You must not remove any copyright notices, trademark notices or other proprietary legends of Original Contributor or its suppliers contained on or in the Covered Code, Technology Specifications and Contributed Code Specifications.

This provision speaks for itself.

> N. Relationship. The relationship created is that of licensor and licensee only. You hereby waive the benefit of any law or regulation dealing with the establishment and regulation of franchises or agencies.

This provision is designed to avoid the effect of some state laws that protect agents or franchisees of national or global companies, like McDonald's.

> O. Assignment. This CUSupp and Technology Specific Attachment(s) shall not be assigned by You, including by way of merger (regardless of whether You are the surviving entity), acquisition or otherwise, without Original Contributor's prior written consent.

An assignment is a legal contract under which one party is permitted to substitute for another in a pre-existing contractual relationship, such as a lease or similar agreement. This provision, typical in commercial contracts, provides that such assignments are not permitted without the consent of the Original Contributor. This is the last provision in the CUSupp. As already noted, individual Sun licenses will contain additional terms, which govern either the specific Technology being licensed or the terms under which technology specifications can be distributed. Those specific contracts are not described here.

The SCSL and the CUSupp present a combination of open source and proprietary contract ideas and values. The SCSL is very far from an open source contract in its strict limitations on the use of the licensed code; the bar on any form of commercial use eliminates a great deal of the motivation for participation in open source projects. The CUSupp, while permitting such commercial use, imposes two significant limitations. First, the possible requirement of payment of royalties will certainly limit the availability of the code (depending on the price). Second, the need to remain compliant with Sun's specifications, while encouraging uniformity, will discourage innovation, at least innovation outside the lines envisioned by Sun. Nonetheless, the SCSL is a potentially important experiment in integrating some aspects of open source into a commercial model, with an emphasis on maintaining the uniformity of operation that is the touchstone of Sun's work.

Microsoft Shared Source Initiative

Microsoft has historically wrung great profits from proprietary software licensing. Its business model, along with its substantial profit margins, is completely dependent upon licensing access to the software that it controls. In response to the growing market for open source and free software in the last 15 years, Microsoft has made clear that it has no intention of changing its approach. In fact, its public position and actions seem to signify that the company is becoming more aggressive about its licensing programs and about protecting its intellectual property through strategies such as patent procurement and litigation.

Yet, historically, Microsoft has provided at least some business partners and customers access to its source code, as well as obtained access to the source code of others for inclusion in its products, or for ensuring interoperability. New demands are also growing: as a result of open source, the developer community is increasingly used to having liberal access to whatever source code it needs to conduct business; governments and customers now expect to be able to audit the source code that makes up the products that they depend upon daily; and academics and start-ups alike understand that open source is an efficient way to conduct shared research projects. As the open source movement continues to gain steam, Microsoft, like many other software companies, has felt pressure to provide public access to its source code.

Microsoft cannot easily turn to existing open source licenses and communities in order to solve this problem. Large-scale proprietary software products represent a complex web of legal relationships between all of those who own copyrights, trademarks, and patents that apply not only to the code, but also to arcane elements such as the communications protocols and media formats being used. Were Microsoft to relicense its code, all participants would have to be contacted and terms renegotiated, or else replacement code would need to be written and tested. As described in Chapter 3, when Netscape open source licensed its proprietary Communicator software under the Mozilla Public License, it had to negotiate with third-party providers of code that had been part of the Communicator system and had to rewrite substantial sections of code when some of those providers refused to permit their code to be released under the MPL. This is a difficult process, even for the largest companies.

Beyond the legal difficulties involved, Microsoft's software business model could not possibly sustain the blow to its profit margins that would occur should its software become freely available. Companies that generate income through services or hardware businesses can piggyback directly on open source by refocusing on those aspects of their business. But with almost all of its revenues derived from the licensing of proprietary software, Microsoft needs an approach to source code access that permits it to continue to use its current business model.

The Microsoft Shared Source Initiative is Microsoft's attempt to solve this source code access dilemma. The Shared Source Initiative has many facets, and it is difficult

---

to describe briefly. It can be most simply explained as an umbrella under which Microsoft positions its many different software-licensing practices. On its face, it is a program for facilitating access to Microsoft source code, but, considered more broadly, it is also a lobbying effort aimed at explaining and defending the benefits of strong intellectual property laws to the world at large.

Within this system, Microsoft has defined five key source code licensing attributes:

1. The ability to view and reference source code without changing it
2. The ability to enhance debugging with source code access
3. The ability to modify source code for local use only
4. The ability to distribute products based on modified sources for non-commercial purposes
5. The ability to commercialize products built on modified source code

Using these attributes, Microsoft has carefully tailored a number of software licenses that grant more or less restricted access to the source code for many of its software products, depending upon a number of variables such as what country the licensee resides in; how important the product is to Microsoft's core business; and whether the software is being used for commercial purposes, charitable use, or academic research. For some products, such as Windows, there may be literally dozens of different licensing options.

Because the Microsoft Shared Source Initiative is so complex, and each license is the result of relatively laborious negotiation within Microsoft and between Microsoft and its users and developers—with product and location specificity built into each license—the project has none of the simplicity or transparency of open source and free software licenses. It is, at least at this time, little more than a branded extension of Microsoft's current commercial licensing practices.

Within Microsoft's existing business ecosystem, however, the Shared Source Initiative has already borne copious amounts of fruit. Awareness of the initiative within Microsoft product teams has resulted in standardized and simplified ways for customers, subcontractors, support firms, hardware vendors, academic researchers, and governments to obtain access to code that would have been off-limits or very difficult to access in the past. It has also catalyzed internal analysis and product planning, which has resulted in deeper Microsoft participation in existing open source communities and processes.

Beyond the edges of the ecosystem populated by Microsoft dependents, reaction to the Shared Source Initiative has been much more ambivalent. To many people, the program seems to be little more than a series of carefully scaled permissions governing access to Microsoft's closely guarded source code. Although some of the licenses involved allow for unfettered change and redistribution of underlying code, the code to which these licenses apply is not core application or operating system code. Developers have no real opportunity to make changes to such core assets without first agreeing to very restrictive terms. As a result, the resulting collaboration between Microsoft and external developers bears little relationship to the open source or open source-like development relationships described in this and previous chapters.

Despite its readily apparent lack of enthusiasm for them, Microsoft has been actively following developments in the open source movement and slowly adapting to them via the Shared Source Initiative. Microsoft has begun to use existing open source licenses for some of its newer projects. Although these projects are minor at this point, the trend is very likely to continue because of the great advantages that open source has to offer, even to Microsoft, at least under certain circumstances. Microsoft is also beginning to understand how open source approaches can be "safely" integrated with its traditional business practices, and as a result of this, Microsoft's intellectual property agenda is likely to cause profound change within existing open source practices, through litigation, lobbying, lawmaking, and "coopetition." Although Microsoft's positioning of shared source as an alternative to open source might seem absurd, it should not be lightly dismissed.

 As this book was going to press, Microsoft released its Windows Installer XML (WiX) technology under the Common Public License (CPL), an Open Source Initiative-approved license, at *http:// sourceforge.net/projects/wix/*. This marks a first, though how far Microsoft will go with such projects is yet to be seen.

In terms of placing various licensing models on a spectrum, the GPL or the BSD-model license would fall on one end, depending on the nature of the "freedom" being measured; obviously, the classic proprietary license would fall upon the other, in terms of the restrictions imposed on licensees. In the continuum would fall the Perl, the MPL, the SCSL and the other licenses already described. The Microsoft Shared Source Initiative falls quite near the classic proprietary model in its function: not a surprising result, considering that Microsoft is by far history's largest beneficiary of the proprietary software licensing model. But, nonetheless, it has already, at least with regards to some applications, moved closer to a true open source model, and the Initiative is a project worth watching.

As this book was going to press, Microsoft released its Windows Installer XML (WiX) technology under the Common Public License (CPL), an Open Source Initiative-approved license, at *http://sourceforge.net/projects/wix/*. This marks a first, though how far Microsoft will go with such projects is yet to be seen.

CHAPTER 6
Legal Impacts of Open Source and Free Software Licensing

All of the discussions in earlier chapters have assumed that each of these licenses can be and will be enforced by their licensors, and, ultimately, by the courts. However, two unique problems (in addition to those involved in the enforcement of any contract) affect licensors of software under open source and free software licenses.

First, for each license described in previous chapters, the licensor may not even know who the licensees are. All of these licenses, to varying degrees, put forth the licensed code with an invitation to adopt it and use it, subject to the terms of the respective licenses. These open source and free software licenses do not require notification or other affirmative action to be taken by licensees that would notify the licensor of the fact that the licensee has entered into the contract.* In addition, most of these licenses permit and even encourage the free sublicensing of the licensor's work to other licensees, whose connection to the original licensee can become tenuous as the licensed work moves through multiple generations of licensing before ending up with a particular user.

Second, while some of these licenses require that the licensee engage in some affirmative action to access the licensed work (such as clicking on a button indicating that the licensee agrees to be bound by the terms of the license) prior to permitting access of the licensed work, many of them—like the BSD, MIT, and Apache Licenses—do not. Others, like the GPL and LGPL, do not require such affirmative assent in all cases.

Both of these problems are substantially addressed by the fact that use of the licensed work is contingent on accepting the terms of the license. Unlike other types of contracts, open source and free software contracts impose very few, if any, affirmative obligations (such as the payment of royalties) on licensees, but rather impose restrictions only on the rights granted by the license. This property will operate, most likely, to save the enforceability of these licenses from challenges regarding the absence of mutual consent or consideration that may otherwise arise.

---

* The SCSL, which is not an open source or free software license, although it incorporates some of their principles, does require some form of notification. The Microsoft Shared Source Initiative operates under totally different custom-negotiation principles, so they know who they are dealing with from the outset.

Entering Contracts

Any contract between two or more persons rests on two fundamental assumptions: one, that there is some mutual obligation created by the agreement, which is known as the *consideration*; and two, that there is mutual consent, or a meeting of the minds, as to the terms of the contract, usually described as the *offer* and the *acceptance*. Once an offer that involves the exchange of consideration has been made and accepted, an enforceable contract is created. This principle is, of course, subject to numerous exceptions.

These concepts are capable of any number of variations and any number of hard cases involing these variations provide the subject matter for first-year law students. Basic principles suffice for our purposes. The idea of consideration turns on the fact that each party is undertaking an obligation, even a very minor one, to the other as part of the transaction. If Robert promises to give Sidney $10,000 in one year, and Sidney does nothing and agrees to do nothing, there is no contract, but only a promised gift. The significance of this is that such a promise is not legally enforceable. If Robert does not pay, Sidney cannot legally compel him to pay. However, if Robert agrees to pay Sidney $10,000 in one year if Sidney forbears from drinking alcohol for that entire time, that creates an enforceable promise: if Sidney fulfills her half of the bargain, she can legally compel Robert to live up to his, even though the consideration (abstinence from alcohol) that she promised (and performed) has at most only a very tangential benefit to Robert.

Even the most unrestrictive open source license imposes at least a minimal obligation ensuring that consideration in the legal sense is exchanged and an enforceable contract is created through the license. The MIT License, described in Chapter 2, imposes the following restriction on licensees:

> The above copyright notice and this permission notice shall be included in all copies or substantial portions of the Software.

While this obligation is not onerous, it is real, and failure to abide by it constitutes a breach of the contract. By extension, the more onerous restrictions imposed by the GPL, the BSD, the Apache, and all of the other open source and free software licenses already described impose sufficient obligations so as not to fail as contracts for lack of consideration. The licensor grants a real benefit, the right to use the licensed software, and the licensee agrees to genuine restrictions, i.e., those that are expressed in the license.

Potentially more problematic is the question of mutual consent. In an ordinary commercial contract, this question rarely, if ever, arises. In general, mutual consent can be attacked only in relatively unusual circumstances. In the classic formulation of a contract, the two parties to the contract have met, negotiated, and reached final agreement, embodied in a formal, signed document. Under those circumstances, the consent of either of the parties can be attacked, essentially in only two ways. First, one of the parties can argue that his consent was induced by *fraud*, i.e., that the other party deceived him as to a fact material to the contract. For example, two parties may agree to a contract that provides for the sale of a document signed by Elvis Presley. The genuineness of the signature is critical to the contract. If the buyer can prove that the signature was a forgery and that the seller knew it, he can void the contract—render it of no legal effect—on the grounds of fraud. Second, mutual consent can be attacked on the basis of *incompetence*. In most jurisdictions, a person under the age of 18 cannot enter into a binding contract. Accordingly, if such a person enters into a contract, she can sue to have the contract voided on the basis that she was incompetent to enter into the contract in the first place.

While these circumstances appear in numerous variations and can present difficulties in interpreting contracts and adjudicating disputes that arise from them, they are relatively clear cut assaults on the mutual consent to a contract. However, because of the absence of a writing signed by both parties formally indicating their agreement to a contract, the open source and free software licenses described earlier present a different, and more complex problem.

It has long been accepted that contracts may be formed in the absence of a signed document. Oral contracts, with significant exceptions, are regularly enforced. The familiar "shrinkwrap" license that frequently governs the use of commercial software is more applicable to software contracts. The user purchases the software; the box in which the media containing the software is sold indicates that use of the software is governed by a license; and the purchaser is further informed that breaking the shrinkwrap and opening the box indicates the user's consent to the license agreement. Some courts have upheld the creation of a contract under these terms; other courts have not. A potentially critical distinction, described in more detail later, is the extent to which the purchaser was aware (or could have made himself aware) that the software was provided subject to a license and could have learned the terms of the license that would govern the use of the software.

These questions become more difficult when the product and the license both exist in a virtual space and the offer and acceptance both take place there. There are a number of different contexts in which this kind of offer and acceptance can take place, and small differences can be critical in determining whether a contract is formed. For the following examples, a web site is posited as the locus of the contract, although the same issues could arise as easily with software recorded on a physical medium, such as a CD-ROM.*

In the first example, an icon appears on the introductory screen for a piece of software, indicating that that software is being provided subject to the terms of a license.

---

* Readers interested in a more detailed legal analysis should read the opinion of Judge Alvin K. Hellerstein in *Specht v. Netscape Comm. Corp.*, 00 Civ. 4871 (AKS), 2001 WL 755396 (S.D.N.Y. July 5, 2001).Such contracts arise outside the world of software licensing as well. Ticket stubs—such as those received at coatchecks or parking garages—which typically disclaim any liability for checked items, present similar issues.

A user who wants to view the terms of the license can click on a hyperlink that takes him to a page displaying the terms of the license. Another hyperlink links to the site from which the software can be downloaded. This "browsewrap" license may create an enforceable contract: the user (or purchaser) is at least made aware that the software is produced subject to a license, but he is not required to assent to the terms of the license, or even to look at it, before accessing the licensed work. The enforceability of this kind of contract is, however, subject to dispute and this arrangement may not result in a contract that would be enforced.

The second example, the so-called "clickwrap" license, is more likely to create an enforceable contract. In this variation, the user is required to view, however fleetingly, the terms of the license and to take some affirmative action to agree to its terms, such as by clicking a button that says "Yes, I have read this license and I agree to its terms," before accessing the licensed software. This is the form of license contemplated in some of the licenses described earlier and will generally provide sufficient notice to the user of the terms of the license and require sufficient affirmative action to create an enforceable contract, so long as the other requirements of contract are met, such as the competence of the parties and the absence of fraud.

A variant of the "clickwrap" and "browsewrap" licenses, in which the user only views the license and is not required to take any affirmative action indicating consent to the licensed terms, but where consent is implied from some other action (usually the downloading of the licensed software), may or may not be sufficient to create an enforceable contract. The licensee knows of the license, knows it governs use of the software, and has the opportunity to review it before accessing the software. Nonetheless, the absence of affirmative consent (such as clicking on a text box as required by the "clickwrap" license) is troubling to courts, and correctly so. It seems unfair to enforce terms of a contract to which one of the parties has done nothing to positively affirm.

This issue has obvious application to the open source and free software licenses already discussed. Staying with the MIT License, say, for example, that an ordinary user comes across a piece of code that is subject to this license. The user takes the code and uses it on his personal computer. The user incorporates the code into a program that he is writing. The user distributes the program, either for profit or not. At no point has the user taken any affirmative, symbolic action that would indicate his consent to the terms of the license that is comparable to the act of signing a contract.

Statutory Developments Related to Software Contracts

The Uniform Electronic Transactions Act (UETA), a model law adopted by at least 22 states and under consideration in others, provides as a general matter that a contract may not be denied legal effect simply because the contract is recorded in an electronic medium and not on paper.

E-Sign, a federal law passed on October 1, 2000, operates to a similar effect, in holding that digital signatures on documents are as effective as ordinary written signatures on paper in memorializing an agreement.˙

Neither UETA nor E-Sign purports to alter ordinary state law governing interpretation of contracts.

Another model law, the Uniform Computer Information Transaction Act (UCITA), does modify ordinary state contract laws relating to transactions in software. Although it is intended to facilitate transactions in information and provide for uniform interpretation of contracts governing such transactions, the UCITA has not been widely adopted. Only two states, Maryland and Virginia, have adopted UCITA; a number of states, however, have adopted anti-UCITA statutes. Because UCITA's effect is currently very limited and does not seem likely to spread in the near future, it is not further addressed here.

The Self-Enforcing Nature of Open Source and Free Software Licenses

There is a "savings" logic present in the MIT License (and others) that preserves the effect of the license even in the absence of an affirmative act of consent. This is because open source and free software licenses do not impose affirmative obligations on licensees but rather impose restrictions on the rights granted under the license: such restrictions can be relatively straightforward, as is the case with the MIT License's requirement of reprinting the copyright and permission notice; or somewhat more complex, as with the far-reaching consequences of licensing under the GPL License.*

The GPL License provides a good example of this phenomenon. The typical limitations of proprietary licenses simply do not apply to most applications of GPL-licensed software. For example, installing, using, or even modifying GPL-licensed software implicates no term of that license. Any user is completely free to undertake any of these actions. There are no limitations on the number of installations of the software that a user may undertake and no requirement that the user pay royalties in exchange for use, in sharp contrast to proprietary licenses. Only if the user intends to distribute the original code or modified versions of it does the GPL come into effect.

It is only at this point (and the same is true of the other open source and free licenses already discussed) that questions of enforcement even arise. And it is at this point that the unique strength of these licenses becomes apparent. As already discussed, in the absence of a license, the user would not have even the right to maintain, use, or modify the copyrighted code. Even work that is not specifically identified as being

---

* This section's discussion draws heavily on the essay by Eben Moglen, "Enforcing the GNU GPL" located at *http://www.gnu.org/philosophy/enforcing-gpl.html.*

copyright is protected under the law of the United States and other nations. The user considering challenging the applicability of the license is thus faced with a real dilemma.

On the one hand, the user is free to disclaim the obligations of the license, most likely on the grounds that he never affirmatively agreed to be bound by the license. If he does so, he is not obligated to pay royalties or otherwise conform to any affirmative agreements that the license might require. However, by disclaiming the license—taking the position that no enforceable contract exists between him and the licensor—the user is arguing that the "default" state of copyright exists: that state of protection which applies to any copyrighted work not in the public domain. While free of any restrictions that may derive from the license at issue, such a user finds himself in the unenviable position of lacking all of the fundamental rights granted by the open source or free software license that he wishes to exercise. A user in such a "default" copyright state is barred from distributing or modifying the work (except to the limited extent permitted by fair use), without the permission of the copyright holder, which permission, by disclaiming the license, he has already refused.

If, however, the user wishes to exercise rights under the license, he is compelled to accept with it whatever limitations or restrictions may be contained in the applicable software license. For example, under the GPL, if a user wishes to incorporate GPL-licensed code into his own programs, he is required to license those programs under the GPL and thereby permit the "free" use of them as described in the GPL. As a legal (and a common sense) matter, he may not pick and choose, so as to accept the benefits of the license without its restrictions.

Unlike people who may object to the onerous obligations that could be imposed by "shrinkwrap," "clickwrap," and "browsewrap" licenses (such as, for example, the obligations of paying royalties) and who would disclaim the contract entirely and forego the use of the licensed software if given the choice, users of open source and free software licensed software cannot realistically "walk away." The continued availability of the work that they want to use is contingent on their adherence to the license's terms. While they are free to "walk away," the condition on the abandonment of the restrictions of the license is the surrender of the rights granted by the license.

This feature makes open source and free software licenses remarkably easy to enforce. A licensor can simply tell infringers that infringement vacates their continued rights to the licensed code. As most infringers are aware of the substantial civil and criminal penalties associated with copyright infringement, and desire the rights granted by the license, they will make their behavior conform to the demands of the license. For those infringers unwilling to conform to the terms of the license, even after being put on notice of the license, and who continue to infringe (typically by redistributing the licensed work under an incompatible license, such as a proprietary license), the licensor can directly contact the customers of the illegally licensed software. The original licensor can inform those customers that the same (or substantially similar software) is available under the terms of the original license, which are almost certainly more favorable to that customer. In addition, because the customer is aware of the difficulties and expense associated with relying on software licensed under what is, at best, a highly questionable license, it is probably sufficient to convince such customers to abandon the use of the work distributed in violation of the license. While this involves some degree of administrative and legal sophistication on the part of the licensor, this is generally not a great burden. The Free Software Foundation has policed the GPL License in exactly this fashion for many years with consistent success.

The Global Scope of Open Source and Free Software Licensing

Another issue for open source and free software licenses is their enforcement in jurisdictions outside the United States. The global nature of commerce and the generally free travel of software across national boundaries implicates the enforcement of open source and free software licenses in a number of jurisdictions, not only those in the United States.

International enforcement of copyright laws is frequently lax. While many countries are signatories of treaties that provide for the international enforcement of copyright protection (such as the Berne Convention), such treaties are frequently disregarded. The proliferation of "pirated" DVDs and CDs is a testament to that. The use of file-sharing software frustrates enforcement of copyright even within the United States. Within such a framework, it may seem impossible to enforce the terms of open source and free software licenses, which depend, as just noted, on the foundations of copyright for enforcement across national boundaries.

In many countries, particularly in the "developed" world where most software creation takes place, the enforcement of copyright is routine. While the unauthorized distribution of copyrighted material is commonplace, it is nonetheless difficult for any established company or person to reasonably hope to profit from the illegal distribution of copyrighted material. This is particularly true of software. Users of software, at least commercial users, are generally more concerned with reliable performance and support than with the incremental cost of software. Users expect to be able to rely on a software maker's products and to receive support for that software's application going forward. Providing this reliability and these services requires the existence of a stable, aboveground organization—exactly the kind of organization that is subject to suit and accordingly to the legal enforcement of copyright law.

The question thus becomes whether open source and free software licenses can reasonably be expected to be enforced, as a legal matter, outside the United States. The answer to this question is a slightly qualified yes. Many countries are signatories to the Berne Convention, which provides for copyright protection more stringent in many respects than that provided by United States copyright law. Moreover, as has been the case with the enforcement of proprietary licenses, the existence of some amount of "pirating" or distribution outside the boundaries of a given license, such as with the unauthorized distribution of music, is not fatal to the successful distribution of the licensed work. Even if a certain, substantial, percentage of distribution of work is through illegal channels, the machinery distributing that work is still capable of thriving, creating, modifying, and delivering new work.

This is likely to be particularly the case with open source and free software licensed work, for the reasons already discussed. "Pirating" work generally means nothing more than the distribution of the work itself without the payment of royalties (or other applicable forms of payment) to the creator of the work. "Pirating," in this sense, thus does not violate the restrictions applicable to most open source and free software licenses, which generally do not limit the free (i.e., without charge) distribution of unmodified versions. Only the distribution of modified work in a way inconsistent with the terms of the applicable license really "counts" as a violation of the license.

"Pirating" in this sense is also limited by the fact that the major markets in which software or any other kind of work can be sold at a profit are subject to legal constraints and the enforcement of law. In addition, practical constraints are more likely to limit the extent of such piracy with regards to software than with regards to other forms of expression, such as CDs or DVDs. While a consumer may be willing to take a chance on a five dollar bootleg CD or DVD that she intends to use just for her personal entertainment, such a consumer is much less likely to take such a chance on software, the stability and functionality of which she really must rely on.

These dynamics probably explain the relatively small amount of litigation spawned by open source and free software licenses. While these licenses certainly can be (and are) infringed upon, market forces and social dynamics tend to limit the extent of such infringement, even in the absence of vigorous legal enforcement of the license by the licensor.

The "Negative Effects" of Open Source and Free Software Licensing

Another effect of open source and free software licensing that has already been touched upon is the obstacle that violations of applicable licenses create for the violator of that license. Such violators will find that their own ability to enforce copyrights that arise out of or are related to infringements of the terms of an open source or free software license is seriously compromised. Violations of such licenses put the violators at risk of surrendering the benefits of any actual, copyrightable work that they may have invested in modifying or improving a licensed program.

Taking again one of the least restrictive examples of open source licenses as an example, it becomes apparent that violation of its terms undermines any future copyright enforcement relating to the modified work. The MIT License, described in Chapter 2, imposes the following restriction on licensees:

> The above copyright notice and this permission notice shall be included in all copies or substantial portions of the Software.

This example is equally applicable to the other open source and free software licenses already described in this book, although, obviously, what constitutes such a violation of the license will vary.

Assume that XYZ Corporation develops software based on a program called Duchess, licensed under a license with terms identical to the MIT license. XYZ incorporates large amounts of the Duchess code into its own program, called Vulcan, which is a use clearly permitted by the Duchess license. For purposes of promotion, however, XYZ decides that it would be better served in marketing Vulcan without acknowledging the efforts of the creators of Duchess and launches Vulcan into the market under a proprietary license without including the required copyright and permission notices. After all, XYZ reasons, Vulcan will be released under a proprietary license, without giving anyone else access to Vulcan's source code. The operations and appearance of Vulcan are sufficiently distinct from those of Duchess that it is not apparent that Vulcan is based on Duchess and the functions it performs are dissimilar to those of Duchess. At the time of the software's launch, it seems remote at best that it will ever come to light that XYZ has infringed upon the Duchess copyright by ignoring the MIT License's requirement that the copyright and permission notice be included in Vulcan.

Years pass, and XYZ prospers thanks to sales of Vulcan. One day, another software company, ABC Corp., brings to market a new program, Virgo, that fulfills the same functions as Vulcan but at a lower price. This Virgo software is also based on the Duchess code, but it complies with the Duchess license's requirement that it provide the copyright and permission notice. Virgo, however, has several features that mirror those in Vulcan—strongly suggesting to XYZ that a substantial portion of Virgo's code was taken directly from Vulcan. Moreover, approximately a year before Virgo's release, ABC had hired several of XYZ's programmers who had access to Vulcan's source code.

XYZ now hires lawyers and seriously considers bringing a copyright infringement suit against ABC for infringing its copyright to Vulcan. Seeing Vulcan's market share erode rapidly to Virgo, XYZ begins drafting a complaint against ABC, the first step in initiating litigation. But in the midst of this process, XYZ's lawyers discover XYZ's failure to comply with the Duchess license. They advise XYZ not to bring the lawsuit.

XYZ asks why. The answer is simple. By failing to comply with the requirements of the Duchess license, XYZ has seriously compromised its ability to enforce its copyright to those portions of Vulcan that really are XYZ's own work. Moreover, upon the discovery of XYZ's violation of the Duchess license, Duchess's creators, could sue XYZ for infringement, and one of the potential measures of damages in such a case would be all, or a substantial portion, of the profits that XYZ had realized through sales of Vulcan.

The first result, the compromising of XYZ's ability to enforce its own copyright claims, comes from the equitable doctrine of *unclean hands*. This doctrine holds that a party seeking relief from a court should have engaged in the transaction from which the lawsuit derives fairly and equitably. Following this doctrine, federal courts have held that a copyright claim can be defeated if that copyright was obtained unfairly or inequitably.* While not a foregone conclusion, if XYZ brought such an infringement suit, it would almost certainly be discovered that XYZ itself had infringed on the Duchess copyright by distributing Vulcan without complying with the license. This could result in the invalidation of XYZ's copyright to Vulcan. Having lost the copyright, XYZ would lose its exclusive right to distribute Vulcan.

The second result, following naturally from the first, is that upon the disclosure of XYZ's violation of the Duchess license, Duchess's creators could sue XYZ for infringing the Duchess copyright. Having disregarded the terms of the license, XYZ is in the same position as any other infringer. One possible remedy for such a violation is a measure of damages called *unjust enrichment*. This measure would award in damages those profits that could reasonably be said to flow from XYZ's infringement of the Duchess copyright; a measure that could result in XYZ having to pay over a substantial portion of the profits it earned since it had begun to distribute Vulcan. Again, while such a result is not a foregone conclusion, it is an outcome that XYZ would have to consider in deciding whether to bring a lawsuit.

Given the reasonable possibility that one or both of these results would flow from the lawsuit, either of which would be sufficient to put XYZ out of business, and given the uncertainty involved in bringing a copyright infringement action under even the best of circumstances, the lawyers see no alternative to foregoing the lawsuit. XYZ simply must compete in the marketplace the best it can with the potentially infringing Virgo program. XYZ's lawyers would also likely recommend that XYZ quietly add the permission and copyright notices required by the MIT license to avoid future infringement.

Thus, the failure to comply with the Duchess license, while providing potentially significant short-term benefits to XYZ, ultimately threatened the viability of XYZ's ability to continue an ongoing operation. While such license violations may never be directly discovered, they significantly compromise, as just described, the violator's ability to enforce its own copyright, with potentially dire consequences.

---

* Wrongful action taken in securing a copyright can invalidate that copyright. See *Lasercomb Am., Inc. v. Reynolds*, 911 F.2d 970, 977-79 (4th Cir. 1990). In at least one case, Ashton-Tate had sued Fox Software and the Santa Cruz Operation, alleging that the defendants had infringed upon its dBase line of programs with the sale of their competing FoxBase software, a federal court found that Ashton-Tate had obtained its own copyright deceptively by failing to inform the Copyright Office that its own software was based in significant part on JPLDIS, a public domain program. As a result, the court voided Ashton-Tate's copyright and dismissed the suit. While the court soon reversed itself, the potential for such a severe sanction is real.

The consequences that flow therefrom can be even more serious depending on the license being violated. Under a "copyleft" license like the GPL, a company like XYZ would be in an even more tenuous position. As described in Chapter 3, "copyleft" is a variety of the generational limitation described in Chapter 1, which requires that derivative works be subject to the terms of the GPL and only the terms of the GPL. This requirement is embodied in Section 2(b) of the GPL.

> 2. You may modify your copy or copies of the Program or any portion of it, thus form-ing a work based on the Program, and copy and distribute such modifications or work under the terms of Section 1 above, provided that you also meet all of these condi-tions:
>
> [. . .]
>
> b) You must cause any work that you distribute or publish, that in whole or in part contains or is derived from the Program or any part thereof, to be licensed as a whole at no charge to all third parties under the terms of this License.

The GPL explicitly provides that failure to comply with the terms of the license voids any rights granted by the license.

> 4. You may not copy, modify, sublicense, or distribute the Program except as expressly provided under this License. Any attempt otherwise to copy, modify, sublicense or dis-tribute the Program is void, and will automatically terminate your rights under this License. However, parties who have received copies, or rights, from you under this License will not have their licenses terminated so long as such parties remain in full compliance.

Assuming that the Duchess program from the previous example were licensed under the GPL instead of the MIT License, these provisions of the GPL License would place a company in the position of XYZ in an even more precarious position. If XYZ takes the position that it is not bound by the GPL License, it has no right to incorporate code derived from it in its own program, Vulcan. If XYZ takes the position that it is bound by the GPL License, it must cease distributing Vulcan under anything but the GPL License and must also concede that its previous distributions under a non-com-pliant license constituted an infringement of the Duchess copyright. In such a sce-nario, XYZ is in an even worse position that it would be in the MIT scenario. Unlike the MIT License, there is no "quiet" way for XYZ to ensure compliance with the terms of the Duchess license in the future. XYZ's lawyers are in the difficult position, once the infringement has come to light, of informing XYZ that it must either cease distri-bution of Vulcan or immediately release it under the GPL (and only the GPL) License. Because criminal as well as civil penalties attach to copyright infringement, the contin-ued distribution of Vulcan under a proprietary license could potentially involve XYZ's lawyers in XYZ's own wrongdoing, a result most lawyers seek to avoid.[*]

---

[*] XYZ's lawyers are not obligated to inform anyone of XYZ's wrongdoing and in most jurisdictions would be barred, by the attorney-client privilege, from doing so. However, continuing to aid an ongoing criminal vio-lation is both unethical and dangerous.

While only examples using the MIT and GPL Licenses are described, similar results would follow from distributions of licensed software inconsistent with the terms of the applicable open source or free software license.

Community Enforcement of Open Source and Free Software Licenses

The open source and free software communities are also critical to the practical enforcement of open source and free software licenses. While the discussion so far has focused on the legal and practical reasons why open source and free software licenses tend to be complied with, there is a more fundamental reason why most programmers comply with such licenses. Non-compliance, or at least knowing non-compliance with the terms of these licenses, is simply wrong.

The world of open source and free software licensing is still a relatively small one. As has already been described in previous chapters, the code written under these licenses is mostly the work of volunteers who have dedicated huge amounts of time, and, in many cases, significant parts of their lives to the development and distribution of good code for the benefit of as many people as possible. In the course of writing this code and supporting these projects, these programmers have foregone significantly more lucrative opportunities offered by commercial software companies. Behind the black and white terms and restrictions of these licenses, which have taken up the bulk of this book, is a real principle. Free code, however free may be defined, is a social good in itself. This is the goal that is being pursued. However that goal may be reached, whatever avenue of development is followed, this principle is held above all others.

This principle is deeply felt by this community. The gross violation of it by taking someone else's work and distributing it as one's own is unthinkable. This moral principle is, by itself, responsible for the largest part for the enforcement of open source and free software licenses, not the texts of the licenses themselves, and not the courts that enforce those licenses.*

Even those who have not internalized this principle have good reason to abide by the norms of this community. Violating those norms will incur, at the least, the displeasure of this community. Given the number of people in this community and, perhaps more importantly, the knowledge and capabilities of its members, such a violation can result in the ostracism of the violator. Such a person might find his emails remaining unanswered, being ignored or flamed in usegroups, and being

---

* For more discussion of this principle, see the essay *Homesteading the Noosphere* in *The Cathedral & The Bazaar: Musings on Linux and Open Source by an Accidental Revolutionary*, Eric S. Raymond (O'Reilly 2001) (rev. ed.), and the chapter *The Art of Code* in *rebel code: inside linux and the open source revolution*, Glyn Moody (Perseus Publishing 2001).

excluded from projects, whether under the open source or free software banner, that involve members of this community.*

This does not mean there is a univerally shared view as to the purpose of open source and free software licensing or the best way to realize that purpose. As noted earlier, there are real ideological differences between, for example, the "open source" community and the "free software" community. That said, there is considerable common ground. One principle, which is universally accepted, is that taking someone else's work and modifying or distributing it in disregard of the intent of its creator is wrong.

This should not be confused with the "cross-over" of programmers (and their code) from an open source project to a proprietarily licensed projects. As described at the end of Chapter 2, prominent open source programmers such as Bill Joy and Eric Allman moved from open source to proprietary projects. In Allman's case, he maintained both open source and proprietary distributions of his popular Sendmail program in a way consistent with both the terms and the principles of the original license. Such movement does not (and should not) result in any ill feeling against such individuals.

In sum, while contracts and courts are fundamental to protecting the principles of open source and free software licensing, the real guardians of these principles are programmers (and users) themselves.

Compatible and Incompatible Licensing: Multiple and Cross Licensing

In writing code, a programmer may find that he wants to fuse elements from two or more programs into a new program. The two programs are under different licenses. The question arises: is it possible to take this code, under different licenses, and combine them in one work without violating the terms of either of the two licenses?

While two licenses may appear to be compatible, programmers must ensure that they are, in fact, compatible. Apparently innocuous terms in one or both licenses may make them incompatible with each other. Distribution or modification of programs, including incompatibly licensed code, will result in copyright infringement.

Those undertaking this analysis should note that with some exceptions (such as the GPL and the SCSL Licenses) the licenses described in this book are frequently templates for individual licenses, and their language may not be exactly the same as that

---

* Those interested in the enforcement of social norms that parallel legal restrictions should read *Order Without Law: How Neighbors Settle Disputes*, Robert C. Ellickson (Harvard, 1991). While this book addresses primarily the enforcement of social norms among cattle ranchers in Shasta County, California, its analysis is no less applicable to "virtual" communities such as the open source and free software communities.

described here. Simply because something is described as a "BSD-style" license, for example, does not mean that it is written just like the BSD License or contains exactly the same terms. In every case, a user considering combining works licensed under different licenses should read the licenses at issue very carefully.

It is much easier to describe those licenses that are incompatible than to assert with any assurance that two licenses are compatible. There are several scenarios in which the answers are obvious. If either one of the works is licensed under a proprietary license, the code cannot be combined with work under another license (except through cross-licensing, described later). As a general matter, under a classic proprietary license, the user has no rights to the work other than to use a single copy of it. Ordinarily, she may not even examine the code, much less modify or distribute part of it as a section of another work. Two works under proprietary licenses, even if they are the same license, cannot be modified or distributed together without violating the license(s).

Another example susceptible to quick analysis is the GPL License. GPL-licensed code is incompatible with code licensed under most licenses. As noted in Chapter 3, the second sentence of Section 6 of the GPL reads as follows:

> You may not impose any further restrictions on the recipients' exercise of the rights granted herein.

By combining GPL-licensed code with code under any but the most unrestrictive licenses, the creator of the putative "new program" is imposing a restriction (compliance with the terms of that license) that is not present in the GPL License and which accordingly violates the GPL. (The LGPL is not restrictive but is compatible with the GPL by design.) As noted previously in this chapter, one of the fundamental building blocks of any contract—and all licenses are a form of a contract—is consideration, i.e., the imposition of some obligation on each party. In the open source and free software licenses discussed in this book, the typical transaction involves the licensor agreeing (becoming obligated) to permit certain uses of the licensed work in exchange for the licensee agreeing and becoming obligated to comply with certain restrictions. Accordingly, any license worthy of the name will impose some obligation: if that obligation does not precisely parallel an obligation in the GPL, that obligation is a "further restriction" as far as the GPL is concerned and cannot be imposed on licensees of the GPL code.[*]

---

[*] The LGPL operates in exactly the same way, excluding, obviously, the less restrictive limitations imposed on "hitchhiker" programs that use, and may be distributed with, the LGPL-licensed library.

For a list of licenses that the Free Software Foundation considers to be compatible with the GPL, see *www.gnu.org/philosophy/license-list.html*.

It should be noted that Section 2(b) and Section 6 of the GPL might be read to be so restrictive as to make the GPL incompatible even with those licenses described by the Free Software Foundation as compatible. In the event the GPL-licensed work is not copyrighted by the Free Software Foundation, a person interested in combining such a work with a work under a "compatible" license may wish to take additional precautions, such as contacting the copyright holder of the GPL-licensed work.

This brings us to another realm of quick analysis. Some works are not subject to any license at all. Their creator has either consigned them to the *public domain*—for example, by attaching a Public Domain Dedication to the work, as described in Chapter 4—or the work has lost its copyright protection and entered the public domain by the lapse of time.* Because such public domain works impose no obligations on their users, code that is in the public domain may be combined with code licensed under any license, so long as that license's terms are complied with. Accordingly, a programmer may incorporate public domain code with GPL licensed code, and modify and distribute the resulting work without fear, so long as he complies with the GPL.

After these three straightforward examples, the question of the mutual compatibility of licenses becomes substantially more complicated. In the following situations, programmers (or preferably their attorneys) should examine each of the applicable licenses cautiously.

In general, the "research style" licenses described in Chapter 2 are compatible with each other. Accordingly, a program licensed under the BSD License may be combined with a program licensed under the MIT License, and both released under the licensee's proprietary license so long as each license's restrictions are complied with. In this example, the BSD License would require that its list of conditions be included in the software distribution and that all advertising materials note that the software includes work made by the University of California at Berkeley; the MIT License would require that its copyright and permission notices be distributed with the resulting software, and the proprietary license governing the combined work would contain whatever additional restriction that licensee chose to impose.

"Research style" licenses are also generally compatible with licenses that do not bar the imposition of additional restrictions on the code to be licensed. For example, the Q Public License permits the distribution of modified forms of the licensed work in the form of the original work plus patches. If a user wishes to draw code for a patch from an MIT-licensed program, he is free to do so and to distribute that patch in a manner consistent with both licenses, so long as he complies with the other terms of the Q Public License and encloses the permission and copyright notices required by the MIT License.

Beyond these general observations, it is difficult, if not impossible, to provide precise guidance about what licenses may or may not be compatible with each other. As already noted, many licenses described in this book are really templates and are subject to significant variations in their terms in practice. Programmers who are considering combining code governed by two or more different licenses should proceed cautiously.

---

* As noted in Chapter 4, there are reasonable questions about the binding effect of public domain dedications, such as the one put forward by Creative Commons.

Fortunately, there is another solution, generally available, which is both easier and more reliable than comparing the arcane terms of two separate licenses. This is the phenomenon of cross-licensing.

As the creator of a work, the original licensor retains all of the rights associated with that copyright, subject only to the sale or licensing of those rights to others. The open source and free software licenses described in this book do not require that the creator of a work surrender all of his rights to another. Rather, in each case, the license reflects only a specific, one-time, grant of certain specified rights based on the compliance of the licensee with specified conditions. The licensor does not agree only to license the work under those terms or to those licensees.

Accordingly, such a licensor retains the power and the discretion to license his work under terms other than those contained in the original license. This is cross-licensing. ABC Corp. licenses its program, Mudd, under the pre-1999 BSD License. Several years later, John Smith wishes to incorporate some of the Mudd code into his ongoing free software project, the GPL-licensed Pond, which is based on code from an earlier GPL-licensed program, River, created by Audrey Strauss. Smith understands that the GPL and the pre-1999 BSD Licenses are incompatible. He can resolve this dilemma if either ABC or Strauss is willing to cross-license their programs—i.e., make the program (or a version of it) available under a license other than that which the program was originally provided under. In this case, Smith could go to ABC and ask them to license a version of Mudd under a GPL License so that he can use it in a GPL licensed new version of Pond. Smith could also go to Strauss and ask her to license a version of her River program under the pre-1999 BSD (or other compatible) license so that he can incorporate it in a BSD licensed version of Pond.

While it may seem somewhat presumptious to approach an author of a work, who likely has given at least some thought to the license applicable to the work, to reconsider that decision, open source and software programmers are generally open to the idea of cross-licensing. Given the ethic in the open source and free software communities to favor free distribution of work and to avoid duplication of effort, most programmers would be inclined to give such requests a favorable hearing, at the very least. This possibility is explicitly laid out in some licenses, including the GPL. Section 10 of the GPL, for example, provides as follows:

> 10. If you wish to incorporate parts of the Program into other free programs whose distribution conditions are different, write to the author to ask for permission. For software which is copyrighted by the Free Software Foundation, write to the Free Software Foundation; we sometimes make exceptions for this. Our decision will be guided by the two goals of preserving the free status of all derivatives of our free software and of promoting the sharing and reuse of software generally.

If this option succeeds, all the difficulties and potential uncertainty associated with different licenses pass away. Whatever license is mutually agreeable to everyone involved will control and the coding can go on without fear of future legal problems.

Some open source groups will not cross-license works copyrighted by them. The Apache Software Foundation, for example, does not cross-license its works.

There are also some situations in which cross-licensing is simply not a practical alternative. Some project structures, such as the "bazaar" structure described in the next chapter, permit input into projects by hundreds and possibly thousands of programmers. The Linux (or GNU/Linux) operating system is the quintessential example. Linux is licensed under the GPL and includes the works of thousands of people who made contributions to the project with the belief (assuming that they took the time to develop one) that the resulting work would be licensed under the GPL. In such cases, there is no one person capable of relicensing the work of all these people under a different license, not even Linus Torvalds. Because of the rigidity of the monopoly granted by copyright laws, each one of those contributors could argue, legally, that their contribution can only be used in ways consistent with the terms upon which they agreed to participate in the project. Cross-licensing such projects, while not impossible, is impractical in all but the most unusual situations.

Most open source and free software projects, however, do not present such logistical difficulties. They are maintained by a small number of people, frequently just one person, whose permission to distribute that work under another license can often be gained for no more than the cost of asking.

CHAPTER 7

Software Development Using Open Source and Free Software Licenses

The purpose of open source and free software licensing is to permit and encourage the involvement by licensees in improvement, modification, and distribution of the licensed work. This open development model of software development is the unique strength of the open source and free software movement. While the open source and free software licenses already discussed approach open software development differently, open development is the goal.

This chapter describes the basic principles of software development under open source and free software licenses, including the problems of forking, community development under the bazaar and the cathedral models, how open source and free software projects are initiated and maintained, and the effect that license choices can have on software development. This chapter also briefly discusses the basic principles of drafting contracts, for those who are interested in drafting their own software license.

Models of Open Source and Free Software Development

The open source and free software licensing is driven by the development model, or models, that it is intended to encourage. After all, there is little point to permitting the "free" modification and distribution of a work if people do not actually take the opportunity to modify and distribute the licensed work.

These licenses are intended to permit, and indeed, to encourage the contributions of others to the project. Nonetheless, one of the first open development projects relied, at least at the beginning, on a relatively small number of closely-knit developers. This project was Richard Stallman's plan to develop a complete operating system modeled after the Unix operating system but written entirely in free code.[*]

---

[*] The following discussion draws heavily from the essay of Eric Raymond, "The Cathedral and the Bazaar," in *The Cathedral & The Bazaar: Musing on Linux and Open Source by an Accidental Revolutionary*, Eric S. Raymond (O'Reilly, 2001).

This project created numerous, deeply influential programs, including the widely used Emacs and the GNU C Compiler and, with the arrival of the Linux kernel developed by Linus Torvalds and his associates, resulted in the creation of the first entirely free operating system, the GNU/Linux operating system. Stallman is also the author of the GPL, and the first, and still most important, philosopher of the free software movement.

Nonetheless, the initial projects under the aegis of the Free Software Foundation—the group Stallman founded to serve as the homebase for the nascent free software movement—did not rely on the open development model, to the same extent, for example, as the Linux project did. Part of the explanation for this is purely a matter of circumstance. The great engine of free software development is the Internet. When Stallman had his epiphany as to the importance of keeping software free in the early 1980s, the Internet was still in its early adolescence. While universities and colleges (particularly those associated with the Department of Defense) and scientific institutions had access to it, relatively few individuals did.

Stallman originally announced his intention to create a complete Unix-compatible software system in the fall of 1983. At that time, he had already written the widely popular Emacs editor, and he started to develop a completely free operating system. The frustration that Stallman felt with the increasing strictures placed on free computing and in particular with the application of security protocols, passwords, and "blackbox" binary code that drove him to this project has been well-described elsewhere.[*] After he formally resigned from the Massachusetts Institute of Technology's Artificial Intelligence lab, Stallman dedicated himself to creating various components that would become critical parts of the GNU/Linux operating system: the GNU C Compiler, GNU Emacs, the GNU Debugger, the GNU C Library, and perhaps no less importantly, the GNU Public License.

It is no exaggeration that it was Stallman's original intention, and his practice for a considerable period, to undertake the bulk of the work substantially by himself. An episode from around the time of the beginning of the GNU project demonstrated that this was possible. By 1982, a company named Symbolics had hired away more than a dozen programmers from the MIT AI Lab to develop a commercial version of the Lisp operating system—an operating system developed and maintained by the MIT AI Lab— against a competing company, Lisp Machines, Inc., or LMI, which had also hired numerous MIT hackers. Under its agreement with MIT, Symbolics was contractually required to permit Stallman, as MIT's administrator of the Lisp system, to review the source code but not required to permit MIT to adopt any of that code. Nonetheless, Symbolics, as a matter of custom, permitted Stallman to adopt features from its source code and maintain them in MIT's version of Lisp. Stallman kept MIT's version of Lisp free, and LMI looked to it to see what developments and improvements its competitor, Symbolics, had made.

---

[*] The circumstances surrounding Stallman's decision to begin work on the GNU project are described in *Free As In Freedom: Richard Stallman's Crusade for Free Software*, Sam Williams (O'Reilly, 2002).

In early 1982, Symbolics decided to hold MIT to the terms of the agreement and barred Stallman from incorporating changes from its version of Lisp. Stallman viewed this as a declaration of war. In what is still considered one of the major feats in programming history, Stallman spent much of the next two years matching the new features and additions in Symbolics' Lisp on his own, keeping pace with a much larger team of programmers, feature for feature.

In the period from early 1984 to 1990, Stallman was generating useful and influential programs at a phenomenal rate. In addition to the GNU Emacs, the GNU Debugger, and the GNU C Compiler already mentioned, Stallman developed GNU versions of several Unix programs, including the Bourne shell, YACC, and awk programs. However, in developing these programs, Stallman relied heavily on his own immense facility as a programmer and a relatively small number of collaborators. While the GPL was designed to ensure maximum freedom to users and programmers for programs developed under the license, Stallman himself, as a project manager, maintained relatively tight supervision over each of the GNU projects.

This led, perhaps inevitably, to the first major stumbling block of the GNU project. Stallman, quite deliberately, had organized his operating system around a piecemeal approach in which the tools for the system would be written before the kernel, its central component. By 1990 or so, that kernel was the last major piece not to have been completed. Stallman and the GNU project had been working on a kernel since at least 1987, starting first with a kernel based on Trix, an MIT program. By 1993, however, the GNU project, having abandoned Trix, had gotten bogged down in a micro-kernel called Hurd.

There were a number of issues that slowed the development of Hurd, including the focus by a more mature Free Software Foundation on the theoretical aspects of micro-kernel development; a breakdown in communication between the GNU Debugger group and the group in charge of developing the kernel; "look and feel" lawsuits that had been brought by Apple and Lotus against other operating systems (most notably Microsoft); and perhaps not least, limitations on Stallman's own contibutions, caused by a disability that prevented him from typing.* This temporary setback set the stage for another great open development project, one using a very different development model.

Just two years earlier, in 1991, Linus Torvalds had started work on his own operating system kernel. Originally based on the Minix operating system, itself an "open" operating system designed for teaching purposes, in a famous email on August 25, 1991, posted to the Minix usegroup, Torvalds announced that he was working on a "(free) operating system (just a hobby, won't be big and professional like gnu) for

---

* For a more detailed discussion of the Hurd micro-kernel and the difficulties in its development, see *Free As In Freedom: Richard Stallman's Crusade for Free Software*, Sam Williams (O'Reilly, 2002) at pages 146 and following.

386 (486) AT clones."* By September, Torvalds had released the first version of Linux, Version 0.1. Interest in Torvalds' operating system, at least within the relatively small Minix community, was immediate and intense. Other programmers quickly responded to Torvalds' postings with questions, comments, and suggestions for how to improve the nascent operating system.

These postings set into motion what would quickly become the Linux phenomenon. This process involved, and indeed depended on the contributions of at first dozens, then hundreds, and now thousands of users, debuggers, and programmers. This development model is likely Torvalds' most significant contribution to open source and free software programming—notwithstanding his own considerable organizational and programming abilities. As the project grew in size and complexity, a structure developed organically, with other noteworthy programmers—such as Alan Cox, Dave Miller, and Ted Ts'o—taking on significant roles in managing the burgeoning growth of these projects. These three, and others, act as intermediaries between Torvalds, who remains at the center of the project.

As Eric Raymond put it in his essay "The Cathedral and The Bazaar," "Linus's cleverest hack was not the construction of the Linux kernel itself, but rather his invention of the Linux development model."† As described by Raymond, this development model is dependent on a number of interlocking conditions. The first is the importance of users. Every program needs a constituency of users who use the program, want the program to work, and are sufficiently committed to make at least some effort toward improving it, whether it be by contributing bug reports or patches. The consistent involvement of such users makes the discovery and elimination of bugs easier. The second is the maxim of "release early, release often." By releasing early and quickly incorporating changes from users, project developers keep their user base actively engaged and involved. When a user notices a bug, submits a patch, and then a few weeks (or even days) later sees the improvement he suggested worked into a new release, he sees immediately the benefits of the development model. He has been rewarded, not financially, but by the availability of a better program. This reward, of course, is shared within the entire community of developers. The "release early, release often" strategy also cuts down on the possible duplication of effort by a number of users/programmers working, unknown to each other, to identify and fix the same bug. When a problem is quickly identified and its solution is incorporated into a new release, the number of users (and hence potential debuggers) exposed to that solved problem is reduced.

This debugging strategy takes advantage of the many different perspectives, and different uses, put to the program by a spectrum of users. While a bug may seem difficult to isolate from the perspective of a single programmer, that same bug may, upon

---

* Torvalds' email as reprinted in *rebel code: inside linux and the open source revolution*, Glyn Moody (Perseus Publishing, 2001) at page 42.

† *The Cathedral & The Bazaar: Musing on Linux and Open Source by an Accidental Revolutionary*, Eric S. Raymond (O'Reilly revised ed. 2001) at page 29.

exposure to a hundred different users and programmers, seem immediately obvious to just one of them. As long as that one is sufficiently committed to submit a detailed bug report or a patch, the project has progressed, and probably more quickly and easily than a more tightly focused, but smaller, group of programmers would have reacted.

This debugging perspective does not necessarily address the complex problems of organizing group work on developing source code in the first instance. In such cases, depending on the development model, adding more programmers to a project may not quicken development, but in fact may slow it down as the additional costs associated with communicating information among a larger group of people outweigh the incremental benefit of adding programmers to a project. While the Linux development model has kept direction and focus within a relatively small circle, as may well be necessary for a software project of any size to survive, much less one of the size and complexity of Linux, its openness has been its strength. By encouraging "egoless" contributions that are improvements to an already established workflow, as opposed to redirections of that workflow, the Linux development model avoids much of the drag that can result from the difficulties in social and information engineering in large, traditional, software projects.

This bazaar model contrasts with what Raymond describes as the cathedral model of software development. Software development, in its traditional form, relies on tightly focused, relatively small groups of programmers associated with a single institution or corporation. Such groups sometimes are as small as two or even just one programmer. Unix itself was the creation of legendary hacker Ken Thompson at Bell Labs: it was written in the programming language C, itself written by another hacker, Dennis Ritchie. Both Unix and C were designed to be simple (or at least simpler than their contemporary competitors). This simplicity and their immense popularity made them prototypes for Linux and the GNU programs that came after them.

Their simplicity and portability made them popular among programmers. Despite an almost total lack of interest by AT&T (Bell Labs' corporate parent), Unix and C spread quickly, first inside AT&T and then outside it. By 1980, it was commonplace in universities and research institutions. Unix, the model for the GNU project and Torvalds' Linux project, set the stage for open source development.

Nonetheless, Unix itself never became a truly open development.* Although there were a number of "hot-spot" programming communities—including Berkeley, the AI and LCS labs at MIT, and Bell Labs itself—these communities were largely self-contained, and although relatively large in the number of programmers they had, did not have the mass to support an open development project, even if there was one. The

---

* It is an irony worth noting that the current holder of the rights to Unix, the SCO Group, has sponsored numerous continuing lawsuits against users of GNU/Linux distributions under the theory that some, as of this writing unspecified, portion of these distributions contains Unix code under the copyright held by SCO Group.

absence of such a project was in part due to the legally imposed limitations by trade secrets and copyrights, and movement toward commercialization of software in the late 1970s and early 1980s. The same trends that led to Stallman's Symbolics war and his subsequent exit from the MIT AI Lab were closing doors to open development projects. Software, once given away for free with expensive hardware, was becoming a booming business in itself.

In its traditional form, commercial software development is based on the exploitation of the monopoly created by copyright for competitive advantage. It makes sense in that system to avoid any process that would undermine that advantage, such as, for example, the sharing of source code with thousands of potentially competing strangers. Programmers for commercial concerns do "work-for-hire": the code they write does not belong to them but to their employers. They are routinely required to sign non-disclosure agreements, preventing them from disclosing to anyone else information that is proprietary (i.e., what their employer considers to be proprietary). Such programmers are also frequently asked to sign non-compete agreements, which prevent them from working for their employer's competitors for a year or two (or more) after they leave that employer. In this environment of deliberate concealment of any information that could be of use to the competition, the idea of open source is anathema.

This emphasis on secrecy channeled commercial programmers into cathedral-style models of software development. While such companies are free to hire as many programmers as they may need, even the resources of a company such as Microsoft are limited.* No user base (or almost no user base) would be willing to subject itself to the disclosure restrictions that are required to maintain the commercial advantage software companies want.† Without open source code and knowledgeable (and energized) users, bug reports, to the extent they are submitted, greatly diminish in value to the project. What results is a relatively small group of programmers, as talented as the resources and attractiveness of the company can gather, building the software project essentially in secret and presenting it as a black box to the software-buying public.

This model of software development is not limited to commercial development. The GNU project, while certainly not anywhere near as "closed" as traditional commercial software development, relied heavily on the contributions of a relatively small number of people who were relatively tightly organized. The GNU project did not, at least in its early days, follow a "release early, release often" model. Its ability (or desire) to incorporate bug reports and patches submitted by users outside the project was limited accordingly. This should not be read as a slight to the GNU project.

---

* Microsoft's Shared Source Initiative, briefly described in Chapter 5, is driven in large part by its attempt to engage with this problem, that is to say, to involve as large a group of developers and users in its process without surrendering its legal rights under copyright law.

† The Sun Community Source License, described in Chapter 5, with its restrictions on distributions outside the community of developers, is a step in that direction.

GNU Emacs has incorporated the suggestions of hundreds of participants over more than 15 years of development and stands as a highly respected model of free software development. In addition, the GPL built a foundation for the open development model.

What really accelerated the full bloom of the Linux development model, however, and the astonishingly rapid development of Linux itself, was what Raymond calls "cheap Internet." While the predecessor of the Internet, ARPANet had been available at most research universities and institutions since the 1970s, the available bandwidth was small and access was limited. The cascading expansion of the Internet from 1990 or so on allowed a whole new realm of users to access it for email, Usenet groups, and surfing the newly developed World Wide Web.

The availability of software archives accessible by the Internet, Usenet groups open to contributors, and most importantly, email to permit communication between project originators, contributors, and users, were all necessary for the success of the Linux development model on the scale that Linux itself has achieved. The legal infrastructure of open source combined with the technical infrastructure of the Internet to make this new approach possible.

The Linux development model is obviously not the only one for developing software. It depends on the commitment and knowledge of its user base to succeed. Such users simply may not be available for every type of program. End user applications (such as video games) have been slow to develop under open source or free software development models.

Nonetheless, the Linux development model is useful (and powerful in its applications) for much more than just Linux itself. The same Linux-style development has been used successfully for a large number of programs.

While the choice of a particular license is an important factor, it is far from the only factor in determining the development of any given project. Both Linux and the GNU project's many developments were created under the same license, the GPL.* Nonetheless, as just described, they follow very different patterns of development. The circumstances surrounding the development of a project, and, in particular, the personalities of those involved and the technology available to its originators, developers, and users, can have far more to do with the success of a project than the choice of a particular license.

The open development model may even keep code "open" that the governing license would permit to be closed, by incorporating it into a proprietary license. For example, as described in Chapter 2, the Apache License permits distribution of modified versions under proprietary licenses. In June of 1998, IBM announced that it would ship Apache as part of its WebSphere group of programs and provide continuing

---

* The very first releases of Linux were released under an open source license of Torvalds' own devising. Torvalds, however, adopted the GPL early on and it has covered every subsequent distribution of Linux.

enterprise level support for it.* As a natural consequence of this adoption, IBM developed its own modifications to the Apache software and distributed them under a license that it had written for this purpose, the IBM Public License. The original Apache license permitted IBM to license its modifications under a proprietary license and not to disclose their source code, and the IBM Public License did nothing to limit its ability to do so. Nonetheless, IBM continued to publish its source code and to freely permit the adoption or modification of its own work. The reason for this was simple. If IBM kept its code proprietary, eventually its version of Apache would depart from the standard Apache version. Future modifications to the standard version would become more difficult to port to IBM's version. IBM would lose the benefits of the open development process for its own version of Apache, as users and potential contributors would have less incentive to contribute bug reports or patches to it—particularly when a strong competitor, such as standard Apache, existed in the same marketplace.

In short, if IBM wanted to remain a contributor to the process (as well as a beneficiary in the fullest sense), it had to contribute, or at least not to keep whatever contributions it had already made to itself. Regardless of the terms of either of the applicable licenses, IBM's or Apache's, to get the full benefits of open source development, IBM had to live by open development rules.

Forking

By maintaining its own Apache development as an open development project, IBM avoided creating a fork. Forking occurs whenever a software project splits. While the two versions may remain entirely or partially compatible for some period of time, inevitably the unique (and now distinct) histories of each one's development will push them apart.

Forks can happen for many different reasons and may have entirely healthy consequences. A very simple piece of code may be developed by a group of programmers to do, for example, packet-switching. One half of the group may decide to follow a development tree leading toward making the simple packet-switching program into a complex database, and the other half may want to make the same program into a video-on-demand server for use in cable television systems. Such forks can occur without rancor and without any real concern for duplicative or unnecessary programming; the two future developments are so starkly different that mutual compatibility is of no concern.

Forks in more mature projects, however, are much more capable of producing undesirable results. For example, in 1993, the GNU Emacs project forked. Jamie Zawinski led a group of other developers on a line separate from that of Emacs' creator

---

* The circumstances surrounding IBM's decision to support Apache are described in *rebel code: inside linux and the open source revolution*, by Glyn Moody, (Perseus Publishing, 2001) at page 205 and following.

Richard Stallman and the GNU project. In part, this fork was driven by real differences as to the best course of future development for Emacs, but it also may have been the result of personality conflicts and concerns with the progress of Emacs development. Some felt that Stallman was relying too much on his own efforts and those of other programmers from the GNU project, thereby slowing development of Emacs. The fork was successful in the sense that two Emacs development projects resulted; as of this writing, both projects are continuing with no indication that this fork will ever close.

Forks in mature projects are properly feared. In addition to creating hard feelings, such forks undermine the foundation of the open development process. They split the user base as well as the programmers that contribute to the project. Given the importance of users to open development, this is a result to be avoided. While two open development projects may remain sufficiently similar for some period of time that modifications and bug patches can be ported from one project to another, at some point, the developments will have diverged sufficiently such that porting a solution from a competing project is no easier than developing that same solution from scratch. This duplication of effort and division of the development community for what, after all, are likely to be two very similar programs, argues strongly against such a fork, except under exceptional circumstances.

Given the serious consequences of forking, it is not unreasonable to look to licenses to prevent or at least to decrease the probability of such forks. While no open source or free software license is fork-proof, they do provide varying levels of protection against such forks.* Some licenses, such as the Apache and Perl Licenses, rely largely on the reputation of the project developers to avoid forks, but they also include some terms that shore up that defense against forks. Other licenses, such as the GPL, at least hinder forking by requiring that developers distribute or modify the licensed code only under "open development" terms. However, by permitting non-open development of code developed under them, code licensed under the MIT or the BSD License may be more prone to forking than code licensed under other licenses.

The network security program Kerberos was released under a variation of the X license that operates substantially like the MIT and BSD licenses. As described in Chapter 2, Microsoft adopted Kerberos and implemented it in its Windows 2000 (and subsequent) operating systems in a version that contained proprietary extensions for communicating with Microsoft servers. This was a fork in that because of these extensions, Microsoft's version of Kerberos is on a separate development plane than the MIT-distributed version of Kerberos and will likely continue to develop more proprietary extensions as Microsoft expands it. This was the result of the use of the X license, which has no terms that would prevent this development.

---

* Proprietary licenses are unforkable. There is no development by anyone other than the licensor and accordingly no possible foundation for a fork. Licenses such as the Sun Community Source License, while not open source licenses, head off forking by designating an official version by compliance testing and by prohibiting the commercial distribution of other versions.

As described in Chapter 2, the Apache License does not prevent the incorporation of its code into code licensed under another license, including a proprietary license. The Apache license does, however, include provisions protecting the Apache name. Specifically, the Apache license, Version 1.1 (as well as Version 2.0), prevents the use of the name Apache in connection with the work being distributed without permission, through Sections 4 and 5.

> 4. The names "Apache" and "Apache Software Foundation" must not be used to endorse or promote products derived from this software without prior written permission. For written permission, please contact apache@apache.org.
>
> 5. Products derived from this software may not be called "Apache" nor may "Apache" appear in their name, without prior written permission of the Apache Software Foundation.

Through this relatively simple device, maintaining a monopoly over the name—if not the licensed code—and maintaining a dynamic high quality distribution, the Apache Software Foundation has remained as the center of Apache development and avoided any forks of consequence.

A similar strategy works in the Artistic License that applies to Perl. As described in Chapter 4, the Artistic License defines both a Copyright Holder and a Standard Version of the program. Contributors to a program so licensed must either permit their modifications to be incorporated into the Standard Version, abstain from public distributions of their version of the work, or clearly document the changes in their version. While forking is possible under this license, the likelihood that any such fork would create a major competitor to the Standard Version is substantially reduced. Indeed, these provisions of the license—along with the steadfast commitment to Perl of its creator, Larry Wall, and his reputation in open source and free software development—have prevented any significant forks from developing in Perl to date.

The GNU GPL limits the likelihood of forks by prohibiting non-open development models for projects that incorporate GPL-licensed code. Every development project under the GPL can accordingly draw freely from every other project. After a fork of a GPL project, each leg of the project remains free to draw on the work of the other—to the extent such work may be available*—a process that may hasten the closing of such a fork and permit the reunification of the forked project. This is obviously not foolproof, as seen in the example of GNU Emacs.

Accordingly, while the choice of license certainly can have some effect on preventing forks, the nature of the open development model is conducive to forking. Permitting open access to source code and encouraging development by outsiders both allows for and creates incentives for the development of forks. Addressing forks is less a question of adopting the proper license, as any open source or free software license permits forking in some way, and is more a question of project development.

---

* While the GPL requires that code derived from GPL-licensed code also be distributed under the GPL, a developer can avoid "sharing" the code she has developed by simply not distributing it.

Choosing an Open Source or Free Software License

Choosing an open source or free software license is more often the result of circumstances than the unfettered discretion of a particular programmer. While each of the licenses described in this book (which represent only a selection of the open source and free software licenses in use) presents its own advantages and disadvantages, in many situations, the decision as to which license to apply will already have been made.

A typical route to involvement in an open source or free software project comes from contributing to an already existing project. Whether by submitting a patch to Linux or a bug report to a less well-established open development project, consideration of the license applicable to the project is generally a secondary consideration at most. A user submitting a bug report does not generally care about the license of the program to which the bug report applies. So long as that user can reasonably expect some benefit from the submission of the bug report, usually in the form of an improved program, that user will make a submission.

Users frequently make even more substantial contributions to open development projects without much more consideration. Again using Linux as an example, scores of programmers have submitted and continued to submit patches or more substantial contributions to Linux without troubling themselves to any great extent about the terms of the GPL applicable to Linux.

A programmer may undertake even more substantial responsibilities for an open development project by helping to maintain it or even taking a leadership role, without choosing the license applicable to the development. In the world of open source and free software, projects are frequently handed down, and the "successor" lead programmer takes over a project from the project's initiator. In such situations, the project comes with the license under which it was originally written. While a successor project leader could in theory insist that a new license apply to the project, the administrative and legal difficulties would have to weigh against such a switch. Even if the original project leader were agreeable, the new project leader would most likely need to secure the consent of every programmer who had contributed to the project under the previous license. After all, they had made their contributions with the understanding (to the extent that they had one) that what they contributed would be licensed under the license originally applicable to the project. Depending on the number of contributors, this could be a considerable hurdle.

Even for "new" open source or free software projects, the choice of a license may substantially be determined by license choices made by others. After all, given the nature of the open development model, it is frequently unnecessary to create a new program from scratch. Whatever the program's function, it is likely that someone, somewhere, has done something similar. By scanning SourceForge.net or other similar sites, someone considering an open source project can see whether a sufficiently similar project is already underway. Such a search might turn up an already existing open source project so similar to the one being considered as to make a new project unnecessary. In any event, prior work on similar projects in many situations will provide a foundation for a new project. In such a case, the developer has to consider carefully the license applicable to the pre-existing project.

Depending on the license, the developer may or may not have the ability to choose a different license to apply to the new project. If that pre-existing project uses an MIT or BSD-type license, the developer can use virtually any license, so long as the proper notification and disclaimer provisions are included. On the other hand, if the pre-existing project were licensed under the GPL, the developer would have little choice but to license his or her own project under the GPL or to get permission from the author to use a different license. As discussed in the previous chapter, different licenses provide different levels of compatibility with other licenses. Given a potential conflict between the provisions of two different licenses, it is the better practice to avoid the conflict entirely, either by developing the project under the same license as the pre-existing project, or by obtaining explicit permission, if possible, from the creator(s) of the pre-existing project to cross-license that project under the license to be used in the new project.

Accordingly, in many situations, a developer's choice of license is constrained by choices made by his predecessors. In fact, this is the intended purpose—described as having a "viral" effect on licensing decisions—of one of the most popular of the open source and free software licenses, the GPL.

In those situations in which a developer is in fact starting from scratch or from code whose license is amenable to change, the decision as to license will probably be largely a matter of personal preference. The factors that might influence this decision include: how frequently used and well-known the license is; how readily comprehensible that license is; and finally, and perhaps most importantly, the license's philosophy, and, in particular, the extent to which the license allows with code developed under other licenses, including proprietary licenses.

In choosing any license to apply to a new project, developers should strongly consider relying on those licenses already well-known in the development community. This makes the project much more transparent to other developers and potential contributors who will probably have a better grasp of the principles of the BSD, MIT, Apache, MPL, and GPL Licenses, than they would of the Monongahela Copper Mining Institute Database License, v8.3. To the extent that licensing issues are important to contributors, using a license already known to them reduces barriers to entry and will likely make for a more successful project.

For much the same reason, using licenses that are written more clearly and which do not contain ambiguous or unusual terms will also help a project succeed. The BSD and MIT Licenses are models in this regard. The Apache License Version 1.1 is both clear and well-known in the development community, and Version 2.0 is becoming more familiar. The GPL and MPL Licenses, while considerably more complex, are well-written and their principles are well-understood. Developers should avoid licenses that seem ambiguous, unduly confusing, or poorly written.

The most important decision in choosing a license will be the choice between a GPL License and a less restrictive license. A full discussion of the disagreement between the two camps is beyond the scope of this book. However, to put it briefly, the GPL is premised on the belief that non-free software is to be avoided and that free software development projects should be set up to encourage open development models of software development and to discourage reliance on software not developed under an open development model, including all proprietary-licensed software. By requiring that any code developed from or based on GPL-licensed code be GPL-licensed, the GPL creates a strong incentive for programmers to license their code under a GPL License, in the form of access to all the code already GPL-licensed.

The argument in favor of less-restrictive licenses—such as the MIT, BSD, Apache, and MPL Licenses—is that open development model of software development is not inconsistent with the development of software under other models, including proprietary models. The fact that one line of a program, such as the Sendmail program described in Chapter 2, is developed under a proprietary license, does not undermine the open development model, in this view. The more developers and users that are involved in working on particular code, the better, even if some of that development takes place in "closed" development models under proprietary licenses.

In sum, there is no ready answer as to which license is the best for a given project. While a certain license may be better suited for a project, particularly when a substantial amount of work has already been done under that license, such decisions depend largely on circumstances and on the taste of the project developer.

Drafting Open Source Licenses

As should be evident from the previous discussion, drafting a new open source license is probably not the best place to start for most open source projects. In addition to the extra time and expense associated with drafting any legal document, the use of a new license will discourage potential contributors from participating in the project. Those contributors who are concerned about licensing implications will want to read and understand the license. Particularly in the case of long or complex licenses, this may present a substantial barrier to entry.

If you choose to do it, however, the first step in drafting an open source license should be retaining a competent and experienced attorney to undertake the task. While many open source licenses have been drafted by non-lawyers, the drafting of any contract, particularly one with the complexities inherent in open source software licenses, should be undertaken by someone with professional knowledge and experience.

After securing counsel, the next step should probably be devising the basic mechanics of the license. The new author should give serious thought to what the function of the license is intended to be. With open source and free software licenses, the key issue will generally be the generational limitations placed on distribution and modification of the licensed work by licensees. Many of the possible limitations have already been described. The MIT and the BSD Licenses, for example, require only that the text of the license be included in the subsequent distribution and that the required attributions be made. The GPL imposes much more substantial limitations: any distribution or modification of the work by licensees must be consistent with the terms of the GPL. If a licensee wishes to modify and distribute the work, he or she must license future users of that modified work under the GPL. The MPL imposes somewhat similar restrictions for modifications to the licensed work, but it permits either the original or the modified work to be distributed as part of a "Larger Work" under another license, including a proprietary license.

The number of potential variations is nearly infinite. The Open Source Definition, described in Chapter 1, imposes some specific requirements for a license that the author wants to have certified as compliant by the Open Source Initiative.

A brief summary of those requirements follows here. An open source license must permit an open development model to be applied to the licensed work, in that the source code must be provided or otherwise made available with the executable version of the code. The license must permit free modification of the licensed work and free distribution of both the original and the modified work. The license cannot discriminate in its application against any person or group of persons or any field of endeavor.

Of course, a license need not be compliant with the Open Source Definition to be an effective license. But if the intent is to draft an "open source license," failure to comply with the Open Source Definition is a pretty good sign that the drafter is not headed in the right direction. Beyond the fundamentals of the Open Source Definition, there is considerable scope for creativity and ingenuity in drafting licenses.

Many of the licenses described in this book, such as the Apache License, v2.0, and the MPL, begin with long, comprehensive lists of definitions. While not necessary, using such definitions can avoid unnecessary repetition of the same language throughout the license. A definitions section can also avoid accidental, and apparently inconsequential, variations in phrases or sentences that are supposed to be identical. Such variations can lead to potentially serious problems in interpreting the license, as users and contributors, and possibly lawyers, judges, and juries, attempt to determine whether the use of slightly different language was accidental or intentional.

Disclaimer of warranties and limitation of liabilities clauses are virtually universal in open source licenses. While certainly not required by the Open Source Definition, they are prudently included in such licenses to protect the licensor and any potential contributors from liability. Such clauses are not unique to open source licenses— many commercial software licenses contain similar terms.

The use of choice of forum and choice of law clauses is relatively uncommon in open source licenses, but there are many situations in which such clauses could be advantageous to the licensor, particularly for "developer-centric" licenses, such as the Apache License, v2.0, and the Perl License. With such licenses, it is anticipated that the project will remain primarily under the control of its initial developer. That developer may want to choose a local forum and the application of local law for the convenience of the developer in the event any dispute arises under the terms of the license. For example, a developer located in Boston may want to identify the Massachusetts state courts located in Boston as the forum for any dispute under the license and for Massachusetts law to control the interpretation and enforcement of the license. When considering the use of such clauses, developers should consult with a lawyer to make sure that the law that they are choosing to govern the license will interpret and enforce the license consistent with the developer's understanding. Laws vary significantly among different locales: it is certainly possible that a New York court would reach a different conclusion than a Massachusetts court as to how a contract should be interpreted.

One final area that a developer should give some thought to addressing is the applicability of patents to the licensed work. In order to prevent patent litigation to the extent possible, it is probably worthwhile to include a clause in the license that grants specific permission for users to exercise a royalty-free right to any patents held by the licensor, and, depending on the terms of the license, any subsequent contributors.

 For a list of licenses that the Open Source Initiative has approved as conforming to their expectations of open source, and for information about their process for approving licenses, visit *http://opensource.org/licenses/*.

Creative Commons Attribution-NoDerivs License

This work is licensed under the Creative Commons Attribution-NoDerivs License. A summary of the license is given below, followed by the full legal text.

You are free:

- to copy, distribute, display, and perform the work
- to make commercial use of the work

Under the following conditions:

Attribution. You must give the original author credit.

No Derivative Works. You may not alter, transform, or build upon this work.

- For any reuse or distribution, you must make clear to others the license terms of this work.
- Any of these conditions can be waived if you get permission from the copyright holder.

Your fair use and other rights are in no way affected by the above.

Creative Commons Legal Code

Attribution No-Derivs 2.0

CREATIVE COMMONS CORPORATION IS NOT A LAW FIRM AND DOES NOT PROVIDE LEGAL SERVICES. DISTRIBUTION OF THIS LICENSE DOES NOT CREATE AN ATTORNEY-CLIENT RELATIONSHIP. CREATIVE COMMONS PROVIDES THIS INFORMATION ON AN "AS-IS" BASIS. CREATIVE COMMONS MAKES NO WARRANTIES REGARDING THE INFORMATION PROVIDED, AND DISCLAIMS LIABILITY FOR DAMAGES RESULTING FROM ITS USE.

License

THE WORK (AS DEFINED BELOW) IS PROVIDED UNDER THE TERMS OF THIS CREATIVE COMMONS PUBLIC LICENSE ("CCPL" OR "LICENSE"). THE WORK IS PROTECTED BY COPYRIGHT AND/OR OTHER APPLICABLE LAW. ANY USE OF THE WORK OTHER THAN AS AUTHORIZED UNDER THIS LICENSE OR COPYRIGHT LAW IS PROHIBITED.

BY EXERCISING ANY RIGHTS TO THE WORK PROVIDED HERE, YOU ACCEPT AND AGREE TO BE BOUND BY THE TERMS OF THIS LICENSE. THE LICENSOR GRANTS YOU THE RIGHTS CONTAINED HERE IN CONSIDERATION OF YOUR ACCEPTANCE OF SUCH TERMS AND CONDITIONS.

1. **Definitions**

   a. **"Collective Work"** means a work, such as a periodical issue, anthology or encyclopedia, in which the Work in its entirety in unmodified form, along with a number of other contributions, constituting separate and independent works in themselves, are assembled into a collective whole. A work that constitutes a Collective Work will not be considered a Derivative Work (as defined below) for the purposes of this License.

   b. **"Derivative Work"** means a work based upon the Work or upon the Work and other pre-existing works, such as a translation, musical arrangement, dramatization, fictionalization, motion picture version, sound recording, art reproduction, abridgment, condensation, or any other form in which the Work may be recast, transformed, or adapted, except that a work that constitutes a Collective Work will not be considered a Derivative Work for the purpose of this License. For the avoidance of doubt, where the Work is a musical composition or sound recording, the synchronization of the Work in timed-relation with a moving image ("synching") will be considered a Derivative Work for the purpose of this License.

   c. **"Licensor"** means the individual or entity that offers the Work under the terms of this License.

   d. **"Original Author"** means the individual or entity who created the Work.

   e. **"Work"** means the copyrightable work of authorship offered under the terms of this License.

   f. **"You"** means an individual or entity exercising rights under this License who has not previously violated the terms of this License with respect to the Work, or who has received express permission from the Licensor to exercise rights under this License despite a previous violation.

2. **Fair Use Rights.** Nothing in this license is intended to reduce, limit, or restrict any rights arising from fair use, first sale or other limitations on the exclusive rights of the copyright owner under copyright law or other applicable laws.

3. **License Grant.** Subject to the terms and conditions of this License, Licensor hereby grants You a worldwide, royalty-free, non-exclusive, perpetual (for the duration of the applicable copyright) license to exercise the rights in the Work as stated below:

   a. to reproduce the Work, to incorporate the Work into one or more Collective Works, and to reproduce the Work as incorporated in the Collective Works;

   b. to distribute copies or phonorecords of, display publicly, perform publicly, and perform publicly by means of a digital audio transmission the Work including as incorporated in Collective Works.

   c. For the avoidance of doubt, where the work is a musical composition:

      1. **Performance Royalties Under Blanket Licenses.** Licensor waives the exclusive right to collect, whether individually or via a performance rights society (e.g. ASCAP, BMI, SESAC), royalties for the public performance or public digital performance (e.g. webcast) of the Work.

      2. **Mechanical Rights and Statutory Royalties.** Licensor waives the exclusive right to collect, whether individually or via a music rights society or designated agent (e.g. Harry Fox Agency), royalties for any phonorecord You create from the Work ("cover version") and distribute, subject to the compulsory license created by 17 USC Section 115 of the US Copyright Act (or the equivalent in other jurisdictions).

   d. **Webcasting Rights and Statutory Royalties.** For the avoidance of doubt, where the Work is a sound recording, Licensor waives the exclusive right to collect, whether individually or via a performance-rights society (e.g. SoundExchange), royalties for the public digital performance (e.g. webcast) of the Work, subject to the compulsory license created by 17 USC Section 114 of the US Copyright Act (or the equivalent in other jurisdictions).

4. **Restrictions.** The license granted in Section 3 above is expressly made subject to and limited by the following restrictions:

   a. You may distribute, publicly display, publicly perform, or publicly digitally perform the Work only under the terms of this License, and You must include a copy of, or the Uniform Resource Identifier for, this License with every copy or phonorecord of the Work You distribute, publicly display, publicly perform, or publicly digitally perform. You may not offer or impose any terms on the Work that alter or restrict the terms of this License or the recipients' exercise of the rights granted hereunder. You may not sublicense the Work. You must keep intact all notices that refer to this License and to the disclaimer of warranties. You may not distribute, publicly display, publicly perform, or publicly digitally perform the Work with any technological measures that control access or use of the Work in a manner inconsistent with the terms of this License Agreement. The above applies to the Work as incorporated in a Collective Work, but this does not require the Collective Work apart from the Work itself to be made subject to the terms of this License. If You create a Collective Work, upon notice from any Licensor You must, to the extent practicable, remove from the Collective Work any reference to such Licensor or the Original Author, as requested.

b. If you distribute, publicly display, publicly perform, or publicly digitally perform the Work or Collective Works, You must keep intact all copyright notices for the Work and give the Original Author credit reasonable to the medium or means You are utilizing by conveying the name (or pseudonym if applicable) of the Original Author if supplied; the title of the Work if supplied; and to the extent reasonably practicable, the Uniform Resource Identifier, if any, that Licensor specifies to be associated with the Work, unless such URI does not refer to the copyright notice or licensing information for the Work. Such credit may be implemented in any reasonable manner; provided, however, that in the case of a Collective Work, at a minimum such credit will appear where any other comparable authorship credit appears and in a manner at least as prominent as such other comparable authorship credit.

The above rights may be exercised in all media and formats whether now known or hereafter devised. The above rights include the right to make such modifications as are technically necessary to exercise the rights in other media and formats, but otherwise you have no rights to make Derivative Works. All rights not expressly granted by Licensor are hereby reserved.

5. **Representations, Warranties and Disclaimer**

UNLESS OTHERWISE MUTUALLY AGREED TO BY THE PARTIES IN WRITING, LICENSOR OFFERS THE WORK AS-IS AND MAKES NO REPRESENTATIONS OR WARRANTIES OF ANY KIND CONCERNING THE MATERIALS, EXPRESS, IMPLIED, STATUTORY OR OTHERWISE, INCLUDING, WITHOUT LIMITATION, WARRANTIES OF TITLE, MERCHANTIBILITY, FITNESS FOR A PARTICULAR PURPOSE, NONINFRINGEMENT, OR THE ABSENCE OF LATENT OR OTHER DEFECTS, ACCURACY, OR THE PRESENCE OF ABSENCE OF ERRORS, WHETHER OR NOT DISCOVERABLE. SOME JURISDICTIONS DO NOT ALLOW THE EXCLUSION OF IMPLIED WARRANTIES, SO SUCH EXCLUSION MAY NOT APPLY TO YOU.

6. **Limitation on Liability.** EXCEPT TO THE EXTENT REQUIRED BY APPLICABLE LAW, IN NO EVENT WILL LICENSOR BE LIABLE TO YOU ON ANY LEGAL THEORY FOR ANY SPECIAL, INCIDENTAL, CONSEQUENTIAL, PUNITIVE OR EXEMPLARY DAMAGES ARISING OUT OF THIS LICENSE OR THE USE OF THE WORK, EVEN IF LICENSOR HAS BEEN ADVISED OF THE POSSIBILITY OF SUCH DAMAGES.

7. **Termination**

   a. This License and the rights granted hereunder will terminate automatically upon any breach by You of the terms of this License. Individuals or entities who have received Collective Works from You under this License, however, will not have their licenses terminated provided such individuals or entities remain in full compliance with those licenses. Sections 1, 2, 5, 6, 7, and 8 will survive any termination of this License.

   b. Subject to the above terms and conditions, the license granted here is perpetual (for the duration of the applicable copyright in the Work). Notwithstanding the above, Licensor reserves the right to release the Work under different license terms or to stop distributing the Work at any time; provided, however that any such election will not serve to withdraw this License (or any other license that has been, or is required to be, granted under the terms of this License), and this License will continue in full force and effect unless terminated as stated above.

8. **Miscellaneous**

   a. Each time You distribute or publicly digitally perform the Work, the Licensor offers to the recipient a license to the Work on the same terms and conditions as the license granted to You under this License.

   b. If any provision of this License is invalid or unenforceable under applicable law, it shall not affect the validity or enforceability of the remainder of the terms of this License, and without further action by the parties to this agreement, such provision shall be reformed to the minimum extent necessary to make such provision valid and enforceable.

   c. No term or provision of this License shall be deemed waived and no breach consented to unless such waiver or consent shall be in writing and signed by the party to be charged with such waiver or consent.

   d. This License constitutes the entire agreement between the parties with respect to the Work licensed here. There are no understandings, agreements or representations with respect to the Work not specified here. Licensor shall not be bound by any additional provisions that may appear in any communication from You. This License may not be modified without the mutual written agreement of the Licensor and You.

   Creative Commons is not a party to this License, and makes no warranty whatsoever in connection with the Work. Creative Commons will not be liable to You or any party on any legal theory for any damages whatsoever, including without limitation any general, special, incidental or consequential damages arising in connection to this license. Notwithstanding the foregoing two (2) sentences, if Creative Commons has expressly identified itself as the Licensor hereunder, it shall have all rights and obligations of Licensor.

Except for the limited purpose of indicating to the public that the Work is licensed under the CCPL, neither party will use the trademark "Creative Commons" or any related trademark or logo of Creative Commons without the prior written consent of Creative Commons. Any permitted use will be in compliance with Creative Commons' then-current trademark usage guidelines, as may be published on its website or otherwise made available upon request from time to time.

Creative Commons may be contacted at *http://creativecommons.org/*.

Index

We'd like to hear your suggestions for improving our indexes. Send email to *index@oreilly.com*.

About the Author

Andrew M. St. Laurent is an experienced lawyer with a long-time interest in intellectual property, particularly software licensing.

Colophon

Our look is the result of reader comments, our own experimentation, and feedback from distribution channels. Distinctive covers complement our distinctive approach to technical topics, breathing personality and life into potentially dry subjects.

The cover image of a shootout at the railway is a 19th-century engraving from Dover's *American West.*

Marlowe Shaeffer was the production editor and copyeditor for *Understanding Open Source and Free Software Licensing.* Philip Dangler was the proofreader. Mary Brady and Darren Kelly provided quality control. Julie Hawks wrote the index.

Emma Colby designed the cover of this book, based on a series design by Hanna Dyer and Edie Freedman. Emma Colby produced the cover layout with Quark-XPress 4.1 using Adobe's ITC Garamond font.

David Futato designed the interior layout. The chapter opening images are from the Dover Pictorial Archive; *Marvels of the New West: A Vivid Portrayal of the Stupendous Marvels in the Vast Wonderland West of the Missouri River,* by William Thayer (The Henry Bill Publishing Co., 1888); and *The Pioneer History of America: A Popular Account of the Heroes and Adventures,* by Augustus Lynch Mason, A.M. (The Jones Brothers Publishing Company, 1884). This book was converted by Julie Hawks and Joe Wizda to FrameMaker 5.5.6 with a format conversion tool created by Erik Ray, Jason McIntosh, Neil Walls, and Mike Sierra that uses Perl and XML technologies. The text font is Linotype Birka; the heading font is Adobe Myriad Condensed; and the code font is LucasFont's TheSans Mono Condensed. The illustrations that appear in the book were produced by Robert Romano and Jessamyn Read using Macromedia FreeHand 9 and Adobe Photoshop 6. The tip and warning icons were drawn by Christopher Bing.